The Evolution of Civilizations

Carroll Quigley

The Evolution of Civilizations

An Introduction to Historical Analysis

Carroll Quigley

Liberty Fund

© 1961 by Carroll Quigley. Foreword and Selective Bibliography © 1979 by Liberty Fund, Inc. All rights reserved, including the right of reproduction in whole or in part in any form. Brief quotations may be included in a review, and all inquiries should be addressed to Liberty Fund, Inc., 11301 North Meridian Street, Carmel, Indiana 46032. This book was manufactured in the United States of America.

First edition published in 1961 by the Macmillan Company, New York. Second edition published 1979 by Liberty Fund, Indianapolis, Indiana. This edition is reprinted by arrangement with Macmillan Publishing Co., Inc.

Library of Congress Cataloging in Publication Data

Quigley, Carroll
   The evolution of civilizations.

   Bibliography: p. 423.
   Includes index.
   1. Civilization—History. 2. History—Methodology
I. Title
CB59.Q5 1979 909 79-4091
ISBN 0-913966-56-8
ISBN 0-913966-57-6 (pbk.)

13 21 22 23 24 C 9 8 7 6 5
21 22 23 24 25 P 14 13 12 11 10

libertyfund.org

To the Memory of Two
Who Still Guide My Way:
My Father, a Saint, and
My Mother, a Spartan
1880–1957

Contents

Diagrams, Tables, and Maps

Foreword
By Harry J. Hogan

The Evolution of Civilizations expresses two dimensions of its author, Carroll Quigley, that most extraordinary historian, philosopher, and teacher. In the first place, its scope is wide-ranging, covering the whole of man's activities throughout time. Second, it is analytic, not merely descriptive. It attempts a categorization of man's activities in sequential fashion so as to provide a causal explanation of the stages of civilization.

Quigley coupled enormous capacity for work with a peculiarly "scientific" approach. He believed that it should be possible to examine the data and draw conclusions. As a boy at the Boston Latin School, his academic interests were mathematics, physics, and chemistry. Yet during his senior year he was also associate editor of the *Register*, the oldest high school paper in the country. His articles were

Dr. Hogan, now retired, has been a professor, administrator, and lawyer. He received his B.A. magna cum laude *from Princeton University, his LL.B. from Columbia Law School, and his Ph.D. in American history from George Washington University. His articles have appeared in the* American Bar Association Journal, *the* Journal of Politics, *and other periodicals.*

singled out for national awards by a national committee headed by George Gallup.

At Harvard, biochemistry was to be his major. But Harvard, expressing then a belief regarding a well-rounded education to which it has now returned, required a core curriculum including a course in the humanities. Quigley chose a history course, "Europe Since the Fall of Rome." Always a contrary man, he was graded at the top of his class in physics and calculus and drew a C in the history course. But the development of ideas began to assert its fascination for him, so he elected to major in history. He graduated *magna cum laude* as the top history student in his class.

Quigley was always impatient. He stood for his doctorate oral examination at the end of his second year of graduate studies. Charles Howard McIlwain, chairman of the examining board, was very impressed by Quigley's answer to his opening question; the answer included a long quotation in Latin from Robert Grosseteste, bishop of Lincoln in the thirteenth century. Professor McIlwain sent Quigley to Princeton University as a graduate student instructor.

In the spring of 1937 I was a student in my senior year at Princeton. Quigley was my preceptor in medieval history. He was Boston Irish; I was New York Irish. Both of us, Catholics adventuring in a strangely Protestant establishment world, were fascinated by the Western intellectual tradition anchored in Augustine, Abelard, and Aquinas that seemed to have so much more richness and depth than contemporary liberalism. We became very close in a treasured friendship that was terminated only by his death.

In the course of rereading *The Evolution of Civilizations* I was reminded of the intensity of our dialogue. In Quigley's view, which I shared, our age was one of irrationality. That spring we talked about what career decisions I should make. At his urging I applied to and was admitted by the Harvard Graduate School in History. But I had reservations about an academic career in the study of the history that I loved, on the ground that on Quigley's own analysis the social decisions of importance in our lifetime would be made in ad hoc irrational fashion in the street. On that reasoning, finally I transferred to law school.

In Princeton, Carroll Quigley met and married Lillian Fox. They spent their honeymoon in Paris and Italy on a fellowship to write his doctoral dissertation, a study of the public administration of the Kingdom of Italy, 1805–14. The development of the state in western Europe over the last thousand years always fascinated Quigley. He regarded the development of public administration in the Napoleonic states as a major step in the evolution of the modern state. It always frustrated him that each nation, including our own, regards its own history as unique and the history of other nations as irrelevant to it.

In 1938–41, Quigley served a stint at Harvard, tutoring graduate students in ancient and medieval history. It offered little opportunity for the development of cosmic views and he was less than completely content there. It was, however, a happy experience for me. I had entered Harvard Law School. We began the practice of having breakfast together at Carroll and Lillian's apartment.

In 1941 Quigley accepted a teaching appointment at Georgetown's School of Foreign Service. It was to engage his primary energies throughout the rest of his busy life. There he became an almost legendary teacher. He chose to teach a course, "The Development of Civilization," required of the incoming class, and that course ultimately provided the structure and substance for *The Evolution of Civilizations*. As a course in his hands, it was a vital intellectual experience for young students, a mind-opening adventure. Foreign Service School graduates, meeting years later in careers around the world, would establish rapport with each other by describing their experience in his class. It was an intellectual initiation with remembered impact that could be shared by people who had graduated years apart.

The fortunes of life brought us together again. During World War II I served as a very junior officer on Admiral King's staff in Washington. Carroll and I saw each other frequently. Twenty years later, after practicing law in Oregon, I came into the government with President Kennedy. Our eldest daughter became a student under Carroll at Georgetown University. We bought a house close by Carroll and Lillian. I had Sunday breakfast with them for years and renewed our discussions of the affairs of a disintegrating world.

Superb teacher Quigley was, and could justify a lifetime of prodigious work on that success alone. But ultimately he was more. To me he was a figure—he would scoff at this—like Augustine, Abelard, and Aquinas, searching for the truth through examination of ultimate reality as it was revealed in history. Long ago, he left the church in the formal sense. Spiritually and intellectually he never left it. He never swerved from his search for the meaning of life. He never placed any goal in higher priority. If the God of the Western civilization that Quigley spent so many years studying does exist in the terms that he saw ascribed to him by our civilization, that God will now have welcomed Quigley as one who has pleased him.

In an age characterized by violence, extraordinary personal alienation, and the disintegration of family, church, and community, Quigley chose a life dedicated to rationality. He addressed the problem of explaining change in the world around us, first examined by Heraclitus in ancient Greece. Beneath that constant change, so apparent and itself so real, what is permanent and unchanging?

Quigley wanted an explanation that in its very categorization would give meaning to a history which was a record of constant change. Therefore the analysis had to include but not be limited to categories of subject areas of human activity—military, political, economic, social, religious, intellectual. It had to describe change in categories expressed sequentially in time—mixture, gestation, expansion, conflict, universal empire, decay, invasion. It was a most ambitious effort to make history rationally understandable. F. E. Manuel, in his review of this book for the *American Historical Review,* following its first publication in 1961, described it as on "sounder ground" than the work of Toynbee.

Quigley found the explanation of disintegration in the gradual transformation of social "instruments" into "institutions," that is, the transformation of social arrangements functioning to meet real social needs into social institutions serving their own purposes regardless of real social needs. In an ideologically Platonistic society, social arrangements are molded to express a rigidly idealized version of reality. Such institutionalization would not have the flexibility to accommodate to the pressures of changing reality for which the ideology has no categories of thought that will allow perception, analysis, and handling. But the extraordinary distinction of Western civilization is that its ontology allows an open-ended epistemology. It is engaged in a constant effort to understand reality which is perceived as in constant change. Therefore, our categories of knowledge are themselves always subject to change. As a consequence reform is always possible.

The question today is whether we have lost that Western view of reality which has given our 2,000 years of history its unique vitality, constantly pregnant with new versions of social structure. In *Evolution,* Quigley describes the basic ideology of Western civilization as expressed in the statement, "The truth unfolds in time through a communal process." Therefore, Quigley saw the triumph in the thirteenth century of the moderate realism of Aquinas over dualistic exaggerated realism derived from Platonism as the major epistemologic triumph that opened up Western civilization. People must constantly search for the "truth" by building upon what others have learned. But no knowledge can be assumed to be complete and final. It could be contradicted by new information received tomorrow. In epistemology, Quigley always retained his belief in the scientific method. Therefore, he saw Hegel and Marx as presumptuous, in error, and outside the Western tradition in their analysis of history as an ideologic dialectic culminating in the present or immediate future in a homeostatic condition.

Quigley comments upon the constant repetition of conflict and expansion stages in Western history. That reform process owes its possibility to the uniquely Western belief that truth is continually unfolding. Therefore Western civilization is capable of reexamining its direction and its institutions, and changing both as appears necessary. So in Western history, there was a succession of technological breakthroughs in agricultural practice and in commerce.

Outmoded institutions like feudalism and—in the commercial area—municipal mercantilism in the period 1270–1440, and state mercantilism in the period 1690–1810 were discarded. Similarly, we may also survive the economic crisis described by Quigley as monopoly capitalism in the present post-1900 period.

Yet Quigley perceives—correctly in my view—the possible termination of open-ended Western civilization. With access to an explosive technology that can tear the planet apart, coupled with the failure of Western civilization to establish any viable system of world government, local political authority will tend to become violent and absolutist. As we move into irrational activism, states will seize upon ideologies that justify absolutism. The 2,000-year separation in Western history of state and society would then end. Western people would rejoin those of the rest of the world in merging the two into a single entity, authoritarian and static. The age that we are about to enter would be an ideologic one consistent with the views of Hegel and Marx—a homeostatic condition. That triumph would end the Western experiment and return us to the experience of the rest of the world—namely, that history is a sequence of stages in the rise and fall of absolutist ideologies.

America is now in a crisis-disintegrating stage. In such a condition, absent a philosophy, people turn readily to charismatic personalities. So at the beginning of our time of troubles, in the depression of the 1930s, we turned to Franklin D. Roosevelt. He took us through the depression and World War II. We were buoyed by his optimism and reassured by the strength and confidence of his personality. Within the Western tradition he provided us with no solutions; he simply preserved options. When he died, all

America was in shock. We had lost our shield. Carroll came over to my place that night. We talked in the subdued fashion of a generation that had lost its guardian and would now have to face a hostile world on its own.

Since then we in America have been denied the easy-out of charismatic leadership. It may just be that we shall have to follow the route that Quigley has marked out for us in this book. We may have to look at our history, analyze it, establish an identity in that analysis, and make another try at understanding reality in a fashion consistent with that open-ended tradition.

If so, America, acting for Western civilization, must find within the history of that civilization the intellectual and spiritual reserves to renew itself within the tradition. Striking as was the impact of this book at the time of its first publication, in 1961, its major impact will be in support of that effort in the future. There is hope that in Western civilization the future ideology will be rational. If so, it would be consistent with an epistemology that accepts the general validity of sensory experience and the possibility of making generalizations from that experience, subject to modification as additional facts are perceived. It is that epistemology which was termed moderate realism in the thirteenth century and, in its epistemologic aspects, is now known as the scientific method. Such a rational ideology is probable only if it is developed out of the special history of the West. As appreciation of that spreads, the kind of analysis that Carroll Quigley develops in this book is the analysis that the West must use.

Such an effort would be consistent in social terms with Quigley's view of his own life. He greatly admired his mother, a housewife, and his father, a Boston firechief, and described them as teaching him to do his best at whatever he chose to put his energies. That was their way of saying what Carroll would have described as man's responsibility to understand and relate actively to a continually unfolding reality. He dedicated his life to that purpose.

Preface to the
First Edition

This book is not a history. Rather it is an attempt to establish analytical tools that will assist the understanding of history. Most historians will regard such an effort as unnecessary or even impossible. Some answer must be made to these two objections.

Those who claim that no analytical tools are needed in order to write history are naive. To them the facts of history are relatively few and are simply arranged. The historian's task is merely to find these facts; their arrangement will be obvious. But it should require only a moment's thought to recognize that the facts of the past are infinite, and the possible arrangements of any selection from these facts are equally numerous. Since all the facts cannot be mobilized in any written history because of their great number, there must be some principle on which selection from these facts is based. Such a principle is a tool of historical analysis. Any sophisticated historian should be aware of the principles he uses and should be explicit to his readers about these. After all, any past event, even the writing of this book, is a fact of history, but most such facts, including this book, do not deserve to be mentioned in the narration of history.

If historians are not explicit, at least to themselves, about their principles of selection among the facts of the past and among the many possible arrangements of these facts, all histories will be simply accidental compilations that cannot be justified in any rational way. Historians will continue to write about some of the events of history while neglecting others equally significant or even more significant, and they will form patterns for these facts along lines determined by traditional (and basically accidental) lines or in reflection of old controversies about the patterns of these facts.

This, indeed, is pretty much what we have in history today. In American history, for example, dozens of books examine and reexamine the same old issues without, in most cases, contributing much that is new or different. The central fact of American history is the process by which a society with European cultural patterns was modified by the selective process of emigration from Europe and the opportunity to exploit the enormous, largely virgin, resources of the New World. Yet in most histories of the United States, this subject is hardly mentioned. Instead we have volume after volume of discussion on the rivalry of Jeffersonians and Hamiltonians or on the unrealistic problem whether the American Civil War was a repressible or an irrepressible conflict or on whether the American lapse into isolationism after World War I was caused more by the vindictiveness of Lodge or the inflexibility of Wilson.

To the non-American world the central fact of American history is American technology—what they used to call "Fordism," meaning mass production. Until very recently there was no history of American technology in existence, and even today this vital subject obtains only incidental mention, with an almost total lack of real understanding, in most histories of the United States.

As we have said, the content of most books depends upon accidental factors or, at most, on the rehash of ancient controversies. The Civil War has commanded major attention, but there is little recognition of the real significance of this war; namely, that after giving an impetus to industrialization, it left a residue of emotional patterns that alienated the farmers of the South and the farmers of the West so that the country could be dominated politically by the high finance and heavy industry of the East. This situation, which forms the essential background for such familiar phenomena as the agrarian discontent and third-party movements of the period 1873–1933, as well as the attacks on political machines and the rise of civil service, or the growth of muckraking or progressivism, and of government regulation of business, is rarely presented in adequate fashion as the background that it is. Instead these events are mentioned as if they were merely accidental occurrences related in some obscure fashion to the idiosyncrasies of Americans. And the average college student of American history finishes his study without any idea why the Republican party became the party of big business in 1892–1932, what the Whitneys contributed to American life, or the significant contributions of Joseph Henry or Josiah Willard Gibbs (1839–1903) to the world today.

In the incredible and growing excitement over the Civil War, tradition and stale controversy continue to determine the centers of attention. The Battle of Gettysburg has been fought and refought (with four major books in the last six months), just as if the South ever really had a chance of

winning the war, in this or any other battle, while the Battle
of Petersburg, which is of far greater tactical significance
(since it was a direct foretaste of 1914–18), is almost
totally neglected.

Matters are no better in European history. To mention
only one point, in which I am personally very interested, the
one dominant central fact of European history over the last
thousand years has been the almost steady growth of public
authority and the public services. We could never guess this
from the history books. Or again, reams have been written
on the French Revolution and its origins, yet some of the
most vital points are hardly mentioned. We have been told
repeatedly that the government of the Old Regime was
"absolute" and that the Revolution began because this regime was financially "bankrupt." Few have seen the paradox lying in a situation where an "absolute state" could
not tax its subjects. A colleague on the faculty at Princeton
once stated in conversation as a fact that the Revolution
occurred in France because that country was the most advanced in Europe. When I replied that, in my opinion, the
Revolution came in France because the French government
was one of the most backward in Europe, he was astonished.
I am not trying here to consider this problem; I am simply
trying to point out that this is a problem that certainly
should have been examined in connection with the study of
the French Revolution and that just as surely would have
been discussed in any historical work based on rational tools
of historical analysis. Because such tools have not been
used, study of the French Revolution, like the study of other
matters, has concentrated its attention on those aspects of
the problem that came to be discussed largely for traditional
and accidental reasons. In fact, the chief force directing the

historiography of the French Revolution has not been a determined effort to find what happened but rather has been the party conflicts of the Third French Republic. Once these partisan motivations are rejected, a history of the French Revolution could be written that, with equal justification, would have discussed quite different aspects of the subject. Without principles of selection among the facts and theories, one selection is as well justified as another on any grounds outside tradition.

So much for the historians who say that tools of historical analysis are unnecessary. To the much smaller group of historians who say that such tools are impossible to obtain, I can only offer this book as an attempt. This group of critics is much more difficult to deal with. They are skeptics sophisticated enough to recognize that there is a problem, but not consistent enough to cease being historians when they insist that there is no solution. The only justification they can offer is to fall back on tradition once again. These skeptics recognize the infinity of past facts and the subjectivity of the criteria usually used in making a selection from these facts, but they are content to continue to work with the traditionally acceptable selections from both. I offer them here principles of selection based on the methods used in science, but I recognize the difficulty of the problem of persuading them that I have anything helpful. As skeptics these people are almost impervious to persuasion.

I came into history from a primary concern with mathematics and science. This has been a tremendous help to me as a person and as a historian, although it must be admitted it has served to make my historical interpretations less conventional than may be acceptable to many of my colleagues in the field.

My greatest personal debt to historians has been to Frederic William Maitland and to Charles Howard McIlwain. The former I did not know, although his influence on me has been very great. The latter, my best-loved teacher, remains the model of my professional life.

This book was read in manuscript by Crane Brinton of Harvard and A. L. Rowse of All Souls College, Oxford; it has benefited from their diametrically opposed opinions. To Professor Brinton, as teacher and friend during three decades, I owe many favors. A word of thanks is also due to that great and lamented scholar, the late Donald Cope McKay of Harvard, who, as my undergraduate tutor, first introduced me to ancient history. And finally, no words can express my gratitude to my wife, Lillian Fox Quigley, whose patient and expert assistance has made many rough roads smooth during the quarter century since we first went off to Europe when she was in her teens.

Oxford, England
June 1961

The Evolution of Civilizations

1

Scientific Method and the Social Sciences

During the summer that I was twelve years old, I walked four or five times a week to fish from Hingham Bridge. The distance was about five miles, part of it along a high railroad embankment that had been ballasted with crushed quartz. In this ballast were hundreds of quartz crystals. Each day I stopped awhile to look for a perfect crystal. I found some excellent ones, but never one that could be called perfect. The books I consulted told me that a quartz crystal should be a hexagonal prism with a regular hexagonal pyramid at the end. The ones I found were invariably irregular in some way, with sides of varying sizes, frequently with several crystals jammed together so that, in seeking to share the same material, they mutually distorted each other's hexagonal regularity.

After several weeks of casual searching, I found three or four crystals that were almost perfect, at least at the pyramidal end. But to find these, I had examined and discarded hundreds of distorted crystals. By what right, I asked, did the books say that quartz crystals occurred in regular pyramidal hexagonal prisms when only a small percentage of those found had such a shape? Obviously, the books meant that crystallized quartz has a tendency to take hexagonal form and will do so unless distorted by outside forces. The fact that ninety-nine percent are distorted does not deter the scientist from forming in his mind an idealized picture of an undistorted crystal, or from stating, in books, that quartz crystals occur in that idealized form.

Later, when I studied science in school and college, I found that most scientific "laws" were of this idealized character. They were not statements of what actually happens in the world or of what we observe through our senses, but rather were highly idealized and much oversimplified relationships that might occur if a great many other influences, which were always present, were neglected. I found that the most highly praised "scientific laws" attributed to great men like Galileo or Newton were of this character. It was a blow to discover that Newton's laws of planetary motion did not, in fact, describe the movements of the sun's satellites as we observe them, except in a very approximate way. In some cases, notably that of the planet Mercury, the approximation was by no means close.

Still later, when my interests shifted from the physical sciences to the social sciences, and I worked with students of human society who were generally lacking in any close familiarity with the natural sciences, I found a curious situation. The social scientists usually had erroneous ideas about the methods and theories of natural science, believing them to be rigid, exact, and invariable. Accordingly, they felt that these methods were not applicable to the social sciences. Thus I found that natural scientists were quite prepared to accept as a "law" a rule that was only approximately true or was true in only one case in a hundred, while the social scientists were reluctant to accept any rule that was only approximate or even one that had no more than one exception in a hundred cases.

After years of work in both areas of study, I concluded that the social sciences were different, in many important ways, from the natural sciences, but that the same scientific methods were applicable in both areas, and, indeed, that no very useful work could be done in either area except by scientific methods. In both areas the laws arising from the use of scientific methods will be idealized theories reflecting observed phenomena only approximately, but these theories must be based on our observations; and any wide failure of approximation or any totally inapplicable cases must either be explained in terms of unconsidered outside factors, or the theories themselves must be changed to cover such variant observations. The "laws" of historical change described in this book seem to me to fit the observed cases at least as closely as most of the theories of natural science. Most of the laws I shall mention apply, without exception, or with only slight, explicable divergencies, to all the cases I know. They are then, it would seem to me, as worthy of consideration as the scientific laws on the formation of crystals.

Before proceeding to examine any theories of historical change, we should review what we understand by the term "scientific method." In general, this method has three parts which we might call (1) gathering evidence, (2) making a hypothesis, and (3) testing the hypothesis. The first of these, "gathering evidence," refers to collecting all the observations relevant to the topic being studied. The important point here is that we must have *all* the evidence, for, obviously, omission of a few observations, or even one vital case, might make a considerable change in our final conclusions. It is equally obvious, I hope, that we cannot judge that we have all the evidence or cannot know what observations are relevant to our subject unless we already have some kind of tentative hypothesis or theory about the nature of that subject. In most cases a worker does have some such preliminary theory. This leads to two warnings. In the first place, the three parts of scientific methodology listed above were listed in order, not because a scientist performs them separately in sequence, but simply because we must discuss them in an orderly fashion. And, in the second place, any theories, even those regarded as final conclusions at the end of all three parts of scientific method, remain tentative. As scientific methodology is practiced, all three parts are used together at all stages, and therefore no theory, however rigorously tested, is ever final, but remains at all times tentative, subject to new observation and continued testing by such observation. No scientist ever believes that he has the final answer or the ultimate truth on anything. Rather he feels that science advances by a series of successive (and, he hopes, closer) approximations to the truth; and, since the truth is never finally reached, the work of scientists must indefinitely continue. Science, as one writer put it, is like a single light in darkness; as it grows brighter its shows more clearly the area of illumination and, simultaneously, lengthens the circle of surrounding darkness.

Having gathered all the "relevant" evidence, the scientist may proceed to the second part of scientific methodology, making a hypothesis. In doing this, two rules must be followed: (*a*) the hypothesis must explain all the observations and (*b*) the hypothesis must be the simplest one that will explain them. These two rules might be summed up in the statement that a scientific hypothesis must be adequate and it must be simple. Once again let us confess that these two rules are idealistic rather than practicable, but they remain, nevertheless, the goals by which a scientist guides his activities.

When we say that a hypothesis must be adequate, and thus must include all of the relevant observations, we are saying something simple. But carrying out this simple admonition is extremely difficult. It is quite true that every scientific hypothesis suffers from inadequate evidence—that is, it does not include in its explanation *all* the relevant evidence, and would be different if it did so. It is not easy to tear any event out of the context of the universe in which it occurred without detaching it from some factor that has influenced it. This is difficult enough in the physical sciences. It is immensely more difficult in the social sciences. It is likely that in any society the factors influencing an event are so numerous that any effort to detach an event from its social context must inevitably do violence to it. The extreme specialization of most social studies today, concentrating attention on narrow fields and brief periods, is a great hindrance to our understanding of such special fields, although the fact is not so widely recognized as it should be, since any specialist's work is usually examined only by his fellow specialists who have the same biases and blind spots as he does himself. But a specialist from one area of study who examines the work being done in some other area cannot fail to notice how the overspecialized training of the experts in his new area of interest has handicapped their understanding of that area.

The second requirement of a scientific hypothesis—that it should be simple—is also more difficult to carry out in practice than it is to write down in words. Essentially, it means that a hypothesis should explain the existing observations by making the fewest assumptions and by inferring the simplest relationships. This is so vital that a hypothesis is scientific or fails to be scientific on this point alone. Yet in spite of its importance, this requirement of scientific method is frequently not recognized to be important by many active scientists. The requirement that a scientific hypothesis must be "simple" or, as it is sometimes expressed, "economical" does not arise merely from a scientist's desire to be simple. Nor does it arise from some esthetic urge, although this is not so remote from the problem as might seem at first glance. When a mathematician says of a mathematical demonstration that it is "beautiful," he means exactly what the word "beautiful" means to the rest of us, and this same element is undoubtedly significant in the formulation of theory by a scientist as well.

The rule of simplicity or economy in scientific hypothesis has a number of corollaries. One of these, called "the uniformity of nature," assumes that the whole universe is made of the same substances and obeys the same laws and, accordingly, will behave in the same way under the same conditions. Such an assumption does not have to be proved —indeed, it could not be proved. It is made for two reasons. First, because it is simpler to assume that things are the same than it is to assume that they are different. And, second, while we cannot prove this assumption to be correct even if it is correct, we can, if it is not correct, show this by finding a single exceptional case. We could demonstrate the uniformity of nature only by comparing all parts of the universe with all other parts, something that clearly could never be achieved. But we can assume this, because it is a simpler hypothesis than its contrary; and, if it is wrong, we can show this error by producing one case of a substance or a physical law that is different in one place or time from other places or times. To speak briefly, we might say that scientific assumptions cannot be proved but they can be refuted, and they must always be put in a form that will allow such refutation.

Other examples or applications of the rule of uniformity of nature would be the scientific assumptions that "man is part of nature" or that "all men have the same potentialities." Neither of these could be proved, because this would involve the impossible task of comparing all men with one another (including both past and future men) and with nonhuman nature, but these assumptions can be made under the rule of simplicity of scientific hypothesis or its corollary, the rule of the uniformity of nature. Thus they do not require proof. But, on the other hand, if these assumptions are not correct, they could be disproved by one, or a few clear-cut cases of exceptions to the rule.

Thus, in the final analysis, these rules about scientific hypotheses are not derived from any sense of economy or of esthetics, but rather arise from the nature of demonstration and proof. The familiar judicial rule that a man is to be assumed innocent until he has been proved guilty is based on the same fundamental principles as these rules about scientific hypotheses, and, like these, rests ultimately on the nature of proof. We must assume that a man is innocent (not guilty) until we have proof of his guilt because it is always simpler to assume that things are not so than to assume that they are, and also because no man can prove the negative "not guilty" except by the impossible procedure of producing proof of innocence during every moment of his past life. (If he omits a moment, the charge of guilt could then be focused on the period for which proof of innocence is unobtainable.) But by making the general and negative assumption of innocence for all men, we can disprove this for any single man by the much easier procedure of producing evidence of guilt for a single time, place, and deed. Since it is true that a general negative cannot be demonstrated, we are entitled to make that general negative assumption under the rule of the simplicity of scientific hypothesis, and to demand refutation of such an assumption by specific positive proof.

A familiar example of this method could be seen in the fact that we cannot be required to prove that ghosts and sea serpents and clairvoyance do not exist. Scientifically we assume that these things do not exist, and require no evidence to justify this assumption, while the burden of producing proofs must fall on anyone who says that such things do exist.

The rule of simplicity in scientific hypotheses is by no means something new. First formulated in the late Middle Ages, it was known as "Occam's razor" and was applied chiefly to logic. Later it was applied to the natural sciences. Most persons believe that Galileo and his contemporaries made their great contributions to science by refuting Aristotle. This "refutation of Aristotle," or, more correctly, "refutation of Plato and of the Pythagorean rationalists," was only incidental to the much more significant achievement of making the commonly accepted rules about the universe more scientific by applying to them Occam's razor. This was done by assuming that the heavenly bodies and terrestrial objects operate under the same laws (laws that were later enunciated by Newton). This application of Occam's razor to natural phenomena was a major step forward in making the study of nature scientific. Application of this rule to the social sciences (that is, to phenomena involving subjective factors) still remains to be done, and would provide a similar impetus to the advance of this area of human thinking. It has already been done in judicial procedure (by such rules as the assumption of innocence and the needlessness of proving negatives), and the chief task in American law at the present time is to protect and, if necessary, extend the application of Occam's razor to judicial procedure. Many persons in recent years have felt uncomfortable over the demand that certain persons should "prove" that they are not "communists," but few realized that the unfairness of such a demand rests on the nature of scientific assumption and the nature of proof and, above all, on the violation of Occam's razor.

These rules about the nature of scientific hypothesis are so important that science would perish if they were not observed. This has already happened in the past. During the period 600–400 B.C. in the Greek-speaking world, the Ionian scientists applied these rules about scientific hypothesis by assuming that the heavens and the earth were made of the same substance and obeyed the same laws and that man was part of nature. The enemies of science about the year 400 B.C. made assumptions quite different from those of the Ionians; namely, that the heavens were made of a substance different from those on earth and, accordingly, obeyed different laws, and, furthermore, that man was not part of nature (since he was a spiritual being). They accepted the older idea that the earth was made up of four elements (earth, water, air, fire), but assumed that the heavens were made of a quite different fifth element, quintessence. They admitted that the earth was changeable but insisted that the celestial areas were rigidly unchanging. They claimed that the laws of motion in the two were quite different, objects on the earth moving naturally in straight lines at decreasing velocity to their natural condition of rest, while objects in the heavens moved in perfect circles at constant speed as their natural condition. These nonscientific assumptions, made about 400 B.C. without proof and by violating the fundamental rules of scientific method, set up a nonscientific world view which could not be disproved. The Pythagorean rationalists were able to do this and to destroy science because the scientists of that day, like many scientists of today, had no clear idea of scientific method and were therefore in no position to defend it. Even today few scientists and perhaps even fewer nonscientists realize that science is a method and nothing else. Even in books pretending to be authoritative, we are told that science is a body of knowledge or that science is certain areas of study. It is neither of these. Science clearly could be a body of knowledge only if we were willing to use the name for something that is constantly changing. From week to week, even from day to day, the body of knowledge to which we attribute the name science is changing, the beliefs of one day being, sooner or later, abandoned for quite different beliefs.

Closely related to the erroneous idea that science is a body of knowledge is the equally erroneous idea that scientific theories are true. One example of this belief is the idea that such theories begin as hypotheses and somehow are "proved" and become "laws." There is no way in which any scientific theory could be proved, and as a result such theories always remain hypotheses. The fact that such theories "work" and permit us to manipulate and even transform the physical world is no proof that these theories are true. Many theories that were clearly untrue have "worked" and continue to work for long periods. The belief that the world is a flat surface did not prevent men from moving about on its surface successfully. The acceptance of "Aristotelian" beliefs about falling bodies did not keep people from dealing with such bodies, and doing so with considerable success. Men could have played baseball on a flat world under Aristotle's laws and still pitched curves and hit home runs with as much skill as they do today. Eventually, to be sure, erroneous theories will fail to work and their falseness will be revealed, but it may take a very long time for this to happen, especially if men continue to operate in the limited areas in which the erroneous theories were formulated.

Thus scientific theories must be recognized as hypotheses and as subjective human creations no matter how long they remain unrefuted. Failure to recognize this helped to kill ancient science in the days of the Greeks. At that time the chief enemies of science were the rationalists. These men, with all the prestige of Pythagoras and Plato behind them, argued that the human senses are not dependable but are erroneous and misleading and that, accordingly, the truth must be sought without using the senses and observation, and by the use of reason and logic alone. The scientists of the day were trying to reduce the complexity of innumerable observed qualities to the simplicity of quantitative differences of a few fundamental elements. This is, of course, exactly what scientists have always done, seeking to explain the subjective complexity of qualitative differences, such as temperature, color, texture, and hardness, in quantitative terms. But in doing this they introduced a dichotomy between "appearance" and "reality" that became one of the fundamental categories of ancient intellectual controversy. All things, as the scientists said, may be made up of different proportions of the four basic elements—earth, water, air, fire—but they certainly do not appear to be. The same problem arises in our own day when scientists tell us that the most solid piece of rock or metal is very largely made up of empty space between minute electrical charges.

The Pythagoreans argued that if things are really not what they seem, our senses are at fault because they reveal to us the appearance (which is not true) rather than the reality (which is true). This being so, the senses are undependable and erroneous and should not be used by us to determine the nature of reality; instead we should use the same reason and logic that showed us that reality was not like the appearance of things. It was this recourse to rational processes independent of observation that led the ancient rationalists to assume the theories violating Occam's razor that became established as "Aristotelian" and dominated men's ideas of the universe until, almost two thousand years later, they were refuted by Galileo and others who reestablished observation and Occam's razor in scientific procedure.

The third part of scientific method is testing the hypothesis. This can be done in three ways: (*a*) by checking back, (*b*) by foretelling new observations, and (*c*) by experimentation with controls. Of these the first two are simple enough. We check back by examining all the evidence used in formulating the hypothesis to make sure that the hypothesis can explain each observation.

A second kind of test, which is much more convincing, is to use the hypothesis to foretell new observations. If a theory of the solar system allows us, as Newton's did, to predict the exact time and place for a future eclipse of the sun, or if the theory makes it possible for us to calculate the size and position of an unknown planet that is subsequently found through the telescope, we may regard our hypotheses as greatly strengthened.

The third type of test of a hypothesis, experimentation with controls, is somewhat more complicated. If a man had a virus he believed to be the cause of some disease, he might test it by injecting some of it into the members of a group. Even if each person who had been injected came down with the disease, the experiment would not be a scientific one and would prove nothing. The persons injected could have been exposed to another common source of infection, and the injection might have had nothing to do with the disease. In order to have a scientific experiment, we must not inject every member of the group but only every other member, keeping the uninjected alternate members under identical conditions except for the fact that they have not been injected with the virus. The injected members we call the experimental group; the uninjected persons we call the control group. If all other conditions are the same for both groups, and the injected experimental group contract the disease while the control group do not, we have fairly certain evidence that the virus causes the disease. Notice that the conditions of the control group and the experimental group are the same except for one factor that is different (the injection), a fact allowing us to attribute any difference in final result to the one factor that is different.

The nature of experimentation with controls must be clearly understood, because it has frequently been distorted from ignorance or malice. A number of years ago a book called *Science Is a Sacred Cow* made a malicious attack on science. In this work the method of experimental science was explained somewhat like this: on Monday I drink whiskey and water and get drunk; on Tuesday I drink gin and water and get drunk; on Wednesday I drink vodka and water and get drunk; on Thursday I think about this and decide that water makes me drunk, since this is the only common action I did every day. This perversion of scientific method is the exact opposite of a scientific experiment. In this performance we assumed that all conditions were different except one, and attributed cause to the one condition that was the same. In scientific method we establish all conditions the same except one, and attribute causation to the one factor that is different. In the perversion of scientific method we made an assumption that was not proved and probably could not be proved—that all conditions, except drinking water, were different—and then we tried to attribute causation to the one common factor. But there never could be only one factor the same, since, as an experimental animal, I was breathing air each day and doing a number of other common actions, including drinking alcohol.

There would, perhaps, be no reason to pay attention to this perversion of science if it were an isolated case. But it is not an isolated case. Indeed, the book in question, *Science Is a Sacred Cow,* attracted undeserved attention and was publicized in America's most widely read picture magazine as a worthy book and a salutary effort to readjust the balance of America's idolatry of science. The magazine article in question reprinted extracts from the book, including the section on experimental method, and seriously presented to millions of readers the experimental proof that water is an intoxicant as an example of scientific method.

Scientific method as we have presented it, consisting of observation, making hypotheses, and testing, is as applicable to the social sciences as it is to the natural sciences. To be sure, certain variations in applying it to the social sciences are necessary. But this is equally true of various parts of the natural sciences. These variations are most needed in testing hypotheses. Even in the natural sciences we frequently cannot use two of the three kinds of testing: we cannot use forecasting in the study of earthquakes or geology in general; we cannot use controlled experiments in these fields or in astronomy. But these deficiencies do not prevent us from regarding geology or astronomy, seismology or meteorology as sciences. Nor should similar deficiencies, especially difficulty in forecasting and the impossibility of controlled experimentation, prevent us from applying the scientific method to the social sciences.

The applicability of scientific method to the study of society has also been questioned on the ground that theories of the social sciences are too changeable. We are told that every generation must rewrite the history of the past or even that every individual must form his own picture of history. This may be true to some extent, but it is almost equally true of the natural sciences. Science is a method, not a body of knowledge or a picture of the world. The method remains largely unchanged, except for refinements, generation after generation, but the body of scientific knowledge resulting from the use of this method or the world picture it provides is changing from month to month and almost from day to day. The scientific picture of the universe today is quite different from that of even so recent a man as Einstein, and immensely different from those of Pasteur and Newton. And even at a given moment the body of knowledge possessed by any single scientist or the world picture he has made from that knowledge is quite different from that possessed by other scientists. Yet such persons are all worthy to be called scientists if they use scientific method. The same is true in the social sciences.

The one major difference between the natural sciences and the social sciences is the assumption, made in the former, that human thoughts cannot influence what happens. This is an assumption, justified by the rule of simplicity, although few persons recognize that it is. There is a considerable body of evidence that human thoughts can influence the physical world, but this evidence, segregated into such fields as parapsychology or the psychic world, is not acceptable to the natural sciences. As a result, phenomena such as poltergeist manifestations (largely because they cannot be repeated on request) go unexplained and are generally ignored by the natural sciences. The latter continue to assume that physical processes are immune to spiritual influences.

In the social sciences, on the other hand, it is perfectly clear that human thoughts can influence what happens; and, · accordingly, the social scientist must face the more complicated situation created by this admission. Thus we assume that a rock, dropped from a high window, will fall even if everyone in the world expected it to rise or wanted it to rise. On the other hand, we are quite prepared to see the price of General Motors common stock rise if any large group of people expects it to rise. In a somewhat similar fashion, expectation of a war or desire for a war will make war more likely.

This difference between the social sciences and the natural sciences makes it possible to draw up fairly definite conditions distinguishing between the two: the natural sciences are concerned with phenomena where we do not expect subjective factors to influence what happens, while the social sciences are concerned with phenomena where subjective factors may affect the outcome.

In this book we are concerned with the social sciences thus defined, and particularly with the effort to apply a scientific method of observation, formulation of hypotheses, and testing to such phenomena. The enormous size of this field has made it advisable to curtail our attention to the process of social change, especially in civilizations.

2

Man and Culture

At certain seasons of the year great turtles come in from the sea to deposit their eggs on tropical beaches. They return to the sea immediately, leaving their eggs to hatch in due time from the heat of the sun. Eventually the little turtles emerge from their shells, push up through the warm sand, and head for the sea. There, guided by a sure instinct and without any need for instruction or learning, they take care of themselves, seeking food where it may be found and avoiding the dangers which are everywhere. Enough survive to maturity to maintain this species of turtle in existence.

The ability of this species of turtle to survive depends upon two factors: (1) so many eggs are hatched each year that, even with heavy losses of the young, a sufficient number reach maturity; (2) these turtles are able to grow up without learning or instruction because their nervous systems are connected up and functioning as soon as they emerge from their shells. The newly hatched turtle is not so much an immature turtle as a small turtle. With the exception of his reproductive instincts, a newly hatched turtle is as fully equipped with a functioning muscular and nervous system as is an adult turtle.

Living things that can care for themselves in this way and for this reason are not unfamiliar. Insects do so and so too do such animals as chicks and ducklings. But man is constructed on an entirely different plan. When a baby is born, it is quite incapable of taking care of itself, and remains relatively helpless for years. Indeed, it would seem that twenty or more years are necessary before a human being reaches maturity.

The helpless condition of the newborn human arises from the fact that his neurological and muscular systems are largely undeveloped and uncoordinated. His nervous system in particular is like the telephone system of a great city in which almost none of the connections from phone to phone or from phone to switchboard are closed. Of course, this comparison is by no means perfect, for the human nervous system is much more complicated, much more adaptable, and much faster than any telephone system. The human brain alone, as a kind of central switchboard, has millions of neural connections. Other millions are distributed throughout the body. The way in which these are connected up, or even the fact that they come to be connected up at all, depends on what happens to the child, how he is trained, and how he grows. The things he is capable of becoming originally we can speak of as his potentialities; the things he does become, as the result of experience and training, we can speak of as actualities. The sum of his potentialities we call human nature, while the sum total of his actualities we call human personality. It is quite clear that human nature (potential qualities) is very much wider than human personality (actually developed qualities). Indeed, we might assume that everyone, at birth (or even at conception) has the potentiality for being aggressive or submissive, selfish or

generous, cowardly or brave, masculine or feminine, pug-
nacious or peaceful, violent or gentle, and so forth, and that
which of these potential qualities becomes actual (or to
what degree it does so) depends, very largely, on the way
in which each person is trained or on the experiences he
encounters as he grows up. The fact that there are societies
or tribes in which almost everyone is aggressive (like the
Apaches) and that there are other closely related tribes in
which almost everyone is submissive (like the Zuñi), and
the fact that infants, taken from one such tribe and reared
in the other, grow up to have in full measure the typical
characteristics of their adopted tribe would seem to indicate
both that all such people are potentially about the same at
conception and that their personalities are largely a consequence of the way in which they are reared. If this is so, it is
clear that the way in which people are brought up is very
important. This is, of course, evident from the consideration
already mentioned; namely, that humans are helpless at
birth and must be cared for and trained during a period of
many years. The way in which they are cared for and trained
depends very largely on the personalities of the people
whom they encounter as they are growing up, but these
personalities again depend on the way in which these adults
were reared. Thus there appear in any society certain patterns of action, of belief, and of thought that are passed on
from generation to generation, always slightly different both
from generation to generation and from person to person in
any single generation, but possessing a recognizable pattern.

This pattern depends not only on the way people are
trained to act, to feel, and to think but also on the more concrete manifestations of their social environment, such as
the kind of clothes they wear, the kind of shelters in which

they live, the kind of tools they have for making a living, the kind of food they eat and how they eat it, the kind of toys they have to amuse themselves, as well as the kind of weapons they have to defend themselves. All of these things, patterns of action, feeling, and thought, as well as concrete objects used in these activities, are known in the social sciences as culture. This culture forms the environment in which a child grows up as the natural environment surrounds the baby turtle as it grows up in the sea. Man is surrounded by natural environment, to be sure; but it is much more remote from him than from the turtle, for, in man's case, culture intervenes as a kind of insulation between him and his natural environment. In fact, the surrounding environment of culture penetrates both into him as a person and into his natural environment, changing both. His neurological reactions in behavior, in feeling, and in thought are largely determined by his cultural environment, and at the same time this cultural environment modifies his natural environment by such activities as heating his home, cooking his food, cutting down forests, draining swamps, killing off animals, and generally modifying the face of the earth.

We have said that the individual's reactions in behavior, in feeling, and in thought (what we call his personality) are largely determined by his cultural environment. At the same time, his personality is part of the cultural environment of those people whom he meets. And, as already said, only by such relationships is his personality developed from his human nature. All this makes a human being so different from a turtle that nothing very relevant to human behavior can be learned from the study of turtle behavior. With the turtle we are dealing with a twofold situation: the turtle and his environment. With the human being we are dealing with a threefold situation: the human being surrounded by his culture and both together surrounded by the natural environment—and by other cultures. Where a turtle lays dozens of eggs and hopes that some turtles from those eggs can be carried to maturity by obedience to fairly rigid instincts, the human has almost no rigid instincts, and adapts his personality to his culture. The culture in turn must adapt itself to the natural environment. Thus, if the natural environment changes, the turtle must change his nature, while man merely changes his culture (and thus his personality). But this beautifully flexible relationship requires such a long period of training and learning during which human nature becomes a human personality and the individual becomes able to care for himself, that humans are dependent upon their parents for many years. Accordingly, humans have few offspring, and each offspring is very valuable, since the survival of the species does not depend (as with turtles) on the more or less accidental survival of a very few out of the many reproduced, but depends instead on the ability to bring up almost all who were born and to train them so that they can take care of themselves, have the intelligence to modify their culture (including their personalities) when it becomes necessary to adapt to the environment, and at the same time develop the capacity to use the freedom to change their behavior (which this whole situation assumes) in such a way that it will be beneficial to themselves and to the group on which they depend for the continuation of their culture.

All this leads us to certain tentative assumptions about human nature, about the nature of culture, and about the nature of human society. In regard to human nature, it would seem that we have to deal with two things: (*a*) a wide range of potentiality and (*b*) a drive to make these potentialities actual. The range of these potentialities seems to run a full gamut from the most concrete and material activities, such as eating or moving about, through a broad belt of emotional and social activities to a fairly broad range of spiritual and intellectual activities. It would be rash to say that this range of potentialities has very specific qualities or needs in it or that there are any intrinsic dividing lines separating one potentiality from another. A study of human personalities and human cultures would seem to indicate that these potentialities blur into one another, that each person has opposing (and even incompatible) extremes of each potential quality, and that there can be a good deal of substituting of one potential quality for another as these qualities develop into actual characteristics. Any divisions we may make in this gamut of human potentialities are probably arbitrary and imaginary. We might divide the range into two: physical and spiritual; or into three: physical, emotional, and intellectual; or into four (*a*) material needs, such as food, clothing, shelter; (*b*) sex; (*c*) gregarious needs, such as companionship; and (*d*) psychic needs, such as a world outlook, psychological security, or the desire to know the "meaning" of things. We could, indeed, divide this gamut into forty or into four hundred divisions or levels, since the reality with which our words seek to deal is a subtle, continuous, and flexible range quite beyond our ability to grasp clearly or fully. This range of human potentialities will sometimes be divided in this book, for purposes of historical analysis, into six levels, as follows: (1) military, (2) political, (3) economic, (4) social, (5) religious, (6) intellectual, although this division will always be made with the full realization that it could, with good justification, be made otherwise as five, seven, sixty, or six hundred levels.

This range of human potentialities is also the range of human needs because of man's vital drive that impels him to seek to realize his potentialities. This drive is even more mysterious than the potentialities it seeks to realize. Throughout history men have given various names to this drive, and there have been endless disputes about its names and about its extent and nature. The Classical Greeks, like Aristotle, sought to ignore it by merely assuming that everything had a purpose and that everything by its very nature sought to achieve its purpose. This is generally known as a teleological explanation (from the Greek word *teleos,* meaning purpose or goal). In the Christian Middle Ages this teleological approach was somewhat modified by the belief that, while everything had a purpose, things were drawn to seek to fulfill these purposes by the love of God. About the year 1600 men began to place this drive inside men (driving them on) rather than outside (drawing them on) as before 1600. Spinoza about 1670 called this drive the "soul." About 1818 Schopenhauer called it "will." About 1890 Bergson called it "the vital urge," while at the same time Freud called it "sex." Throughout this later period many natural scientists called it "energy." Without getting into any controversy about the merits of these various terms, we can agree with them all that there does seem to be some force driving men to seek to realize their potentialities.

Before going further to examine how these efforts produce both culture and societies, let us try to sum up our conclusions regarding the divisibility of the range of human potentialities by the following diagram in which the distance between the line *AB* and the line *CD* represents this range.

The various columns represent various ways in which it might be divided. This range as a whole we shall call "the dimension of abstraction":

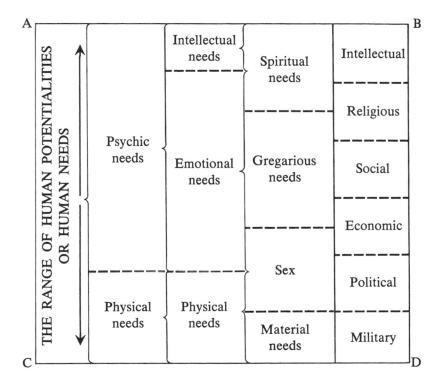

When these potentialities of human nature are realized, they become the characteristics of human personality. This is very helpful, for we cannot directly observe or study human nature, and are compelled to make assumptions as to what it must be like from our studies of human personality. Since the characteristics of human personality emerge from the potentialities of human nature as a result of experience and training, and since each person's experience and training are different, each personality is different. At the same time, since each person in the same society is brought up in the same culture and thus tends to have similar experiences and similar training, most of the persons in a society tend to have a basic personality pattern, with similar general characteristics either emphasized or subdued.

Not only is human personality formed by the social environment; the social environment (or culture) is largely made up of the personalities it has created. In this way culture is passed down from generation to generation, always somewhat changed but always largely the same. From this point of view culture is known as the social heritage, passing on from generation to generation by teaching and learning, most of it unconscious.

When a child is first trying to walk, he may fall without actually hurting himself. What happens in the next few moments may contribute considerably to the formation of his future personality. If an adult swoops down on him, full of sympathetic sounds and commiseration, he may decide that he is hurt and begin to cry. This could easily become one of the earliest steps toward forming a personality that reacts to the unexpected with self-pity. On the other hand, such a fall might lead some neighboring adult to say: "Get up, Jimmy, and try again. You must be more careful and watch where you are going." This could easily be an early step toward self-responsibility and self-reliance. Frequently, after such a fall, the child, if ignored, will be frustrated and resentful. Struggling to his feet, he may strike out at the nearest person or at some inanimate object. Again the reactions of surrounding adults depend upon the personality patterns of the culture, and serve to mold the developing personality of the child. There are societies where a frustrated child who strikes at an innocent bystander might be admired: "Look at that spirit; isn't he the little man!" This serves to encourage the development of a culture based on personalities of irrational aggressions. If, on the other hand, a child who displays an early response of aggression to frustration is immediately stopped, has his hands slapped to discourage such a reaction, and is sternly warned: "You fell because you were not careful and did not watch what you were doing. Mrs. Jones had nothing to do with your fall, so don't you dare strike at her . . . ," in such a case the child's personality will be turned from aggression to self-responsibility.

Episodes such as this occur many times a day in every society. When they occur, the people involved react to them in accordance with their own personality structures. Few of the persons involved in such a situation stop to think that they are involved in a teaching situation and are helping to mold the society of the future by helping to mold the personality of one of its members. In highly integrated societies, such as most primitive tribes, the outcome of each such episode as this will be similar because the adults involved have similar personality structures and, as a consequence, the children growing up, who occasion such incidents, will experience similar reactions and will themselves develop similar personality structures, whatever these may be. In a more complex and more disintegrated society, such as our own, the personality structures of adults are already so varied that it is difficult to say how they would react to the event we have described. Thus quite different reactions might occur, and the children who are at the center of these episodes, by experiencing different reactions will grow up with different personalities, thus continuing and probably increasing the disintegration of the society's behavior patterns. There can be no doubt that we could have predicted the social response to any act of childish aggression a century or more ago with some assurance: the child would have been punished. But today it would be impossible to guess what might happen; and, just as the possible reactions have become more varied, so the personalities developed from such reactions have become more diverse and the society itself has become less integrated.

The culture of a society consists of much more than the personalities of the people in the society. It consists of all the material things they use, such as the dwellings, tools, and clothing already mentioned. It consists of patterns of action, feeling, and thought. It consists of established social relationships between one person and another as well as between persons and objects. It consists of all kinds of fine, subtle, and changeable interrelationships between people and between goups, relationships and feelings that are sometimes obvious but are frequently unobserved, reactions that are so long established (and thus so "natural") that they are neither noticed nor questioned. Each individual in a society is a nexus where innumerable relationships of this character intersect. Taken as a whole, these innumerable relationships (many of them deeply imbedded in his neurological system) form a status, which was slowly created as he grew up and will be abruptly destroyed when he dies. The gap created in the fabric of society by the death of an individual is slowly closed as some of the ruptured relationships are healed over; many others are taken up by different persons; and the many social functions that formed the previous status are taken over by a number of quite separate persons.

Culture is thus a very subtle and very complex thing. From one point of view it is the cushion between man's purely animal nature and the natural environment. From another point of view it is the social heritage passed down from generation to generation. From another point of view it is a complex medley of personalities, material objects, patterns of behavior, subtle emotional relationships, accepted intellectual ideas and intellectual assumptions, and customary individual actions. From any point of view it is constantly changing, and forms the chief subject of study in all the social sciences.

This culture is both adaptive and persistent. It is adaptive because it is able to change, and it is persistent because it will not change without cause. The causes of such social change are both internal and external to the culture. They include the geographic, the biologic, and the cultural environment. The geographic environment includes such things as terrain and climate. Obviously, culture must adapt itself to these; consequently, the Eskimos have quite a different culture from the Arabs of the desert or the jungle Negroes. And it is equally clear that as geographic conditions change, cultures must change too. When all of Europe was under glacial conditions, the cultures there must have been different from what they became when all of Europe was under thick forests (about 8000 B.C.) or under temperate conditions (about 1000 B.C.). The cultures in Europe adapted themselves to these changes.

Similarly, culture adapts itself to changing biologic conditions. When the herring swarmed in the North Sea in the late Middle Ages or the buffalo swarmed on the North American plains in the early nineteenth century, the people living in these areas had cultures adapted to these conditions. But when the herring disappeared or the buffalo were largely exterminated, the people of northern Europe or the

Indians of the Great Plains had to adapt their cultures to such changing biologic environment.

In a similar fashion, but to a much greater degree, cultures must adapt themselves to changing cultural environments. These latter include the culture itself as well as other different cultures. When a culture changes because one part of it must adapt itself to a different part of the same culture, we say that it is self-adaptive. Thus, when a culture gets a different weapon (as when the Indians on the Great Plains obtained the horse after 1543 or obtained guns after about 1780), the religious, intellectual, social, economic, political, and military aspects of the culture are changed by this new acquisition. At the same time a culture must adapt itself to other cultures, as the culture of Western civilization has to adapt itself to the culture of Soviet Russia or as the people of Tahiti or the people of China had to adapt their cultures to the culture of Western civilization during the nineteenth century. When a culture is not able to adapt itself to changes in its geographic, biologic, or cultural environment, it may perish, just as the cultures of the American Indians or the culture of the ancient Carthaginians perished when these peoples were unable to adapt themselves to the impact of Western civilization or to that of Classical civilization. It is worth noting that when animals (like the dinosaurs) are incapable of adapting their physical structure to changes in the environment, the species perishes; but man (who has the insulation of culture between his physical structure and his environment) merely undergoes destruction of his culture instead of destruction of his species when his culture cannot adapt itself to changes in the environment.

It sometimes happens that a culture is unable to adapt itself to changes in part of itself. For example, a change in weapons (which is part of culture) may be so drastic (like the atom bomb) that the other parts of the same culture, such as the economic and political systems, cannot adapt themselves to this military change and the culture will perish. This means that cultural changes are not necessarily progressive, but are frequently irrational, retrogressive, and destructive. A culture may even commit suicide. For example, at a remote period the culture of the Aztec people in Mexico changed on the religious level by the introduction of human sacrifices to one of their gods. The military level adapted itself to this religious change by changing its tactics from an effort to kill the enemy to an effort to capture the enemy (so that captives could be used as religious sacrifices). This change injured the culture's ability to defend itself because the Aztecs no longer fought to defend themselves or to kill their enemies, but fought to capture them for sacrifices. When the Spaniards under Hernando Cortez arrived in Mexico in 1519, the Aztec defense was much hampered by the fact that they were fighting to capture while the Spaniards were fighting to kill.

Because culture is adaptive to itself, it is *integrative;* but, because it is also adaptive to diverse external influences as well as to the human drive to realize human potentialities, no culture ever becomes *integrated.* By "integrative" we mean that the different parts of a culture adapt themselves to one another and tend to become increasingly an interlocking unified system in which each part fits snugly into all the surrounding parts. But this result is never reached, for, at the very moment that one part of culture is adapting itself to another part to become more closely fitted to it, it is becoming less adapted to some third part which is also changing under influences from some other source. Thus no culture ever becomes integrated. This is a good thing, because a fully integrated culture would be rigid and would resist change so completely that it would become incapable of adapting itself to changes in its external environment on the one side and incapable of fulfilling man's drive to realize his potentialities on the other side. A fully integrated culture would be like the dinosaurs, which had to perish because they were no longer able to adapt themselves to changes in the external environment. Accordingly, culture is made up of loose-fitting parts that are only partially adapted to one another, to the environment, and to human needs, and are constantly changing in response to shifting pressures from these three directions. It is able to survive just because it is not rigidly integrated.

So far, we have spoken about culture. This is the part of reality with which history is concerned, but it is only part of the whole picture that historians must examine. The rest of this picture is made up of the persons whose activities created the culture. It must always be remembered that culture is the consequence of persons seeking to realize their potentialities sufficiently to satisfy their inner drives. Without human beings there would be no culture. It is equally true that without culture there would be no humans (but only animals, in direct contact with their natural environment). The whole combination of human beings plus their culture we call by various names such as societies, social groups, or even civilizations. These terms have different meanings that we shall examine in a moment. Before we do, we should sum up the stage we have reached in our discussion.

We could write our last conclusion as an equation, thus:

$$\text{society} = \text{humans} + \text{culture}$$

The society is surrounded by its natural environment to which it adapts itself by changes in its culture. Thus the whole relationship might be represented by a diagram:

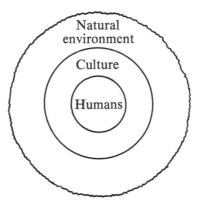

The rigid lines between these concentric circles (like the plus mark in the equation just given) are misleading, because culture is not rigidly separated from the human beings on the one hand and from the environment on the other. Rather it penetrates into both. In fact, much of culture is inside human beings because it takes the form of trained neurological reactions, developed muscles, emotional reactions, ideas both clear and vague, and the established patterns of acting that make the difference between human personality and human nature. Human personality is the part of culture that is inside human beings and can be observed. Also inside human beings, but beyond the limits of our observation, is human nature. Such human nature is made up of potentialities and the drive (or drives) to express these. What these potentialities or drives are we cannot know from observation but only from inferences based on our observations of personality.

In addition to personality (which is inside human beings), culture has manifestations outside human beings. This external culture consists of networks of human relationships, of concrete tools and instruments (called artifacts), and of symbols for communication or expression.

In order to develop their potentialities so that human personalities emerge from latent human nature, human beings establish relationships with one another. As the child develops, these relationships are extended from such fundamental relationships as those with mother and nurse to those with parents, siblings, and teachers, to those with friends, with the opposite sex, with business relations, with representatives of the government (like the police, the tax collector, and the draftboard), and with one's fellow citizens and fellow soldiers. All these relationships, as part of culture, form groups of human beings. Of these groups there are many different kinds. We shall distinguish four different kinds at this point: (1) social groups, (2) societies, (3) producing societies, and (4) civilizations. All are made up of aggregates of human beings with their personalities and external culture.

3

Groups, Societies, and Civilizations

The social sciences are usually concerned with groups of persons rather than with individual persons. The behavior of individuals, being free, is unpredictable. There is more hope of success when we deal with the activities of aggregates of persons because in such aggregates the unpredictable behaviors of individuals tend to cancel each other out and become submerged in the behavior of the group as a whole. While the behavior of such a group may not be predictable, it is less free to change and can, accordingly, be extrapolated in a way that individual behavior does not allow. The same situation exists in the physical sciences, where we are quite unable to predict the behavior of any individual molecule or particle, but can, with assurance, predict the changes that take place in any large aggregate of molecules. These relationships, in the physical sciences, can be stated in the form of "laws" concerning the pressure, volume, size, state, and temperature of aggregates of molecules.

With aggregates of persons we can state no laws comparable to those found in the physical sciences, although we can point out tendencies. For example, if an aggregate of persons in a stable group undergoes a rise in standards of living we can expect a tendency toward an increase in population for the group as a whole, even when we cannot say of any individual in the group that he will have more children or even any children at all. Moreover, we can study the nature and distribution of the increased supply of wealth to determine its effects on the numbers of children in various subgroups within the main group. But in the social sciences, where we must be satisfied with tendencies rather than with laws, we can analyze the working out of such influences and tendencies only if we have a fairly clear idea of the nature and structure of the social groupings involved. This is quite different from the natural sciences where laws about the behavior of aggregates could be made long before men had any clear idea of how such aggregates were made up.

The statement that we can enunciate rules of social tendencies only if we have fairly clear ideas about the nature of social groupings makes it necessary for us to confess that the nature of groups is one of the matters on which there has been wide disagreement in the past. In general men's ideas on this subject could be placed in three classes: (1) those who believed that social groups were merely collections; (2) those who believed that social groups were organisms; and (3) those who denied that social groups were either collections or organisms but argued that they were *sui generis,* a particular kind of aggregate of their own.

The distinctions between these three points of view on the nature of social aggregates could be expressed roughly as follows. A collection is no more than the sum of its parts, and the parts are interchangeable within the collection. An organism is more than the sum of its parts (since they have patterns of relationships), and the parts, being fitted to their position and role in the whole, are not interchangeable. The third class, made up of those who maintain that a social group is *sui generis,* occupy a middle ground between the "collectionists" and the "organicists" since they say that the whole is more than the sum of its parts but that the parts (that is, the individuals in the group) are interchangeable in their functions and positions.

A discussion such as this about the nature of social groups may seem to be a merely academic dispute of little practical significance, but, as a matter of fact, it has been profoundly significant throughout human history. Those who have seen human groups as organisms, from the ancient Greeks to Hitler, have derived from this point of view certain corollaries about the relations of the individual to the group that have been destructive of individualism and of human liberties. For in an organism the parts exist for the sake of the whole and are subordinate to it; they must be sacrificed if necessary for the welfare of the whole. Thus Aristotle says that a man cannot live apart from the state, as an animal could or a god could, because a man cut off from the state is like a thumb cut off from a hand: it is no longer a thumb but merely looks like a thumb. In saying this he is using an organic analogy which explains the totalitarian character of the Greek *polis* or of the later Roman *imperium.* Both were as prepared to sacrifice the individual to the state as we would be to cut off a cancerous thumb in order to save the whole organism.

On the other hand, the argument that a social group is only a collection and thus simply an aggregate of individuals with no established patterns of relationships and with no aims or purposes beyond those of the individuals who make it up is equally pernicious of human values. For a collection can have no established traditions or any purposes of its own and can expect no spirit of sacrifice or of public service from its members; instead, it must expect its members to be as competitive in their relations with one another as they would be toward any member of an outside group.

The middle ground that regards a social group as an aggregate of its own distinctive type avoids the difficulties both of totalitarian organicism and of the rampant individualism of the collectionists. Because of their belief that the whole has pattern, and thus is more than a mere aggregation of individuals, holders of the middle ground are able to preserve social tradition and to encourage devotion to the whole as an entity with its own distinctive values; but by their insistence that individuals are interchangeable within the whole they are able to protect the ultimate value of the individual and to infer that the whole exists for the sake of the individual, and not the opposite, providing him with opportunities to develop his higher potentialities through social cooperation in a way that would not be possible in a mere collection of individuals.

From centuries of argument on these matters there has begun to emerge a sufficient consensus for us to say that students of the social sciences today tend to avoid either of the extreme positions of organicism or individualism and tend to agree that social groups are aggregates of a special kind subject to their own rules and characteristics. Accordingly we must seek to define a social group and to show the various types of these that can exist. There are three basic types of such social aggregates: (1) social groups, (2) societies, and (3) civilizations.

A social group is an aggregate of persons who have had relationships with one another long enough for these to have become customary, and for them to come to regard themselves as a unit with well defined limits. The essential thing about a group is that its members can say who is in it and who is not. The term covers such aggregates as a class in history, a football team, a fraternity, a university, a business concern, a parish or church, a political party or a state. All these groups come into existence gradually as relationships are established and mutual recognition grows. When a class in history or a football squad assembles for the first time, it is not a group, but simply an aggregate of persons, and the group comes into existence only gradually. In fact, it continues to develop as long as it is of any social significance.

A society is a group whose members have more relationships with one another than they do with outsiders. As a result, a society forms an integrative unity and is comprehensible. It is the vehicle of the culture we were talking about before. A society has a culture because it is a unity, and it is a unity because its members have more relationships with one another than with outsiders. A group does not have any culture of its own; the culture of a group is the culture of the society in which the group is. By some stretching of the use of words, the personalities of the members of a group might be regarded as the culture of the group; but culture consists of more than personalities (since it also includes external culture), and the personalities of any group have more relationships with people who are outside the group than with people inside the group, if for no other reason than the fact that these personalities developed by means of relationships with outsiders long before these personalities joined the group. If this were not true, and the personalities of the members of the group had been developed by means of relationships within the group, then this aggregate of which we are speaking is a society and not a group.

It is sometimes difficult for some people to distinguish between a group and a society because they fail to see the most fundamental relationships among people. It is frequently helpful to think of some of the varied relationships that can exist among people. If this is done, it becomes clear that the Zuñi Indians or the Japanese about 1850 were societies, but that a history class, a football team, or a corporation is a group. The Zuñi or the Japanese were societies because they had their religious, intellectual, social, economic, and political relations with other members of the same group. The members of a class, of a football team, or of a corporation have most of these relationships with outsiders. Members of such a group have their religious relationships with the whole Christian tradition, while their intellectual relationships are with the whole tradition of Western culture; their social relationships are with outsiders to the group, such as parents, sweethearts, or friends; their economic relationships are with the whole capitalist economic world and beyond (for example, they drink coffee for breakfast); and their political relationships are with all their fellow citizens and even outside that. In such a wide-flung nexus of relationships, the relatively narrow range of mutual relationships possessed by members of the same class, the same team, or the same corporation shows clearly that these latter are groups and not societies.

The real problem in distinguishing between groups and societies arises when we look at modern political units like the state or nation. Most states, such as Canada, France, Italy, Cuba, or the United States, are not societies but groups because their members' relationships with one another are only political and social, while their religious, intellectual, and economic relationships are in a much wider context. The religious ideas of people in the countries mentioned are expressed in terms of monotheism, the Christian ethical and doctrinal systems, the deity as a masculine being located in the sky, and so forth. There is nothing specifically Canadian, French, or American in these ideas. On the other hand, they are quite different from the religious ideas of peoples in a different society. These latter might be expressed in terms of a female deity residing within the earth, or of nonhuman shape, or demanding human sacrifice, and so on. Similarly, the eating patterns of peoples in all the countries mentioned are very similar: they cook their food, eat bread made from wheat, drink coffee, prefer steaks, and are rather unlikely to be found eating raw blubber or fried locusts. Similarly, they all trace family descent through the father, practice monogamy, have private property, seek profits, accept the scientific tradition, use explosives as weapons, and so on. These similarities are so much more numerous and so much more important than the dissimilarities between these countries that the personality patterns and the general outlook on the universe that bind these people together into a single system of relationships make them have more relationships with one another across political frontiers than they do with members of any single group within such frontiers. The fact that Canadians have more relationships outside Canada than inside it means that Canada could not be understood or even described without using terms like *Christian, scientific, industrial, monogamous, nationalism, Protestant, capitalism, parliament, democracy, railroads, rifles, ballots, radioactivity,* and such. None of these terms, nor the things which they

represent, is of Canadian origin nor can they be understood
in purely Canadian terms. The need to use them in describing Canada means that Canada can be understood only as
part of the larger system from which these words (and the
objects they represent) arise. This large system is, as we
shall see, Western civilization; Canada can only be understood as a political group within Western culture.

This distinction between groups and societies (with the
former defined as an aggregate whose members have more
relationships with outsiders than with one another) means
that a society is a comprehensible unit, while a group is not
a comprehensible unit. A group can be known but it cannot
be comprehended, because comprehension involves knowledge of a major part of the relationships existing in an aggregate. Such knowledge is not possible within a group because
many of the relationships of the members of a group go
outside the group to members of the larger unit, the society,
of which the group is a part.

If a man from Mars, who knew nothing of our customs
but who could, in some mysterious fashion, communicate
with us, were suddenly to appear in the midst of a social
group, among a football squad at practice or in the middle
of a church service, or in a classroom during a lecture, he
would find it utterly impossible to comprehend what was
going on from explanations, no matter how detailed, of the
interrelationships of the members of that group. His most
obvious questions—"What are these persons doing?" "Why
do they do it?" "What do they eat?" "Where does their
clothing come from?" "What happens when one of them
dies?"—or any others of an endless variety of questions
could not be answered except by reference to persons, objects, ideas, or customs outside the group itself. Indeed, it is
a safe rule that no significant questions about anything in-

side a group can be answered except by reference to things outside the group.

On the other hand, when a stranger suddenly arrives in a different society, as R. F. Fortune arrived among the Dobu, B. Malinowski among the Trobriand Islanders, Captain Cook among the Polynesians, Pizarro among the Incas, or Marco Polo among the Chinese, it is possible to obtain explanations and understanding of what is going on if there are communication and sufficient time. Thus, such a society is a comprehensible aggregate, while no social group is comprehensible, using that adjective in its real meaning as referring to something that can be "grasped together."

Since a society is comprehensible, while a group is not, most political units (being groups) are not comprehensible units. Political units are comprehensible only when a single political unit covers the whole of a society. This is frequently not the case, although it is usually true of the more primitive societies organized in tribes. The Zuñi, for example, like many of the other Indian tribes, were both a political unit and a society. Japan and China were, about 1850, comprehensible political units because they were separate societies. In most advanced societies it will be found that the religious, intellectual, social, economic, and even military patterns are roughly coterminous with each other and with the outline of the society as a whole. But in such a society the political units usually cut across these other patterns. We can know a great deal about such political units, but we cannot understand them because understanding requires knowledge of a major portion of the patterns of relationships in society as a whole.

As we examine numerous societies like that of the Eskimos, the Zuñi Indians, the Chinese, the Hottentots, or our own Western civilization, we see that there are two different kinds of such societies: (*a*) parasitic societies and (*b*) producing societies. The former are those which live from hunting, fishing, or merely gleaning. By their economic activities they do not increase, but rather decrease, the amount of wealth in the world. The second kind of societies, producing societies, live by agricultural and pastoral activities. By these activities they seek to increase the amount of wealth in the world. As we shall see later, the distinction between these two kinds of societies is of most fundamental importance. Man was a parasite from his first appearance on the earth, perhaps as long as a million years ago. Only with the discovery of the techniques of agriculture and domestication less than ten thousand years ago did it become possible for man to be a producer, and, even during the last ten thousand years, there have been more parasitic societies (like the Sioux or the Eskimos) than there have been producing societies (like the Zuñi or the Chinese).

If we concentrate our attention on the producing societies that have existed during the last ten thousand years, we see again that there are at least two distinct kinds. There are simple producing societies like the Zuñi (with agriculture), or the Masai (with pastoral herds), and there are much more complex societies that we call "civilizations" (like the Chinese, the Aztecs, or ourselves). The distinction between a civilization and an ordinary producing society is not easy to draw, and it is too early in our discussion to seek to draw it at this time. However, it is clear that most of the civilizations with which we are familiar have had both writing and city life. Accordingly, as a temporary definition, we might say that a civilization is a *producing* society that has writing and city life.

We might sum up our definitions to this point by saying that aggregates of persons may be divided into (*a*) collections, (*b*) groups, or (*c*) societies. The members of a collection, coming casually together in time and place, have no established relationships. The members of a group do have relationships sufficiently established to be able to identify who is or who is not a member of the group, but they have the major portion of their total relationships with persons who are not members of the group. A society, on the other hand, is made up of persons who have the major part of their relationships with one another. It may be either parasitic or producing, and if it is a producing society it may or may not be a civilization. These rather simple but very significant distinctions can be summed up in a table:

AGGREGATES OF PERSONS
A. Collections
B. Groups
C. Societies
    1. Parasitic societies
    2. Producing societies
        a. Simple tribes or bands
        b. Civilizations

When we examine these three kinds of societies (parasitic, producing, and civilizations), we see that there have been very many parasitic societies, a much smaller number of producing societies, and very few civilizations. As for the relative numbers of each, we might say that there have been hundreds of thousands of the first, at least thousands of the second, but not more than two dozen civilizations. Since our chief concern in this book is with our own society, which is a civilization, the rest of this book will be concerned with the nature of this particular kind of society only.

Of the two dozen civilizations, all of which existed during the last ten thousand years, seven have been alive in recent years, while the rest, amounting to approximately seventeen in number, lived and died long ago. All of them, both living and dead, can be divided into three groups depending upon the carbohydrate plant they produced as an energy food. There were three such foods: maize, rice, and grain (wheat and barley). In the maize group were two civilizations: (*a*) the Andean civilization, which began about 1500 B.C., culminated in the Inca Empire, and was destroyed by outside invaders about A.D. 1600; (*b*) the Mesoamerican civilization, which began about 1000 B.C., culminated in the Aztec Empire, and was destroyed by similar invaders about A.D. 1550. Both of these civilizations were derived from a common source, a producing society which was not a civilization, probably situated in some hilly area in the northern part of South America.

The "rice" group is somewhat misnamed since the chief carbohydrates which supported it in the earliest period and have continued to be used since were millet and wheat. This group has at least three (and perhaps as many as six) civilizations in it. Only an expert on the history of the Far East could speak with confidence on this subject. Since this is not one of our chief areas of interest, we shall oversimplify the situation by listing no more than three civilizations. Of these the earliest, Sinic civilization, rose in the valley of the Yellow River after 2000 B.C., culminated in the Chin and Han empires after 250 B.C., and was largely disrupted by Ural-Altaic invaders after A.D. 400. From the debris of this Sinic civilization there emerged two other civilizations: (*a*) Chinese civilization, which began about A.D. 400, culminated in the Manchu Empire after 1644, and was destroyed by European intruders in the period 1790–1930; and (*b*) Japanese civilization, which began about the time of Christ or a little earlier, culminated in the

Tokugawa Empire after 1600, and may have been completely disrupted by Western intruders in the century following 1853.

The earliest civilizations are to be found neither in the maize group nor in the rice group, but in the much more important group of "grain civilizations." This group is more important not only because it contains the first civilizations to come into existence but also because it contains such a large number of civilizations, seventeen at least. The earliest civilizations were derived from a number of closely related producing societies that we shall call the Neolithic Garden cultures, or, less accurately, the Painted Pottery Peoples. The latter were the first peoples to have agriculture, and thus formed the earliest producing societies in history. At the risk of considerable oversimplification, we might say that these earliest agriculturalists appeared in the hilly terrain of western Asia, probably not far from Armenia, about nine thousand years ago. Because they knew nothing about replenishing the fertility of the soil, they practiced "shifting cultivation," moving to new fields when yields declined in their old fields. In consequence, they expanded steadily, reaching Denmark and Britain in the west and China in the east before 2000 B.C., that is to say, within five thousand years. In the course of this movement they found, in various alluvial river valleys, sites adapted to permanent large-scale settlement because, in such valleys, the annual flood replenished the fertility of the soil by depositing a layer of fertile sediment; and, accordingly, the need for "shifting cultivation" ended and the possibility of permanent, eventually urban, settlements was offered. This possibility was realized in four alluvial valleys of the Old World, in Mesopotamia during the sixth millennium B.C., in the valley of the Nile shortly afterward, in the valley of the Indus River early in the fourth millennium B.C., and in the Huang Ho Valley of China late in the third millennium B.C. The last of these has already been mentioned as the source of the Sinic civilization, which was the parent of the Chinese, Japanese, and probably other Far Eastern civilizations.

The first civilization, known to us as the Sumerian or Mesopotamian civilization, began after 6000 B.C., reached a peak of achievement about 1700 B.C., and ended in a series of empires of which the last was the Persian. That empire and the civilization of which it was the political aspect were destroyed by outside invaders, the Greeks under Alexander the Great, after the end of the fourth century. Parallel with this, a quite different civilization in the Nile Valley reached its peak about 2300 B.C., established its greatest geographic extent as the Egyptian Empire a millennium later, and was destroyed by the same Greek invaders in the few generations following 330 B.C.

While this was going on, other civilizations appeared, flourished, culminated in their respective empires, and perished at the hands of outside invaders in a strikingly similar process. In the Indus Valley the Indic civilization began about 3500 B.C., reached a peak of achievement about 2200 B.C., culminated in a political empire that we might call the Harappa Empire, and was destroyed by the Aryan invaders who came into the Indian subcontinent from the northwest after 1700 B.C. From the wreckage of this culture, there was constructed a quite distinct civilization, which we may call Hindu. This reached a peak of achievement about 100 B.C., and culminated in a series of empires of which the last, called the Mogul Empire, was established early in the sixteenth century. This empire and the civilization of which it formed a part were destroyed by European invaders in the centuries following 1700. From the wreckage of this Hindu civilization a new civilization seems to be coming into existence in our own time.

Returning to the Nearer East we can see that a number of different civilizations appeared there, largely from Mesopotamian inspiration. On the island of Crete the earliest civilization outside an alluvial valley began to form toward the end of the fourth millennium B.C. It reached its peak in the Minoan period, about 1500 B.C., and ended with the Mycenaean Empire, destroyed by the Dorian invaders in the twelfth century B.C.

In Anatolia, in the second millennium B.C., rose and fell the shortest-lived of all civilizations. Known as the Hittite civilization, this had its beginnings after 2000 B.C., reached its widest imperial extent about 1300, and perished a few generations later from the onslaughts of invading Iron Age intruders, cousins of the Dorians who were simultaneously destroying Cretan civilization.

In the Levant, during the same period, there appeared, under Mesopotamian stimulus, a civilization we might call Canaanite. Beginning before 2000 B.C., it reached its greatest extent, from the Red Sea to Spain, about 900 B.C., and ended with that empire which, called Punic by the Romans and Carthaginian by us, was known to themselves, more accurately, as Canaanite. It perished from Roman invasion before 100 B.C.

From the wreckage of Cretan civilization there began to grow, about 1000 B.C., a new civilization with which we are well acquainted. Known as Classical civilization, or Mediterranean civilization from the sea whose shores it occupied, it reached its greatest peak in the century divided at 400 B.C., and finally culminated in the Roman Empire. It was destroyed, as is generally known, by the Germanic "barbarian invaders" in the fifth century of our era. From its wreckage emerged three civilizations: (*a*) Western civilization, which may culminate in an American empire; (*b*) Orthodox civilization, which seems to be culminating in the Soviet empire; and (*c*) Islamic civilization, which did culminate in the Ottoman Empire, and was disrupted by intruders from Western civilization in the first half of the present century.

In this enumeration we have named sixteen civilizations. Of these, two existed in the New World, three in the Far East, one in Africa, and the others in the rest of Eurasia. With careful study it would be possible to distinguish approximately eight more civilizations divided about equally between the Near East and the Far East. We refrain from attempting to do this because the facts are not clear and any conclusions would be disputable. The Near East and the Far East in the history of civilizations are like complex masses of quartz from which numerous crystals protrude in various directions. The number of crystals in the mass might be disputed, and there would surely be disagreement about which portions of the main mass of quartz should be attributed to each crystal. It is possible that detailed study of the problem, like microscopic examination of the quartz, might help to solve this problem, but for our purpose the task is not worth the effort. Just as it is possible for adjacent molecules in the quartz mass to be oriented in diverse directions so that they should, perhaps, be attributed to different crystals, so it is possible (and indeed is well established) that individual persons living next to each other in, let us say, Palestine in the thirteenth century B.C., should from their personal orientations be attributed to Hittite civilization or to Egyptian civilization or to Canaanite civilization or even to Mesopotamian civilization. Such attribution of individuals to civilizations is no matter of any historical significance and need not concern us here. Nor need we worry, at this time, about the eight or more additional civilizations that have existed at various times in Ethiopia, Cambodia, Indonesia, or Tibet. Let us study the nature of civilizations, as a scientist would study the nature of crystals, by examining the more clearly demarked and less controversial examples of our subject.

Leaving aside for the moment the two civilizations found in the New World, we can arrange the fourteen Old World civilizations into a pattern to show their chief cultural connections. Many other connections, which we do not show on the diagram, exist in fact and can be inserted by the cognizant reader. It is to be noted that four of the early civilizations are cultural descendants of the Neolithic Garden cultures, which were not themselves civilizations (since they lacked both writing and city life):

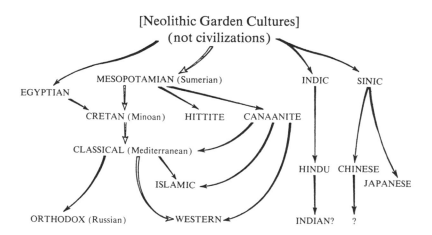

In this diagram the family tree of our own Western civilization (a lineage involving three generations between the Neolithic Garden cultures and ourselves) has been marked with a double line. The meaning behind these lines and the other cultural connections shown on the diagram will be indicated later.

For later reference the following table gives the name, approximate dates, the name of the culminating empire, and the outside intruders who terminated its existence for the sixteen civilizations mentioned:

NAME	DATES	EMPIRE	INVADERS
Mesopotamian	6000–300 B.C.	Persian	Greeks
Egyptian	5500–300 B.C.	Egyptian	Greeks
Indic	3500–1500 B.C.	Harappa	Aryans
Cretan	3000–1100 B.C.	Minoan	Dorians
Sinic	2000 B.C.–A.D. 400	Han	Huns
Hittite	1900–1000 B.C.	Hittite	Phrygians
Canaanite	2200–100 B.C.	Punic	Romans
Classical	1100 B.C.–A.D. 500	Roman	Germans
Mesoamerican	1000 B.C.–A.D. 1550	Aztec	Europeans
Andean	1500 B.C.–A.D. 1600	Inca	Europeans
Hindu	1500 B.C.–A.D. 1900	Mogul	Europeans
Islamic	600–1940	Ottoman	Europeans
Chinese	400–1930	Manchu	Europeans
Japanese	100 B.C.–A.D. 1950 (?)	Tokugawa	Europeans
Orthodox	600–	Soviet	?
Western	500–	?	?

4

Historical Analysis

We have already mentioned our belief that civilization is an object that can be studied in a scientific way just as a quartz crystal can be studied. In such a study we must, like the student of crystals, examine in a comparative way a large number of examples—even, ideally, all the examples available. But it is obvious that a civilization is a much more complicated object than a crystal. Let us be explicit about that word "complicated." A civilization is complicated, in the first place, because it is dynamic; that is, it is constantly changing in the passage of time, until it has perished. Furthermore, a civilization is part of the social sciences; that is, it contains subjective elements, and these are usually the more important elements in the culture. Accordingly, in a civilization, unlike a crystal, what people think or feel can influence what exists, changing the object completely in the process. In the third place, many aspects of a civilization are continua, existing in such subtle gradations and in such varied degrees of abstractness that the divisions we make in it, in the course of our analysis, and the words we use as symbols to refer to our analytical divisions reflect only very roughly the situation that exists in the reality itself. All three of these difficulties are important, but the third, which is frequently ignored in discussions of these matters, requires a little further examination—for that reason, at least.

Much, if not all, of the physical world consists of continua. To say this is equivalent to saying that much of the physical world is irrational. It exists and it operates, but it does these things in ways that cannot be grasped by our conscious rational mental processes. This can be seen most easily if we consider first a few examples of continua in the physical world.

How many colors are there in a rainbow? Some answer three—red, yellow, blue. Others answer six—red, orange, yellow, green, blue, violet. When I was a child in school, for some unknown reason, we were told that there were seven colors, the teacher inserting "indigo" between blue and violet. The proper answer, of course, is that the number of colors in the rainbow is infinite. This in itself is something we cannot grasp in any rational way. But let us consider what it means.

In the first place it means that there is, in the rainbow, no real line of division between any two colors. If we wish to draw a line we may do so, but we must recognize that such a line is imaginary—it may exist in our minds, but it does not exist in the rainbow itself.

Moreover, any line that we draw is arbitrary, in the sense that it could have been drawn with just as much justification somewhere else, perhaps only a hairbreadth ·away. If we draw a line between red and orange and another between orange and yellow, we may call the gamut between those two lines orange, but, as a matter of fact, the color is quite different on either edge of that gamut. We may decide that orange is a narrower range than the gamut between our two lines and, accordingly, slice off the margins of the orange gamut, calling the severed margin on one side yellow-orange and the severed margin on the other side red-orange. But once again the color is not the same across any of these three ranges. In fact, it is impossible to cut off any gamut in a rainbow, no matter how narrow we make it, in which the color is the same across the width of the gamut. We can move no distance, however infinitesimally small it may be, across the rainbow without a change in color. This means that the number of colors in the rainbow is infinite. But it also means that the number of colors in any portion of the rainbow is infinite. That is, there are as many shades of orange as there are colors in the whole rainbow, since both are infinite. Now, this is a truth that we cannot understand rationally. It seems contrary to logic and reason that we could add all the existing shades of red and yellow to all the existing varieties of orange without increasing the number of color varieties we have. The reason is not so much that infinity added to infinity gives infinity as that there are no different varieties of colors at all, because there are, in fact, no dividing lines in the rainbow itself. When we use the plural terms "colors" and "shades" in reference to a rainbow, we are implying that there are different colors and accordingly that there are divisions in the rainbow somehow separating one shade from another and thus entitling us to speak of these in the plural. Since there are no such lines of separation, we would be more accurate if we spoke of the rainbow in the singular as "a continuum of color." But, of course, we could not do this consistently because it would make it impossible to think about or to talk about the colors of any objects. Since the continuum changes across its range, it is distinctly different in color from one portion to another, just as dresses, flowers, or neckties are different in color from one another. If we are going to talk about these very real differences, we must have different words for the different colors involved. Thus we must give different color terms to different portions of the rainbow's gamut. The important truth to remember is that, while the differences beween colors are real enough, there are no real divisions between colors: these are arbitrary and imaginary.

As is well known, the gamut of radiations of visible light that we call the rainbow is not an entity in itself but is an arbitrary and imaginary portion cut out of a much wider gamut of electromagnetic radiations. The variety of colors in the rainbow arises from the fact that the radiations of visible light come at us in wave lengths of different frequency. As the wave lengths of these radiant forms of energy get smaller (and thus their frequency gets larger), we observe this difference as a shift in color toward the blue end of the visible spectrum; as the wave lengths get longer (and the frequency less), we observe a color shift toward the red end of the spectrum. If this shift of wave length continues, the radiation may pass beyond the range to which our eyes are sensitive. Beyond the red we can notice these radiations as heat (infrared); beyond the violet we might have difficulty noticing the radiations directly, but their consequence would soon appear as a kind of sunburn on our skin. Once again there is no dividing line between the visible gamut of radiations and the ultraviolet on one side and the infrared on the other side. Some persons can "see" further into these than others can, and other forms of living creatures can "see" further into one or the other range than any human could. Bees, for example, are fully sensitive to ultraviolet radiations, while humans are generally so insensitive to these that they consider glass windows, which cut off most ultra-violet, as being fully transparent.

The gamut of radiant energy is much wider than the three subgamuts we have mentioned. Beyond the invisible ultra-violet are other radiations of even shorter wave length, including soft X rays, hard X rays, and finally the very high-frequency gamma waves released by nuclear explosions. Going the other way in the radiation range, we find that there are radiations of increasing wave length beyond the infrared which we call heat. These radiations of lower frequency and longer wave length include those used to carry our radio and television broadcasts. While we sit here reading, quite unaware of their passage, these radiations are going through our bodies. They are different from the visible light that allows us to see to read only in the wave lengths and energy content of the radiations.

This great gamut or range of energy radiations, from the shortest gamma waves at one end to the longest broadcast waves at the other end, forms a continuum. The difference between a deadly gamma radiation and an enjoyable television broadcast, like the difference between red and blue, is a very real difference, but it is only a difference of wave length (and thus a difference of distance) and not a difference of kind. Accordingly, no real lines of demarcation exist in the gamut itself, and the whole range forms a single continuum.

The quality of being a continuum that exists in the range of electromagnetic radiations is not a quality that has anything to do with energy or with radiations, but is true simply because these radiations exist in space and differ from one another because of space distinctions, namely, their wave lengths. This spectrum is a continuum, and therefore irrational, because space is a continuum, and therefore irrational.

The irrationality of space sounds a little strange to most of us because we are so familiar with space that we rarely stop to think that we do not really understand it. But the irrational quality of space (which arises from the fact that space is infinitely divisible) is one of the early discoveries of ancient intellectual history. By 2000 B.C. the Babylonians were familiar with the fact that the square of the hypotenuse of a right-angle triangle is equal to the sum of the squares of the other two sides. Introduced to the Greeks in a generalized form by Pythagoras before 500 B.C., this statement came to be called the "Pythagorean theorem." Unfortunately, Pythagoras also taught that reality was rational and that the truth can be found by the use of reason and logic alone, without any need for observation through the senses, which would merely serve to confuse us. This rationalist method for discovering the nature of reality was accepted by Socrates and Plato (and, in his earlier period, by Aristotle) and led to the death of ancient science by contributing to a denigration of observation, testing of hypotheses, and experiment. It is one of the great ironies of history that thinkers like Pythagoras and Plato helped to kill ancient science by propagating the belief that observation was not necessary since reality was rational, and therefore its nature could be found by the use of reason and logic alone, long after a pupil of Pythagoras, Hippasus of Metapontium, had used the Pythagorean theorem to demonstrate that space (and thus reality) is irrational.

The demonstration of the irrationality of space arose from

the proof that the diagonal of a square is incommensurable with its side. We would say that, if the side of a square is one unit long, its diagonal, by the Pythagorean theorem, is $\sqrt{2}$ units long. And the square root of 2, we say, is an irrational number. But few of us really know what we mean by the word "irrational" in this sense. There are three ways of looking at it, each a slightly different way of looking at a quite irrational situation. We sometimes say that $\sqrt{2}$ is an endless decimal which begins with 1.41421 . . . and continues forever in an infinite series of digits which never ends and never repeats itself. Or we could say that $\sqrt{2}$ is a number which cannot be expressed as a fraction—that is, as a ratio between two rational numbers. But both of these statements are simply alternative ways of talking about the utterly irrational fact that there is no common unit of distance, no matter how small we make it, which will go into the side of a square a certain number of times and will also go into the diagonal of the square a round number of times without anything left over. Rationally we would think that if we took as a unit of measurement a distance which was infinitely small—like one-sextillionth of a cat's whisker or even one-sextillionth of that or however small a unit was needed—that we could eventually find a unit so small that it would go evenly into both the side and the diagonal. But the fact is that there is no unit, however small, which will go evenly into both distances, so that there is no common unit between them, and we must say that they are incommensurable. But this is not a situation that is rationally comprehensible to our conscious reasoning powers, and it is quite nonlogical. But it is true.

This quality of irrationality of space is not something exceptional, either in space or in other aspects of reality.

The radius of a circle is similarly incommensurable with its circumference; the irrational relationship between the two distances is signified by the ratio we call π. This quality of irrationality rests on the fact that space is infinitely divisible; no matter how close together we make two points, the number of points between them remains infinite. The infinite colors of the rainbow, like the incommensurability of a square and its diagonal or of a circle and its radius, are simply applications of this irrational quality of space.

A similar irrational quality is to be found in time. We usually think of time as a succession of intervals. It is really a continuous flow, and any intervals we may choose to put into it, be they seconds, hours, or centuries, are arbitrary and imaginary. And in consequence, any conclusions we derive or any inferences we may draw from such intervals may be mistaken. We have twenty-four hours in the day as a purely conventional arrangement going back to our early ancestors in the Neolithic Garden cultures who had a number system based on twelve and passed on to us, as relics of that system, such arrangements as twelve eggs in a dozen, twelve inches in a foot, twelve pennies in a shilling, twenty-four parts in a carat, twelve ounces in a pound of gold, twelve deities on Mount Olympus, and many other odd facts of which one of the most pervasive today is that teen-age begins with thirteen. From the Neolithic belief that day or night should each have twelve parts we derived our twenty-four-hour day, but since these divisions are arbitrary and imaginary, we could with equal justification have a day of ten hours or of twenty-three or twenty-five hours.

Most of us are familiar with the paradoxes of Zeno, especially with the one about a race between Achilles and a tortoise. Zeno argued that if the tortoise got a head start, Achilles could never catch up with him even if he could run much faster. Zeno felt that if the tortoise was a certain distance ahead when Achilles started, the tortoise would move forward a little farther while Achilles was covering the handicap distance and would, thus, still be ahead when Achilles finished the handicap distance. Accordingly, Achilles must keep on running to overcome the new increment, but by the time he had made up that increment the tortoise would have moved forward a new amount and would still be slightly ahead. According to Zeno, this process would continue forever, the tortoise advancing a decreasingly small amount while Achilles was making up the tortoise's previous increment. A mathematician might say that the distance between the two would approach zero as a limit but would reach that limit only after an infinite number of intervals (either of time or of distance) and that Achilles would, accordingly, not catch up in any finite number of intervals.

The explanation of this paradox of Zeno's rests on the fact that the space and time through which the contestants are running are both continua, but Zeno, by treating them as if they were a succession of intervals, introduced an untrue condition, and from this contrary-to-fact assumption (that time or space exists as a sequence of intervals) he derived a contrary-to-fact conclusion (that Achilles can never catch up).

Such paradoxes are good examples of the methodological rule that logic and rationality do not apply to continua. As we shall show later, this is one of the basic rules of historical method (although, it must be confessed, few historians give it much thought).

Space and time are not the only continua. Another familiar example is the system of real numbers. Since this is a continuum, we can state a rule: no two numbers can be

placed so close together that there is not an infinite number
of numbers between them. For example, between 3 and 4
are an infinite number of numbers. One of these is π. As we
have said, π is irrational, and, accordingly, although it is a
very exact number we cannot write it with the ordinary ten
symbols used in writing numbers. If we say that π is 3.14,
we do not refer to a single number but are really saying that
π is one of the infinite number of numbers in the gamut from
3.135 to 3.145. In that gamut we could indicate that π was
in a much narrower gamut (which still contains an infinite
number of numbers) by writing its value as 3.141592. This
refers to the infinite number of numbers in the gamut of
numbers ranging from 3.1415915 to 3.1415925. Since the
value of π is known to over a thousand decimal places, we
can define the gamut of numbers within which π lies more
and more narrowly simply by carrying the numerical expression for π to more decimal places. But each gamut, no
matter how narrow it gets, refers to an infinite number of
numbers, because the system of real numbers is a continuum.

To those who are not familiar with mathematics, all of
this discussion of $\sqrt{2}$ and of π may seem very strange, unreal, and unapplicable to anything with which they are
concerned. I hope to show that the remarks I have just made
about numbers are applicable not only to statements we all
make about many familiar things but also to history.

A moment's thought will show that any statement about
any continuum is just the same kind of statement as that
which we have just made about π. Just as any value we may
give to π refers to a gamut containing an infinite number of
numbers and this gamut can be made narrower by carrying
our statement of the value of π to more decimal places, so
any statement about any color refers to a gamut that con-

tains an infinite number of colors. Thus the word "orange" does not refer to a single color (any more than 3.14 refers to a single number), but rather refers to the gamut of colors between red and yellow. If we narrow this gamut by speaking of "yellow-orange," we still are referring to an infinite number of colors. And we could make the gamut narrower by referring to "orange yellow-orange" or to "yellow yellow-orange," thus bisecting the previous gamut. This process could be continued indefinitely, just as the value of π can be carried to more decimal places. The value, however, of carrying either very far is not large.

We have been talking about rainbows, numbers, and space-time in order to establish what we mean by a continuum. Now we can define the term in the sense that we shall use it in discussing history. "A continuum is a heterogeneous unity each point of which differs from all the surrounding points but differs from them by such subtle gradations in any one respect that no boundaries exist in the unity itself, and it can be divided into parts only by imaginary and arbitrary boundaries."

We might add that some continua are perfect while others are highly imperfect, the distinction being that a perfect continuum has an infinite number of gradations between any two boundaries drawn in it, no matter how closely together they are drawn, while an imperfect continuum has a finite number of gradations between at least some of the boundaries drawn in the continuum. For example, the gamut of variations of light intensity during any twenty-four-hour period is a perfect continuum. But the "races" of mankind, however defined, are an imperfect continuum. For the variations in any standard we set as a criterion for race can be no more numerous than the number of individual human persons on the earth (that is, no more than a few billion variations) instead of the infinite number we expect to find in a perfect continuum. If, for example, we set color of skin as the criterion of "race," and we were to arrange the human beings on the globe in some magical fashion in a long line with the blackest black man at one end and, next to him, the second blackest man, and so on, in ascending order of light reflection from their skin surfaces, until we passed through all the blacks, browns, reds, yellows, and whites to end up with the whitest white man on the globe, possibly an albino Norwegian—if we were to do this, I feel confident there would be no place on that long line where any two adjacent persons would have any difference in skin color sufficient to be distinguished by any normal physical process. We might then decide that men, based on skin color, form a single race. Or, if we insist on having more than one race, we might simply divide the line at its midpoint and settle for two races—the "lights" and the "darks." But however many races we decided upon, there would be no discernible difference in skin color between any two adjacent persons between whom we drew a boundary line. Nevertheless, in the final analysis, this range of skin color would represent an imperfect continuum, because the variation of skin color between any two boundary lines or in the range of mankind as a whole would be numerable and not infinite.

We might, on the other hand, arrange mankind in a line on the basis of height. In that case we would have several billion variations over a total height difference of no more than seven or eight feet, giving an average difference between any two adjacent persons of no more than one fifty-millionth of an inch, a difference which is, once again, too slight to be discernible by any normal procedures and is, indeed, considerably less than the normal increase and de-crease of any one person's height caused by rest and exercise during a day. Indeed, if we tried to arrange the persons of the world in order by height we would find the daily changes in individual height to be relatively so much greater than the average height differences between individuals that persons would be compelled, from their constantly changing heights, to change their positions in the line by hundreds of thous-ands and even millions of persons at relatively short inter-vals. If we were to use such a criterion as height as a measure of race, we could do so only so long as people were locally segregated into groups of obviously different average heights. As soon as people began to move about or mix socially, the classification would break down. And we could never classify racially, on this basis, any isolated individual.

We deal with continua rationally either by dividing them into arbitrary intervals to which we give names, or by giving names to the two ends of the continuum and using these terms as if the middle ground did not exist at all. This last method is called "polarizing a continuum," and is frequently done even when the greatest frequency of occurrence is in the middle range. When the telephone rings in the sorority house because someone wants a "blind date," the sisters at once ask the vital question, "Is he tall or short?" They ask this question even though it is perfectly obvious that the majority of men are neither tall nor short but are nearer the middle range. Such polarization of continua is so common and so familiar that we come, frequently, to accept our categories as real instead of being arbitrary and imaginary, as they usually are. An accident report asks, "Day or night?" although accidents are most frequent when it is neither day nor night, but dusk. Many questionnaires polarize continua by asking us to check: "White—Colored?" "Man—Woman?" "Pro—Con?" In English law this is done in the distinctions between "Adult—Juvenile" or "Sane— Insane." In the social sciences it is done in such contrasts as "monopoly—competition" in economics, "democratic— authoritarian" or "totalitarian—liberal" in politics. We have already done it several times in this book, as in the dichotomy between natural science and social science or between objective and subjective. The familiar polarization of man into spirit and flesh dominated religious ethics for centuries.

This practice of slicing continua into parts or even into dual poles and giving names to these artificial categories is necessary if we are to think about the world or to talk about it. But we must always remain alert to the danger of believing that our terms are real or refer to reality except by rough approximation. Only by making such divisions can we deal in a rational way with the many nonrational aspects of the world.

We could, of course, renounce any desire to deal with the world rationally and content ourselves with successful nonrational dealings with it. We can deal with the irrationality of space, time, quantity, number, race, color, and so forth, simply by action. Merely to walk, or to run like Achilles, is to deal with the irrationality of space and time and to discover, by action, who will win in a race. When we merely walk along, talking with our friends, we are, by walking, dealing successfully with space and time. No one could ever walk rationally. Simply stand still and make an effort to walk rationally. What is the first thing to do? And what should be done next? What messages must be given to which muscles and in what sequence? We do not know, and we could not do such a complicated mental operation quickly enough to walk by any rational thinking process.

When we approach history, we are dealing with a conglomeration of irrational continua. Those who deal with history by nonrational processes are the ones who make history, the actors in it. But the historian must deal with history by rational processes. Accordingly, he must be aware of the processes and difficulties to which we have referred when we try to deal with continua rationally. For history deals with changes in society. And all changes, occurring in time, involve continua. Both society and culture are, even if static, concerned with continua. Indeed, a society is a continuum of continua in five dimensions.

When we say that a society or a civilization exists in five dimensions, we are referring to the fact that it exists in the three dimensions of space, the fourth dimension of time, and the fifth dimension of abstraction. All of these are easy to understand except the last. Let us look, for a moment, at this fifth dimension of abstraction. It is clear that every culture consists of concrete objects like clothes and weapons, of less tangible objects like emotions and feelings, and of quite abstract things like ideas. These form the dimension of abstraction. For example, in Western civilization we have such items as the following: (*a*) automobiles, (*b*) romantic love, (*c*) nationalism, (*d*) Beethoven's string quartets, and (*e*) the integral calculus. All of these are clearly products of Western civilization and could not have been produced by any other culture. They are of different degrees of abstractness and, accordingly, we can say that Western culture exists in a fifth dimension, the dimension of abstraction. This is the same dimension as the gamut of human needs to which we previously referred. However, it is wider than this gamut. It may be similarly divided into six levels, in a rough and approximate fashion. These divisions are arbitrary and imaginary, and even the order in which we list the levels is partly a matter of taste. These levels are, from the more abstract to the more concrete: (1) intellectual, (2) religious, (3) social, (4) economic, (5) political, and (6) military. Each of them could, if necessary, be subdivided into innumerable sublevels, as, for example, the economic into agriculture, commerce, and industry or into production, distribution and consumption. Such varied divisions and subdivisions are made possible by the fact that the reality is much more subtle and complex than are the categories of our thinking processes.

Assuming such a sixfold division of culture, it becomes possible to make a rough diagram of the history of any culture by letting the vertical axis represent the dimension of abstraction and the horizontal axis (from left to right) represent the passage of time. Thus:

	1500	1600	1700	1800	1900	2000
Intellectual						
Religious						
Social						
Economic						
Political						
Military						

In the above diagram we have represented the changes in culture from 1500 to 2000. The changes that take place in any single level (however we divide it or subdivide it) we shall call "development." Thus we may speak, for example, of the "intellectual development" or of the "military development" of a culture. The process of change on any single level we shall speak of as "historical development" (always remembering that the divisions between levels are arbitrary and imaginary and that we can make as many or as few as we like, because the levels really merge into each other).

Since the levels of culture arise from men's efforts to satisfy their human needs, we can say that every level has a purpose. Assuming the sixfold division we have made, we can speak of six basic human needs: (1) the need for group security, (2) the need to organize interpersonal power relationships, (3) the need for material wealth, (4) the need for companionship, (5) the need for psychological certainty, and (6) the need for understanding. To satisfy these needs, there come into existence on each level social organizations seeking to achieve these. These organizations, consisting largely of personal relationships, we shall call "instruments" as long as they achieve the purpose of the level with relative effectiveness. But every such social instrument tends to become an "institution." This means that it takes on a life and purposes of its own distinct from the purpose of the level; in consequence, the purpose of that level is achieved with decreasing effectiveness. In fact, it can be stated as a rule of history that "all social instruments tend to become institutions." The meaning of this rule will appear as we discuss its causes.

An instrument is a social organization that is fulfilling effectively the purpose for which it arose. An institution is an instrument that has taken on activities and purposes of its own, separate from and different from the purposes for which it was intended. As a consequence, an institution achieves its original purposes with decreasing effectiveness. Every instrument consists of people organized in relationships to one another. As the instrument becomes an institution, these relationships become ends in themselves to the detriment of the ends of the whole organization. When people want their society to be defended, they create an organization called an army. This army consists of many persons with different duties. Each person takes as his purpose the fulfilling of his duties, but this soon leaves no one in the organization with the purpose of the organization as his primary purpose. The purpose of the organization—in this case, to defend the society—becomes no more than a secondary aim for everyone in the organization. Defense becomes secondary to discipline, keeping authority in channels, feeding and paying the troops, providing supplies or intelligence, and keeping visiting congressmen, or the people as a whole, happy about the army, the personal comforts of the soldiers, and so on. Moreover, as a second reason why every instrument becomes an institution, everyone in such an organization is only human and has human weakness and ambitions, or at least has the human proclivity to see things from an egocentric point of view. Thus, in every organization, persons begin to seek their own advancements or to act for their own advantages: seeking promotions, decorations, increases in pay, better or easier assignments; these begin to absorb more and more of the time and energies of the members of an organization. All of this reduces the time and energy devoted to the real goal of the organization and injures the general effectiveness with which an organization achieves its purposes. Finally, as a third reason why every instrument becomes an institution, the social conditions surrounding any such organization change in the course of time. When this happens the organization must be changed to adapt itself to the changed conditions or it will function with decreased effectiveness. But the members of any organization generally resist such change; they have become "vested interests." Having spent long periods learning to do things in a certain way or with certain equipment, they find it difficult to persuade themselves that different ways of doing things with different equipment have become necessary; and, even if they do succeed in persuading themselves, they have considerable difficulty in training themselves to do things in a different way or to use different equipment.

Military history offers numerous examples of the institutionalization of instruments. The Roman army, which had conquered most of the known world by means of the legion, was unable, and probably unwilling, to transform itself into a force of heavily armed cavalry when this became necessary in the late fourth century of our era. As a result, the Roman army, and the civilization it was supposed to defend, were wiped from the earth by the charging horsemen of Germanic barbarians, beginning with the dreadful defeat at Adrianople in 378. The inability of fighting men to reorganize their ideas and their forces from infantry to cavalry was one of the vital factors in the replacement of pagan Classical civilization by Christian Western civilization.

In the centuries from A.D. 700 to 1200, cavalry in the form of the medieval knight became as established in military tactics as the Roman infantry had ever been. In 732 the Saracens, whose relentless advance had begun in Arabia a century before, were defeated by the cavalry of Charles Martel at Tours, and the Christian West was saved from

Moslem conquest. By 1099 the Western counterattack had reached in apex in the capture of Jerusalem. In the three-century interval between these two victories, Germanic and Frankish cavalry, under Charlemagne, Otto the Great, and others, had saved Western culture from numerous pagan threats. Methods of fighting from horseback had become well established, almost formalized, and had begun to assume those chivalric embellishments that contributed so much to the institutionalization of this method of warfare. Noble youths, as we all know, spent years in jousting and tournaments to achieve the skill considered necessary for success on the field of battle.

The supremacy of the medieval knight was still unquestioned in the early decades of the fourteenth century. The defeat of French chivalry at the hands of bourgeois infantry before Courtrai in 1302 was dismissed by the losers as an inexplicable and unrepeatable accident. On the Celtic fringe of Britain, similar defeats at the hands of lower-class long-bow men were more readily recognized for what they were, a new and successful tactic, and bowmen were incorporated into the English armies. By means of this innovation, English mercenary armies were able to inflict a series of disastrous defeats on French feudal forces in the century following the opening of the Hundred Years' War in 1338. The inability of the French knights to analyze their defeats is one of the best examples we have of the reactions of an institutionalized force to weapons innovation. Of the numerous blinders on their eyes, the most significant perhaps was their inability to conceive that men of low birth could kill men of noble blood from a distance. A similar inability, in the same period, made it impossible for the noble cavalry of

Burgundy and of the Hapsburgs to analyze their defeats at the hands of Swiss pikemen.

The advent of gunpowder and the intensification of fire-power made cavalry obsolescent in the early nineteenth century and obsolete before the end of that century, yet by 1900 cavalrymen were still dominant in many armies and enormous resources were devoted to an army that was, by that time, largely worthless. As early as the Crimean War (1854–56) the poet Tennyson saw that it was a blunder to send cavalry charging against gunfire. The American Civil War should have shown clearly the demise of offensive cavalry and even the fraudulent nature of its claim that it was, at least, "the eyes of the army." Yet the postwar reminiscences of officers were filled with the exploits, largely based on institutionalized self-deception, of military men. Reviewing some of these reminiscences, in its issue of October 31, 1868, the *Army and Navy Journal* said: "The day of the saber is over. The late civil war in America, which taught so much both in military and naval science, made it manifest that cavalry as cavalry had finished its work. Already fifty years before, at Waterloo, the havoc made in the matchless 'Old Guard,' the consummation and ideal of cavalry, by the English infantry, had destroyed the prestige of heavy cavalry on the actual battlefield. But since then, the perfection of rifled arms, both in infantry and artillery weapons, has made its downfall absolute. It is a question of shock against shock; and, with 'modern arms of precision,' a compact body of infantry can empty every saddle in a charging squadron before it arrives to where sabers can be used." Leaving aside, for the moment, the fact that firepower, as these words were written, had also condemned any

"compact body of infantry," we must emphasize the fact
that these remarks on the role of cavalry went largely un-
heeded in military circles. By the end of the century cavalrymen, in all armies except the French and the Germans, were
organizing, both formally and informally, to maintain the
role of cavalry in military forces and to secure promotions
for fellow cavalrymen.

The talent "experts" have for seeing what they expect to
see or what they are trained to see rather than what is there
to see is nowhere better shown than in the tactical discussions preceding World War I. In giving evidence before the
Royal Commission on the [Boer] War in South Africa, that
intrepid cavalryman Douglas Haig announced firmly, "Cavalry will have a larger sphere of action in future wars." That
was in 1904. Fourteen years later, as British commander in
chief in France (having succeeded in that post another
cavalryman, Sir John French), Haig had to cooperate with
the commander in chief of the American Expeditionary
Force, also a cavalry general, John Pershing. Pershing's
obsession with the importance of cavalry made it necessary
for him to carry on two wars, one against the Germans and
another, almost equally virulent, against Peyton C. March,
Chief of Staff in Washington. Much of this struggle, in
which Pershing, as a public hero, was generally successful,
was concerned with the control of transatlantic shipping
space, which Pershing wanted to utilize for horses and
fodder, while March sought to reserve it for men and
ammunition.

In an analysis of this problem in 1935, the military historian Liddell Hart wrote: "French, Germans, Russians, and
Austrians had unexampled masses of cavalry ready at the

outbreak of war. But in the opening phase they caused more trouble to their own sides than to the enemy. From 1915 on, their effect was trivial, except as a strain on their own country's supplies: despite the relatively small number of British cavalry, forage was the largest item of supplies sent overseas, exceeding even ammunition, and thus the most dangerous factor in aggravating the submarine menace; while by authoritative verdict, the transport trouble caused in feeding the immense number of cavalry horses was an important factor in producing the Russian collapse."

Nor does the story of cavalry complete the picture of how military institutions distort men's picture of reality to the injury of their stated aims. A more significant and more frightful example is to be seen in the bayonet. This steely blade was made obsolete by increased firepower almost as rapidly as the cavalry's saber, yet the change went equally unobserved by most experts. In fact, the cause of the obsolescence of both saber and bayonet, the great increase in firepower, especially from machine guns, went equally unobserved. According to the book, as taught in military schools and training manuals, victory in battle was achieved by methods perfected by Napoleon, as analyzed by Clausewitz (1780–1831). On this basis orthodox expertise established that victory was to be achieved by the three successive stages of artillery barrage, bayonet assault with infantry, and cavalry pursuit with saber. To this, near the end of the nineteenth century, the Frenchman Charles Ardant du Picq added the murderous addendum that all three of these stages were really secondary to morale. General Ferdinand Foch, for many years in charge of advanced training of French officers, entrenched these professional and erroneous views by reporting, from his on-the-field studies of the Russian–Japanese War of 1904–05, that machine-gun fire would not reduce the effectiveness of bayonet charges.

A third example of institutionalized thinking in military tactics in this period might be called the doctrine of the "straight front." According to the book, the worst error a commander could make would be to allow his unit to be cut off from his line of supplies and to be caught in a "crossfire." To avoid these errors, it was "imperative" to advance with a straight front against the enemy, even if this required holding back the advance at defensively weak spots and throwing reserves at the enemy's strong points. Simply by reversing this rule in March 1918 (by advancing as rapidly as possible and by throwing reserves at the defensive weak points, thus bypassing and isolating his strong points), Erich von Ludendorff made the most spectacular advances of the war, bursting over Chemin des Dames and being stopped finally, ten weeks later, thirty-four miles from Paris —stopped because he could not bring himself to use his unorthodox methods with full conviction and resources.

As a consequence of the institutionalization of military tactics by devotion to the bayonet, the saber, and the straight front, the early years of World War I saw the largest casualties in history, suffered, in most cases, to advance over a few miles of devastated terrain. In the early months of 1916 almost a million casualties were suffered by both sides in a single battle (Verdun), while later in the same year another battle (Somme) cost 1,200,000 casualties, mostly by bayonet charges against machine-gun fire. When civilians in England tried to force the professional soldiers to use the tank, or civilians in Germany tried to make the professionals use poison gas against machine guns, both were resisted bitterly. When the civilians succeeded in ordering the military to use these innovations, their use was sabotaged by the soldiers. The refusal of the British Command, in 1915, to yield to civilian requests to shift their munition orders from ineffective shrapnel to high-explosive shells for barrages against trench defenses led to an acute intragovernmental crisis that gave impetus to the rise of David Lloyd George. In the American army of 1918 a major part of training time was devoted to bayonet practice. As late as 1940 this was still true, although in the interval the casualty statistics of World War I had shown that the casualty figures from bayonet wounds were microscopic. Noncommissioned officers, skilled in bayonet tactics, were reluctant to abandon something that they knew and could teach, and justified their inertia, in spite of the statistics, on the grounds of the presumed morale-raising attributes of cold steel. From experiences such as these, the French premier, Georges Clemenceau, drew the conclusion that "war is far too important to ever be entrusted to soldiers."

Clemenceau might well have broadened his remark to say that everything is too important ever to be entrusted to professional experts, because every organization of such professionals and every established social organization becomes a vested-interest institution more concerned with its efforts to maintain itself or advance its own interests than to achieve the purpose that society expects it to achieve. As a consequence, old established armies and navies have frequently been defeated by new forces that have not yet become institutionalized. Thus the Greeks defeated the Persians; the new Roman navy defeated the Carthaginian fleet; the English defeated the French chivalry in the Hundred Years' War; the English navy, barely seventy-five years old, defeated the Spanish Armada; Braddock was defeated; the Colonists won the American Revolution; the new French armies of Napoleon defeated the old, bedecorated forces of Austria and Prussia; the new Prussian army of Emil von Roon and Helmuth von Moltke defeated Austria and France in 1866 and 1870; the Boers held off the English for years; and Japan defeated Russia in 1905. Such defeats can be avoided only by constant reform that seeks to reorganize an institutionalized force so that its aim—to defeat the enemy —remains always paramount.

This situation appears in every social organization. Workers join together to get better pay and working conditions. The organizations they form, labor unions, soon take on a life of their own, and the workers begin to wonder if they are not now as much the slaves of the union as formerly they were slaves of the management. The kings of England, long ago, created a representative assembly to consent to taxation. Soon that assembly (Parliament) took on life of its own and ended by decapitating, removing, and ruling kings. A political party was organized in 1854 to protect freedom in the United States and to prevent the extension of slavery. By 1868 it was an organized machine of vested interests, a functioning spoils system, whose chief aim was to perpetuate itself in office and whose chief method for achieving that aim was to end the freedom of the whites in the South. A church is organized to bring men psychological security by linking them with the Deity. A century later it has become a vested institution with wealth and power, and its chief aim is to preserve and expand these valuable prerogatives. A college is organized to train youth in practical and humane achievements; later it has become a whole tissue of vested interests in which standards are lowered and admission qualifications relaxed in order to secure a flow of tuitions that go to meet the institution's expenses. Within its hallowed walls, professors intrigue for promotions and appointments for themselves and their disciples, while a condition of undeclared war goes on between departments and schools to get larger student enrollments in their courses and thus justify bigger slices from the annual university budget. Even in earlier days, professors of the classics resisted efforts to reduce required Latin from four years to two, or to make Greek completely elective, or to abolish compulsory chapel, or to establish a first (elective) course in chemistry without any efforts at any objective analysis of the purposes of these activities or of their role in training youth for later life; that these changes would reduce the established system's control of the college was, in most cases, a sufficient argument to oppose change.

We see fraternities, established to promote fellowship among students, with the passage of time become vested institutions serving to destroy fellowship by dividing the students into uncordial and competitive cliques to the jeopardy of real academic goals. A game called football was invented about 1870 to provide healthful physical exercise for the undergraduates on bright autumn afternoons. Seventy years later the undergraduates who needed exercise most were seated in the stands of a city baseball park on Friday night, with their flasks and their coeds, while on the grass (or mud) below, the undergraduates who needed exercise least pushed each other about under the floodlights.

The process by which football was, almost imperceptibly, transformed from an instrument for providing physical exercise to an institution acting as an obstacle to exercise for many students who loved the game and needed the exercise is as instructive an example of social development as changes in military tactics. The informal games of the 1860s and early 1870s between groups from the same campus led, little by little, to challenges for games with other institutions. This led to travel expenses, more formalized rules, nonpartisan officials, and uniforms. The increase in interest led to larger groups of spectators. What could be more natural than to pass a hat among these spectators to raise money for the players' expenses? Defeats led to desire for revenge, and thus to stricter rules of team membership, practice, and training. All of this led gradually to more formalized coaching. This task rested at first with the captain and more experienced players, but, as established intercollegiate rivalries began to grow, an experienced player of previous years, usually the last victorious captain, was asked to return from the outside world to coach intensively during the week before the "big game." As other colleges adopted this pattern and several "big games" a year emerged, the demands on graduates to return to the campus for coaching duty became more than could be fulfilled. The obvious solution, a full-time paid coach, made it essential to have an established team income. "Passing the hat" among the spectators was replaced by sales of tickets at a fixed price. But sold tickets entitled spectators to a seat, which led very quickly to the building of the first modern stadium (1903). In time stadiums were being built with borrowed funds, with the result that their mortgage charges, along with coaches' salaries and other expenses, made it essential that the stadium's seats, no matter how numerous, must be filled, or nearly filled, on the eight or so Saturdays a year it was used.

Gradually the interests of the spectators and the need for football income became dominant over the interests of any undergraduate who liked football or needed exercise. The team had to win, at least most of the time, and the game had to be spectacular to watch. Scouts looked for able players outside and, in one way or another, persuaded them to come to the scout's college to play football. Financial rewards proved, in many cases, to be powerful persuaders. Thus the game shifted from undergraduates who needed exercise to those who had already had too much exercise. At some institutions, where football incomes were earmarked for educational uses such as for building funds, almost all games were played in baseball parks of large cities remote from the campus, with the result that the team could rarely be seen by its own students. Teams that played on the East Coast, the West Coast, and the Gulf Coast on successive weekends spent much of the autumn traveling and might be away from their college halls for weeks.

When the depression cut attendance in the early 1930s, many games were scheduled in the evening to attract working spectators. For the same purpose the rules were manipulated to give more open play, high scores, and superiority to the offense. By reducing the diameter of the ball, it was made easier to pass and harder to kick, in the belief that spectators preferred passing. Restrictions on passing requiring a minimum distance behind the scrimmage line for the passer or penalizing successive incompleted passes were removed. To keep the ball moving on offense, the referee was instructed to move the ball in fifteen yards from the side lines when it became dead closer than that distance from the sides. At no point in this process did many persons stop to ask themselves, "What is the purpose of football anyway?" But those who look at football's ninety years of development can see quite clearly how an organization which originally rose as an instrument for undergraduate exercise had become something quite different, to the jeopardy of undergraduate exercise.

This process, which we call the institutionalization of instruments, is found in almost all social phenomena. The purpose of music, I suppose, is to provide pleasure from sounds. Various notes are combined together for this purpose and are thus a medium for achieving the purpose of music. But if the same combinations are much used and long continued, they cease to provide pleasure and even cease to be heard. They become "banal." New combinations of sound are devised, usually over the objections of the academician defenders of the older banal combinations who call the innovations "dissonance" or even "discord." But soon the new combinations become accepted, give pleasure, and after much use become banal. They have become institutionalized. Later students, looking back over the development of music, frequently wonder what all the excitement was about. It is difficult for us today to hear the "dissonance" that contemporaries heard in Mozart; we even have some trouble hearing the "discords" with which Stravinsky so shocked the musical world in 1913.

A similar process can be seen in painting, sculpture, architecture, drama, opera, poetry and, indeed, in most human activities. Works that caused riots at their debuts, like Hugo's *Hernani* or Eliot's *Prufrock,* leave us cold or only slightly moved. They have reached a condition equivalent to music's banality. Expressions that were vivid, concrete, evocative, and thus "poetical" when first used become "prosaic." The expression "Let us get under weigh," which once would recall a full-sail vessel getting under the weight of its anchor and thus off to sea, has now become so lacking in these poetic qualities that editors, proofreaders, and even H. W. Fowler insist on spelling "weigh" as "way."

There is of course nothing particularly original in the statement that organizations begin with devotion to a purpose and somehow along the way get turned from that purpose and gradually become a collection of special interests. The historians of religion frequently point out this process by distinguishing between "religion" and "clericalism." To escape this transformation, the Quakers renounced all organizational features, but it can hardly be said that they have been successful in escaping completely from what seems to be an inevitable process of change. Thorstein Veblen devoted much of his analysis of our economic system to a similar process which he contrasted by such dichotomies as industry versus business, workmanship versus vested interests, or the engineers versus the price system.

The process of which we speak was generalized by Charles Péguy in *Notre Jeunesse* when he said, "Everything begins as *mystique* and ends up as *politique*." In his own experience he had seen the idealism and broad humanitarianism of the original Dreyfusards gradually transformed into the selfish grasping at political power of the Combes ministry. The experience seared his idealistic soul to the point where he welcomed death from German guns in 1914. Fortunately for the survival of mankind most of us are not so sensitive as Péguy, for the institutionalization of social instruments is the most widespread of historical phenomena, and no observant person can fail to notice it. We shall point out many examples of this process in the rest of this volume.

When instruments become institutions, as they all do, the organization achieves its function or purpose in society with decreasing effectiveness, and discontent with its performance begins to rise, especially among outsiders. These discontented suggest changes, which they call reforms, just as we see happening in American elementary and secondary education today. When these suggestions are not accepted or are rejected by the established groups who control the criticized organization, conflicts and controversies begin, the discontented seeking to change the organization, while the vested interests seek to maintain their accustomed methods of operation. While all good or all wrong is never entirely on one side in such controversies, discontent and controversy are unlikely to rise to any important level unless the organization is well institutionalized and considerably less effective than the society as a whole expects. Accordingly, when this degree of discontent is reached, the vested-interest groups are generally tending to defend a relatively ineffective system and the "reformers" are, among many mistakes, generally advocating measures that would increase the organization's relative effectiveness in achieving its social purpose.

The strain between the two groups engaged in a struggle such as this will be called, in this book, "the tension of development." From this tension and its ensuing controversy, there may emerge any one (or combination) among three possible outcomes: reform, circumvention, or reaction. In the first case, reform, the institution is reorganized and its methods of action changed so that it becomes, relatively speaking, more of an instrument and achieves its purpose with sufficient facility to reduce tension to a socially acceptable level. In the second case, circumvention, the institution is left with most of its privileges and vested interests intact, but its duties are taken away and assigned to a new instrument within the same society. This second method is much used by the English. The king was left covered with honors, but the task of governing England was taken over by Parliament and ultimately by a committee of Parliament. The Lord Warden of the Cinq Ports has a brilliant uniform and a drafty castle, but the task of guarding the seas of England was given to the Royal Navy in the sixteenth century. The Earl Marshal of England is left with titles and social prestige and still manages the coronation, but the job of leading the army was given to a commander in chief. In the period before the tenth century, when Europe needed defense, an organization called feudalism grew up to provide this need, and performed its task so well that European culture was preserved from the assaults of the Saracens, the pagan Germans, and the eastern raiders. In fact, feudalism performed its task so well that by 1100 Europe was mounting that counterassault that we call the Crusades. But within three hundred years, feudalism had become a vested institution of hereditary privileges and emoluments. It was circumvented by creating in the society a new organization, called the Royal Army, to which the task of defense was given. The privileged vested interests of feudalism were neither reformed nor abolished but were left as a structure of honor and rewards that we call chivalry and the hereditary nobility.

In the third possible outcome, reaction, the vested interests triumph in the struggle, and the people of that society are doomed to ineffective achievement of their needs on that level for an indefinite period. The agrarian system of ancient Rome was an inefficient method of producing food even in respect of the existing technical knowledge, but to reform it would have involved abolition of slavery and division of the large estates. The reformers who wanted to do this were assassinated by the daggers of the landlords, some on the floor of the senate itself. As a result, the economic needs of the Roman system could be met only by the use of other levels, especially by military conquest and by political exploitation of conquered provinces. But in time, both the political and the military organizations became ineffective vested institutions. The result was civil war and eventual conquest by outside barbarians.

When an institution has been reformed or circumvented, there is once again an instrument on the level in question, and the purpose of that level is achieved with relative effectiveness. But, once again, as always happens, the new instrument becomes an institution, effectiveness decreases, tension of development rises, and conflict appears. If the outcome of this conflict is either reform or circumvention, effectiveness increases and tension decreases. If the outcome is reaction, ineffectiveness becomes chronic and tension remains high.

As a result of this process of historical development, the development of each level appears in history as a pulsating movement. Periods of economic prosperity alternate with periods of economic stagnation; periods of religious or intellectual satisfaction alternate with periods of religious or intellectual frustration. Periods of political order or military success alternate with periods of political disorder or military disaster.

This process of historical development takes place on innumerable levels of a society because there are innumerable levels to the culture. But this process is only one aspect of the historical evolution of a society. The other aspect we call historical morphology; it is concerned with the relationships between the different levels of culture in a society.

Before we examine it, we might state, in a formal way, three definitions:

1. Historical development is concerned with the changes that take place on any single level of culture in a society.

2. Historical morphology is concerned with the ways in which one level of culture influences the other levels of culture in the same society.

3. Historical evolution is a resultant of historical development and historical morphology, both acting simultaneously and reacting on each other.

"Morphology" is a word borrowed from biology. It means that the parts of a living organism are adapted to one another. In its most obvious sense it means that a giraffe could not possibly have the neck of an elephant nor could an elephant have the legs of a giraffe. But it also has a more subtle meaning. When we speak of a heavyweight boxer we frequently mention his "best fighting weight." This means that, given his height, reach, age, experience, and all the rest of his specifications, there is an optimum weight for his best fighting ability. If he is over that weight, he is slowed up; if he is under that weight, his blows lack impact. On the other hand, if he is at his best fighting weight, there is also an optimum length for his arms or an optimum height. If his reach or his height varies by much from these optimum points, his fighting ability will suffer. All of these are morphological relationships.

The same kinds of morphological relationships appear in a society. The ability of a society to defend itself on the military level is dependent on its ability to provide domestic order on the political level, wealth on the economic level, companionship on the social level, understanding on the intellectual level, and psychic certainty on the religious level. At the same time the ability of the society to defend itself affects its ability to achieve these five other goals. Thus each level is closely connected with all the others. It would be quite impossible to support a mechanized army without a fairly centralized political system, without a highly industrialized economic system, or without a fairly active scientific tradition on the intellectual level. On the other hand, a military system like feudalism, in which men fought as trained specialists on horseback, could be supported by a completely decentralized political system (in which there was no state at all) or by a purely agricultural economic system, and with an intellectual system which emphasized honor and loyalty rather than knowledge or science. Such a system existed in Western Europe about the year 1100, just as the system indicated in the preceding sentence exists in Europe in the twentieth century.

Just as there is an optimum length for a giraffe's neck (given all his other measurements as fixed), and just as there is a best fighting weight or a best length of reach for a heavyweight boxer (given all his other measurements as fixed), so also there is an optimum point of development on each level of culture (assuming all the other levels have reached fixed points of development). This optimum point for each level in relationship to the development of each other level is the point at which morphological tension is least. This means that time and energy on each level can be devoted to achieving the purpose of each level and need not be used up in interlevel friction because of the need to speed up the development of another level; nor need such energy and time be used in any one level in amounts beyond that which would be required to attain a certain degree of achievement on that level because of the inadequacies of some other level. For example, if the point of development of the political level is morphologically inadequate, more time and energy must be expended on the economic or the military level to achieve a certain amount of production or protection from these levels. All this is really nothing more than a rewording of our previous statement that culture is integrative. And just as we said, at that time, that culture never gets integrated and that it would be a bad thing if it did, so we can say here that morphological tension never reaches zero and that it would be a bad thing if it did (for then the society would be rigidly frozen into an unchanging pattern and would perish).

We can picture this somewhat more clearly with the aid of a diagram. In this diagram we shall mark, very roughly, the point which we believe our Western society has reached on each of the six levels of culture:

Intellectual						X
Religious	X					
Social		X				
Economic				X		
Political			X			
Military					X	

Each of these points is a very rough estimate because each represents the resultant of a large number of sublevels. For example, the point we have indicated on the Intellectual Level represents the resultants of a very advanced science, a very backward art, a fairly mediocre humanities, and other factors. The backwardness of our religious development or of our social developments represents the widespread frustration of these human needs, the low level of our appreciation of the nature of deity, the widespread failure to establish any feeling of relationship between this deity and man's spiritual life and, on the social level, the widespread frustration of men's gregarious needs in a society built on great cities, millions of unrecognized faces in those cities, and a general lack of established, satisfying social relationships.

The advanced point indicated on the economic and military levels indicates the extraordinary success we have had in producing wealth and in directing power against outside societies. Our amazingly high standards of living are proof of the advanced status of the economic level, while the number of outside societies that we have destroyed (from the American Indians and the Australian aborigines to Mandarian China or Mogul India) are witness to our success on the military level. The advanced states of both of these levels are largely due to the even further advanced state of our intellectual level. The fact that the latter is still in advance of the economic or military level means that its morphological influence on them is still tending to pull them forward. On the other hand, the backwardness of these two levels (and, indeed, of the three others as well) in relationship to the intellectual level is tending to hold the development of this last level back. Thus each level acts upon all the others.

The backwardness of our religious and social developments is undoubtedly holding back the development of the intellectual and political levels. At the same time, the relatively advanced state of the intellectual, economic, and military developments of our society is forcing the political development forward, while the backwardness of the political level has a tendency to hold the developments on the military, economic, and intellectual levels back. The backwardness of one level of development in respect of other levels of development is widely recognized among students of society, and is called "cultural lag."

In the specific case we have just mentioned (the cultural lag of the political level), we are also dealing with a widely recognized fact. Our political organization, based as it is on an eighteenth-century separation of powers and on a nineteenth-century nationalist state, is generally recognized to be semiobsolete. We hear demands for a "European federation" or for a "twentieth-century Congress." The breakdown of the separation of powers is evident in the rapid growth of administrative regulation (which disregards such separation). The need to adapt the United States Constitution to the speed of communication of the twentieth century is evident in the Twentieth Amendment, which moved the inauguration date up from March 4 to January 20. The need for further adaptation is clear from the fact that the American Congress still spends hours of its inadequate time on verbal roll-call votes when it could make a permanent-record vote by electricity in a few seconds. The power of vested institutionalism is evident in congressional resistance to a reform that would force congressmen to make a public record of their positions on each bill.

One last example of morphological interrelationships, and that the most extreme, could be found in the relationship of the atomic bomb to Western civilization. This bomb was a product of our advanced development on the intellectual, economic, and military levels. The fact that this great discovery of atomic fission was used for a purely destructive purpose is due to the backwardness of our religious, social, and political levels. But the advanced condition of certain levels, as signified by the bomb, has undoubtedly had profound influences on the three more backward levels and will force them to advance more rapidly. There can be little doubt that the advent of atomic warfare on the military level has had profound effects and will have even more profound effects on the three backward levels. People are, in consequence of its use, turning again to the problem of religion or the inadequacy of our political development. The decentralization of our cities is a process already clearly evident from such forces as improved communications (telephone) and transportation (automobiles), and is reflected in the growth of suburbs and the decrease in metropolitan growth; if the atom bomb speeds up this process, it will probably lead to a considerable advance on the social level. As people disperse from the great beehives of modern cities to the more intimate living of the suburbs and countryside, there will undoubtedly be a considerable improvement in the satisfaction of men's needs for companionship on this social level.

Even in our oversimplified diagram of six levels, it is clear that the process of morphology is a complex one. There are thirty-six interrelationships between the six levels we have, and, since each relationship works both ways, there are seventy-two factors at work. But when we remember that the divisions between these levels are arbitrary and imaginary and that really there are an infinite number of levels, each acting upon all the others, pulling these others forward or backward and being pulled backward or forward in turn, it is clear that the reality of cultural morphology is unbelievably complex. The number of factors at work with an infinite number of levels is infinity raised to the infinite power and multiplied by two. This is a number large enough for anyone.

What happens in a society as a whole, what we called "historical evolution," is a resultant of historical development and morphology acting both independently and upon each other. If a level of development is going through the process of development that we have described—the process of institutionalization of instruments with growing tension —the outcome of such tension, as between reform, circumvention, and reaction, may well be determined by morphological factors. A level, regarded as if it were alone, may have all the factors necessary to produce reform. But the influence of morphology may produce reaction. Something like this occurred in Spain in the period 1930–40. There, all the factors on the political level seemed to be leading toward reform, but the backwardness of the five other levels and the great power of the institutionalized vested interests on those five other levels turned political reform into political reaction.

We have said that the evolution of a society is a resultant of the two kinds of change that we call development and morphology. Let us now turn our attention to this larger issue, the historical evolution of a society, restricting our attention to the kind of society with which we are chiefly concerned, namely, a civilization.

5

Historical Change
in Civilizations

It is clear that every civilization undergoes a process of historical change. We can see that a civilization comes into existence, passes through a long experience, and eventually goes out of existence. We know, for example, that Mesopotamian civilization did not exist about 10,000 B.C.; it did exist about 3000 B.C.; it had ceased to exist by A.D. 1000. Similarly, it is clear that Classical civilization did not exist about 1500 B.C.; it clearly did exist about 500 B.C.; and it had obviously passed out of existence by A.D. 1000. And, finally, it is clear that Western civilization did not exist about A.D. 500; it did exist in full flower about A.D. 1500; and it will surely pass out of existence at some time in the future, perhaps before A.D. 2500. Now, while everyone will probably agree with all this, it would be difficult to obtain agreement on any specific dates on which these events occurred. This difficulty arises from the fact that civilizations come into existence, rise and flourish, and go out of existence by a slow process which covers decades or even centuries, and historians are unable to agree on any precise dates for these events. This is perfectly proper: if Classical civilization came into existence by a slow process and went out of existence by a slow process, it would give a false appearance of rigidity to fix its dates, say at 1184 B.C.–A.D. 476, as has sometimes been done. In the following discussion it should be remembered that the dates given for historical periods are only approximate.

Beyond recognizing that civilizations begin and end, historians are fairly well agreed that, after they begin, they flourish and grow for a while, that eventually they reach a pcak of power and prosperity, and that they weaken and decay before their final end.

This process of evolution of civilizations can only be studied in an effective fashion if we divide it into a number of consecutive periods. We might divide it into two periods, such as "rise" and "decline"; we might divide it into three periods, such as "youth," "maturity," and "old age"; or we might divide it into five or fifty periods. The process of change in the history of any civilization is a continuum and, accordingly, the periods into which we may divide it are arbitrary and imaginary. Thus, it might be argued that one system of periodization is as good as another and, accordingly, we are free to divide it in any way that seems to fit our purpose at the moment. To some extent this is true, as long as we are aware that our periods are subjective, but necessary, divisions.

However, it is not completely true that one periodization is as good as another, although any system of periodization may well be useful for some specific purpose. Obviously, periodization must depend on changes in the society's culture. And, equally obviously, changes in a culture must depend on the causes of these changes. Accordingly, the periodization should, ideally, depend on the causes of the culture changes. This rule has been consistently neglected in all discussion of this subject. Writers tell us that a civilization rises and falls; they divide this process into periods, and they sometimes try to explain why it rises and falls; but they rarely relate their periods of the process of change to their explanation of the causes of the change.

The most popular explanation of the causes of historical change and especially of the rise and fall of civilizations has been by means of some biological analogy in which a people, once young and vigorous, were softened and weakened by rising standards of living, or by a loss of the ideology of hard work and self-sacrifice that had made their rise possible. In most cases little or no effort has been made to correlate this process of change with the various stages through which the civilization was said to have passed. In some cases this "softening of fiber" theory has been presented in a more naïve form by a simple biological analogy in which civilizations, like man himself, were felt to pass through a simple sequence of youth, maturity, and old age. In many cases no real explanation of the process of change has been given at all, the theorists in question being satisfied with attaching names to the various stages of historical change. Giovanni Battista Vico, for example, saw the history of each people as a process by which barbarian vigor slowly developed into rationalism, the period of greatest success being merely the middle period when the two qualities of vigor and rationality were in a fruitful, precarious, and temporary balance, while the decline was due to the final triumph of rationalism over energy. In the late nineteenth century, as biological sciences became more influential, these basic ideas were reserved with varying quantities of biological sauces. The Russian thinker Nikolai Danilevsky attributed the earlier period of vigor to biologic mixture of peoples, and attributed the intermediate ages of greatest achievement to the rise of a state organization that could direct such energies into more productive channels. The final stage of decay is not clearly explained but seems to be attributed to some process of political institutionalization not too remote from the explanation offered here.

At the turn from the nineteenth to the twentieth century, the influences of Darwinian thinking became dominant in theories of civilization dynamics. W. M. Flinders Petrie in 1911 offered a Darwinian version of the theories of earlier writers such as Danilevsky: an earlier period of struggle, based on the vigorous energy of barbarian intruders, was gradually weakened by the enjoyment of rising standards of living which weakened "strife." Enunciating the general rule, "There is no advance without strife," Petrie pictured each cycle as an accelerating decay resulting from a decrease in "strife." This point of view, generally accepted by many of the earlier theorists on this subject, saw the later stages of any civilization as a period of decreasing strife or violence, a conclusion which seems to be sharply at variance with the facts.

To Oswald Spengler, one of the most famous of modern writers on this subject, a similar pattern was evident. He discerned in each people an earlier stage of vigorous creativity that he called "culture" and a later stage of weakening moral fiber and devotion to selfish physical comforts that he called "civilization." As is usual among writers on this subject, no real explanation was provided for this loss of motion, although the pattern was applied to ten different "cultures."

The most famous of recent writers on this subject, Arnold J. Toynbee, has produced the most voluminous and, in spite of its sprawling organization, most satisfactory theory of these processes. He is still strongly influenced by Darwinian biology, and attributes rise and fall of civilizations to the "challenge and response" to "the struggle for existence." In spite of his many improvements over earlier writers, especially in regard to the units to which this pattern applies and the stages through which the pattern takes each unit, Toynbee's theories have several of the prevalent inadequacies of earlier writers, especially in his failure to correlate the stages of change with the process of change and, above all, in his failure to explain why a civilization which has been "responding" to "challenges" successfully for centuries gradually ceases to do so, and decays.

Most of the earlier writers derived their patterns from the study of a relatively few units, and generally based their interpretations very largely on the Greco-Roman experience in Classical antiquity. This reliance on the culture that most of us know best is, of course, to be expected, but has been unfortunate, since the pattern of rise and fall in Classical antiquity is not completely typical, as can be seen from the difficulty most writers have had in deciding whether the Greeks and Romans should be treated separately or together.

Vico derived his pattern from only two examples, Roman and Christian cultures, but most later writers had information, however vague, on a much greater number of cases. Many had no clear idea of the unit we call "civilization," and they confused peoples, political units, societies, and even religions in an indiscriminate fashion, greatly increasing the difficulty of finding patterns of change. Danilevsky spoke of ten historical "types," to which he added Russia as an eleventh in the future. In general his units were linguistic groupings, so that the Greeks and Romans were treated as separate units. Spengler also spoke of ten, but his units were different from Danilevsky's and were made very ambiguous in some cases by being based on spiritual outlooks, such as his famous conceptions of Apollonian (Classical), Faustian (Western), and Magian (post-Classical Near Eastern) cultures. Toynbee saw about two dozen civilizations, not much different from those accepted in this present book.

The pattern of change in civilizations presented here consists of seven stages resulting from the fact that each civilization has an instrument of expansion that becomes an institution. The civilization rises while this organization is an instrument and declines as this organization becomes an institution.

By the term "instrument of expansion" we mean that the society must be organized in such fashion that three things are true: (1) the society must be organized in such a way that it has an *incentive to invent* new ways of doing things; (2) it must be organized in such a way that somewhere in the society there is *accumulation of surplus*—that is, some persons in the society control more wealth than they wish to consume immediately; and (3) it must be organized in such a way that the surplus which is being accumulated is being used to pay for or to utilize the new inventions. All three of these things are essential to any civilization. Taken together, we call them an instrument of expansion. If a producing society has such an organization (an instrument of expansion), we call it a civilization, and it passes through the process we are about to describe. Before we describe this process, however, we should be certain we understand the nature of an instrument of expansion.

The three essential parts of an instrument of expansion are incentive to invent, accumulation of surplus, and application of this surplus to the new inventions. Economists might call these three "invention," "saving," and "investment," but the terms used by economists are generally so ambiguous to noneconomists that we hesitate to use them.

"Incentive to invent" is sometimes difficult for students to grasp because they assume that all societies are equally inventive, or that "necessity is the mother of invention," or that invention is somehow related to innate, hereditary biological talent (so that there are "inventive races" and "noninventive races"). None of these things is true. Some societies, like Mesopotamian civilization or our own Western civilization, are very inventive. Others, like many primitive tribes, or civilizations like the Egyptian, are very uninventive. Nor does "necessity" have much to do with inventiveness. If it did, those peoples who are pressed down upon the subsistence level, or even below it, in their standards of living, like some of the Indian tribes of the Matto Grosso, would be very inventive, which they are not. Or, if invention were in any way related to necessity, the poverty-stricken fellahin of Egypt or Trans-Jordan or the equally hard-pressed coolies of China or the peasants of India would have devised some new and helpful methods for exploiting their available resources. This is far from being the case. Or, again, if biologically inherited talent had anything to do with inventiveness we would not have seen the great decrease in invention by the Chinese in the last thousand years, or the decrease in inventiveness among Anglo-Saxon Americans in the last hundred years, or the sudden appearance of inventiveness among noninventive peoples of eastern European stock when they migrated to America.

Inventiveness depends very largely on the way a society is organized. Some societies have powerful incentives to invent, because they are organized in such a way that innovation is encouraged and rewarded. This was true of Mesopotamian civilization before 2700 B.C., of Chinese civilizations before A.D. 1200, and of Western civilization during much of its history. On the other hand, many societies are organized so that they have very weak incentives to invent. Suppose that a primitive tribe believes that its social organization was established by a deity who went away leaving strict instructions that nothing be changed. Such a society would invent very little. Egyptian civilization was something like this. Or any society that had ancestor worship would probably have weak incentives to invent. Or a society whose productive system was based on slavery would probably be uninventive, because the slaves, who knew the productive process most intimately, would have little incentive to devise new methods since these would be unlikely to benefit themselves, while the slaveowners would have only a distant acquaintance with the productive processes and would be reluctant to invent any new methods that might well require the ending of slavery for their successful exploitation. For these reasons, slave societies, such as Classical civilization or the Southern states of the United States in the period before 1860, have been notoriously uninventive. No major inventions in the field of production came from either of these cultures. The significance of this can be realized when we recall that at the very time that the South was inventing so little, the North, and especially the people of the Connecticut River Valley, were passing through one of the greatest periods of invention in history (cotton gin, mass production and interchangeable parts, steamboat, screw propeller, revolver, electric motor, vulcanizing rubber, sewing machine, anesthesia, and so forth).

"Accumulation of surplus" means that some persons or organizations in the society have more wealth passing through their control than they wish to use immediately or in the "short run." This is so necessary to expansion that it means that some persons must have more than they need, even if others must have less than they need. If a society containing 100 persons is producing 100 square meals a day, it would, perhaps, be "just" for each person to obtain one meal a day, but such a distribution would never allow the society to increase its production of meals except by temporary and accidental increases called "windfalls." If, however, the distribution of square meals in that society is organized so that fifty persons get only half a meal a day, twenty-five persons get one meal a day each, and twenty-five persons get two meals a day each, it might be possible for the society to increase its production of square meals. This could be done if someone invented a better way of producing square meals and if the twenty-five persons who get two meals each a day, consumed only one and a half meals each day and gave the surplus of twelve and a half meals each day to twenty-five of the fifty persons who had only half a meal each in return for their efforts in making the new, more productive, invention. This redistribution of meals to obtain the use of a new invention is what we mean by "investment," the third essential element in any instrument of expansion.

We thus have three possible ways in which the 100 meals produced by this society could be distributed. They could be written as follows:

TYPE A
100 persons at 1 meal each	100 meals

TYPE B
50 persons at ½ meal each	25 meals
25 persons at 1 meal each	25 meals
25 persons at 2 meals each	50 meals
100 persons total	100 meals

With Type A distribution there can be no increase in output even if someone thinks of a new invention, since no one would have leisure to make it. With Type B distribution there may be an increase in output but only if someone thinks of a new invention and if the surplus of meals controlled by the twenty-five richest persons is redistributed to the poorer persons as payment for these poorer ones making the new invention. This would give a third type of income distribution if the surplus was invested in the way mentioned. Thus:

TYPE C

25 persons at ½ meal each	12.5 meals
50 persons at 1 meal each	50.0 meals
25 persons at 1.5 meals each	37.5 meals
100 persons total	100 meals

Every kind of material progress and many kinds of non-material progress depend upon the three factors we have mentioned. This is as true of parasitic societies as it is of productive societies. Let us imagine a solitary savage who lives by hunting and who, by throwing rocks at game from dawn to dusk, averages one rabbit a day. Let us further imagine that this diet of one rabbit a day is just enough to keep him alive until the next day. In such a situation this lonely hunter could not make a bow and arrow, even if he could invent it in his mind, because to make a bow and arrow would take, let us say, ten days' work. Thus this savage has an incentive to invent, even has the necessary invention, but he has no surplus and cannot improve his position. Then let us assume that he throws a rock one day and kills a deer large enough to keep him alive for twelve days. He now has both invention (in his mind) and surplus (the deer). He may live from the deer for twelve days in idleness, or he may use his leisure from hunting to make the bow and arrow he has conceived. In the former case he will be no better off, and may be worse off because of loss of skill in rock throwing as a result of such leisure. In the latter case, on the contrary, his surplus (the deer) is transformed into a bow and arrow by investment, and at the end of ten days he has a new weapon that raises his ability to kill rabbits from an average of one a day to, say, an average of three a day. Of these three he can consume one a day himself, as previously, and support two other savages with the two other rabbits he kills each day. In return for such support, these two could be required to build a hut, to cure rabbit skins, to make additional arrows, and so forth. In this way the new capital equipment, the bow and arrow, has made it possible to raise the standards of living of all three.

It is by some such process as this, but much more elaborate and complex, that civilizations grow, thrive, and expand. Every civilization must be organized in such a way that it has invention, capital accumulation, and investment. Loosely speaking, the term "instrument of expansion" might be applied to the organization for capital accumulation alone, although, strictly speaking, this organization should be called the surplus-creating instrument. This surplus-creating instrument is the essential element in any civilization, although, of course, there will be no expansion unless the two other elements (invention and investment) are also present. However, the surplus-creating instrument, by controlling the surplus and thus the disposition of it, will also control investment and will, thus, have at least an indirect influence on the incentive to invent. This surplus-creating instrument does not have to be an economic organization. In fact, it can be any kind of organization, military, political, social, religious, and so forth. In Mesopotamian civilization it was a religious organization, the Sumerian priesthood to which all members of the society paid tribute. In Egyptian, Andean and, probably, Minoan civilizations it was a political organization, a state that created surpluses by a process of taxation or tribute collection. In Classical civilization it was a kind of social organization, slavery, that allowed one class of society, the slaveowners, to claim most of the production of another class in society, the slaves. In the early part of Western civilization it was a military organization, feudalism, that allowed a small portion of the society, the fighting men or lords, to collect economic goods from the majority of society, the serfs, as a kind of payment for providing political protection for these serfs. In the later period of Western civilization the surplus-creating instrument was an economic organization (the price-profit system, or capitalism, if you wish) that permitted entrepreneurs who organized the factors of production to obtain from society in return for the goods produced by this organization a surplus (called profit) beyond what these factors of production had cost these entrepreneurs.

Like all instruments, an instrument of expansion in the course of time becomes an institution and the rate of expansion slows down. This process is the same as the institutionalization of any instrument, but appears specifically as a breakdown of one of the three necessary elements of expansion. The one that usually breaks down is the third— application of surplus to new ways of doing things. In modern terms we say that the rate of investment decreases. If this decrease is not made up by reform or circumvention, the two other elements (invention and accumulation of surplus) also begin to break down. This decrease in the rate of investment occurs for many reasons, of which the chief one is that the social group controlling the surplus ceases to apply it to new ways of doing things because they have a vested interest in the old ways of doing things. They have no desire to change a society in which they are the supreme group. Moreover, by a natural and unconscious self-indulgence, they begin to apply the surplus they control to nonproductive but ego-satisfying purposes such as ostentatious display, competition for social honors or prestige, construction of elaborate residences, monuments, or other structures, and other expenditures which may distribute the surpluses to consumption but do not provide more effective methods of production.

When the instrument of expansion in a civilization becomes an institution, tension increases. In this case we call this "tension of evolution." The society as a whole has become adapted to expansion; the mass of the population expect and desire it. A society that has an instrument of expansion expands for generations, even for centuries. People's minds become adjusted to expansion. If they are not "better off" each year than they were the previous year, or if they cannot give their children more than they themselves started with, they became disappointed, restless, and perhaps bitter. At the same time the society itself, after generations of expansion, is organized for expansion and undergoes acute stresses if expansion slows up.

The nature of these organizational stresses and tensions arising from a decrease in the rate of a society's expansion can be seen most clearly in contemporary Western civilization. In this society the economic system produces three kinds of goods: (*a*) consumers' goods and services, (*b*) capital goods, which cannot be consumed but which can be used to make consumers' goods, and (*c*) government goods and services, including armaments. In producing each kind of goods, the factors of production, such as land, labor, materials, capital, managerial skills, entrepreneurial enterprise, legal fees, distribution costs, and so forth, must be used and paid for. These costs, including profits for entrepreneurs, have a double aspect. On the one side they represent the costs of producing the goods, and thus determine the final selling price of the goods; this must be sufficiently high to cover these costs. But, on the other hand, these costs represent the incomes of those who receive them and thus represent the purchasing power available to buy the goods offered for sale. If we look, for a moment, only at the flow of consumers' goods, we see that this flow of goods is offered for sale at a price that, by just covering the costs of the goods, is just equivalent to the purchasing power distributed to the economic community as incomes available for buying these goods. But, of course, some incomes are saved. These savings reduce the flow of purchasing power below the level of the flow of consumers' goods at prices sufficient to cover costs of these goods. Thus there is not sufficient purchasing power available to buy the goods being offered at the price being asked, and either goods must go unsold or prices must fall, *unless the money which was held back as savings appears in the market as purchasing power* for consumers' goods. Traditionally, this reappearance of savings as purchasing power in the market occurred through investment—that is, as expenditures for the factors of production to be used to make capital goods. This process provided the purchasing power needed to permit the flow of consumers' goods to go to consumers because investment distributed rent, salaries, wages, interest, profits, and such to the community to form incomes and thus available purchasing power but did not demand purchasing power from the economic community because the producers' goods created by these expenditures were not offered for sale to consumers, as consumers goods were, but, if sold at all, were merely exchanged for the savings of investors. This whole relationship means that our modern economic system cannot produce and consume what it produces unless it also invests (that is, expands).

After centuries of expansion our society is now organized so that it cannot subsist; it must expand or it will collapse. This relationship might be expressed in the rule that, unless savings are invested in producers' goods, there will not be sufficient purchasing power to buy the consumers' goods that are being produced. Of course, as this problem has become increasingly acute in the contemporary period, a third factor has intervened: government spending. Such government spending provides purchasing power just as investment does. When the factors of production are mobilized at government cost to make a nuclear submarine, the community obtains incomes available as purchasing power, and no subsequent claim on this purchasing power is made by government action, since the submarine is not offered for sale. Of course, insofar as this government spending is covered by taxes levied on consumers' purchasing power there is no net increase in such purchasing power; but a considerable part of government spending is covered by taxes on savings (and thus operates like investment) or is not covered by taxes at all (and thus represents a net increase in purchasing power, an inflationary increase when savings are being invested fully).

This rather complicated example of how an expanding society can become so organized for expansion that it enters upon an acute crisis if the expansion rate decreases is worth analyzing, because somewhat similar crises occur in all civilizations when the rate of expansion decreases. And such decrease is the chief result of the institutionalization of the instrument of expansion, something that occurs in every civilization. We shall see many examples of this and of the varied ways this process occurs when we make a more detailed analysis of the evolution of various civilizations.

Our tentative definition of a civilization was "a producing society that has writing and city life." This definition is imperfect because it is descriptive rather than analytical; it is also imperfect because it is not completely true. Western civilization about A.D. 970 had almost no city life, but still was a stage in a civilization. And Andean civilization, even under the Inca Empire, had no writing, but clearly was a civilization. It is now possible to offer a better, if not perfect, definition of a civilization: "a producing society with an instrument of expansion."

Before we go on to examine the consequences when an instrument of expansion becomes an institution, we might point out that the surplus-creating organization that is such an essential part of any instrument of expansion does not need to be the only surplus-creating organization in the society. In all societies there are other, less significant, surplus-creating organizations than the one we have considered part of the instrument of expansion. In Mesopotamian civilization the significant surpluses were accumulated by the Sumerian priesthood from tithes and its own profits, but there can be no doubt that private persons were accumulating surpluses from profits of private enterprise or from the earnings of privately owned slaves or even from voluntary restrictions on their own consumption. These kinds of surplus accumulation may be found in any civilization no matter what preponderance may exist for its "own" instrument of expansion. In 1850, when Western civilization was most completely organized on the basis of private profit, surplus was undoubtedly being accumulated, and invested, from government taxes or from private slavery. And we would not be surprised if the most socialistic civilizations, like the Andean under the Incas or the Russian under the Soviets, had a certain amount of private accumulation from profits.

These variant and incidental types of surplus accumulation are usually of little significance in a civilization, not only for their relatively small volume of savings but even more because they are not usually expended in productive investment but rather are likely to end up in luxury expenditures and are, thus, little more than postponed or transferred consumption. In theory, however, it must be admitted that our statement that "every civilization has an instrument of expansion" could well be understood to mean that a civilization has at least one such instrument. Except for one dubious case, we do not know of any civilization, in its prime of life, that has had more than one significant surplus-creating organization.

We have said that an instrument of expansion, like all instruments, becomes an institution and that as a result *the rate of expansion* begins to decline. This institutionalization of the organization of expansion, which usually takes the form of a decreasing rate of investment (rather than of a decrease in either invention or in accumulation of surplus), leads to a crisis. This crisis, which we have called increasing tension of evolution, arises from the clash between the decreasing rate of expansion, on one hand, and the fact that people's minds and the organization of the society are arranged for expansion, on the other hand. Reserving until later our detailed examination of the forms this crisis takes, we might point out here that it usually gives rise to conflicts between the vested-interest groups that control the uninvested accumulations of surplus (because they control the surplus-creating organization in the society) and are sufficiently satisfied with the existing social organization to desire no change and the great mass of the population who are discontented at the dwindling prospects of expansion.

The growing tension of evolution and the clashes it engenders can result in one of the three possible outcomes to the crisis. These are (1) reform, (2) circumvention, or (3) reaction. We speak of *reform* when the organization of expansion is rearranged so that it ceases to be an institution and becomes an instrument once more. We speak of *circumvention* when the vested-interest groups are left with much of their privileges intact and when a new instrument of expansion (especially a new surplus-accumulating instrument) grows up alongside the older institution and takes over the latter's expansive functions. We speak of *reaction* when the privileged vested-interest groups are able to prevent either reform or circumvention and, in consequence, the rate of expansion continues to decrease. If the outcome is reform or circumvention, the civilization once again has an instrument of expansion and the rate of expansion increases once again. If the outcome is reaction, the decline becomes chronic. There have been several cases where a civilization has succeeded in obtaining reform or circumvention of its institution of expansion, as we shall see in our detailed examination of the process of evolution in individual civilizations. The clearest case to be found is the evolution of our Western civilization, where both circumvention and reform have occurred. As a result Western civilization has had three periods of expansion, the first about 970–1270, the second about 1420–1650, and the third about 1725–1929. The instrument of expansion in the first was feudalism, which became institutionalized into chivalry. This was circumvented by a new instrument of expansion that we might call commercial capitalism. When this organization became institutionalized into mercantilism, it was reformed into industrial capitalism, which became the instrument of expansion of the third age of expansion in the history of Western civilization. By 1930 this organization had become institutionalized into monopoly capitalism, and the society was, for the third time, in a major era of crisis. A detailed analysis of these changes will be provided later.

The process that we have described, which we shall call the institutionalization of an instrument of expansion, will help us to understand why civilizations rise and fall. By a close examination of this process, it becomes possible to divide the history of any civilization into successive stages. We have said that these divisions are largely arbitrary and subjective and could be made in any convenient number of stages. We shall divide the process into seven stages, since this permits us to relate our divisions conveniently to the process of rise and fall. These seven stages we shall name as follows:

1. Mixture
2. Gestation
3. Expansion
4. Age of Conflict
5. Universal Empire
6. Decay
7. Invasion

Every civilization, indeed every society, begins with a mixture of two or more cultures. Such mixture of cultures is very common; in fact, it occurs at the boundaries of all cultures to some extent. But such casual cultural mixture is of little significance unless there comes into existence in the zone of mixture a new culture, arising from the mixture but different from the constituent parts. The process is a little like the way in which a mixture of chemicals sometimes produces a new compound different from the mixing chemicals. In the case we are discussing, the new compound is a new society with a new culture. The contributing societies may be civilizations or merely producing societies (agricultural or pastoral) or merely parasitic societies (with hunting or fishing). Of the millions of cases of such cultural mixture that are occurring all the time, only rarely does there appear a new society. And even more rarely does this new society become organized in such a way that it is a producing society with an instrument of expansion. In the rare case where this occurs, we have the first stage of a new civilization. The fact that there have been no more than two dozen civilizations in almost ten thousand years of cultural mixture of producing societies will indicate how rare this occurrence is.

Since cultural mixture occurs on the borders of societies, civilizations rarely succeed one another in the same geographic area, but undergo a displacement in space. The process may be described somewhat as follows. Within a society, people have little choice as to the ways in which they will satisfy basic needs (or fulfill their potentialities). If they are hungry, they eat the food their associates eat, prepared in the fashion customarily used in their society. If they wish companionship, or a picture of their relationship to the universe or a relationship to God or security or shelter or sex or children or whatever they may wish, they obtain these desires largely in the ways and forms provided by their own society. But on the borders of societies there is a considerable mutual interpenetration of social customs, and there arise, accordingly, alternative ways of satisfying human needs. This is, obviously, particularly true where intermarriage occurs, and where decisions must be taken and choices made as to which customs will be followed. Such choices are imperative in regard to bringing up the children of mixed marriages. When this occurs far enough inside the border of a society for there to be a social majority and consensus, there is no real choice, and, if any effort is made to make a choice, the children themselves will preempt for the local consensus. But in an area of fairly equal mixture, or in an area of unequal mixture where the majority culture is declining and decreasing in prestige, a very real need to make choices arises. These choices in themselves are not very significant in forming a new culture, but two other considerations are important. In the first place, the many choices being made must be morphologically compatible in order to give rise to the necessary amount of integration to permit a body of social custom to arise. And, in the second place, a certain number of families in the same locality must make the same or similar choices. In this way a new society may arise. If this society is productive and if it becomes organized so that it has an instrument of expansion, a new civilization will be born.

As a consequence of these conditions, civilizations have generally arisen on the periphery of earlier civilizations. Canaanite, Hittite, and Minoan civilizations arose on the edges of Mesopotamian civilization. Classical civilization was born on the shores of the Aegean Sea, especially the eastern shore, on what was the periphery of Minoan civilization. Western civilization arose in western Europe, especially in France, which was a periphery of Classical civilization. And on other peripheries of Classical civilization were born Russian civilization and Islamic civilization.

If the new society born from such mixture is a civilization, it has an instrument of expansion. This means that inventions begin to be made, surplus begins to be accumulated, and this surplus begins to be used to utilize new inventions. Eventually, as a result of these actions, expansion will begin. The interval before such expansion becomes evident, but after the most obvious mixture has ceased, may cover generations of time. This period will be called the Stage of Gestation. It is Stage 2 of any civilization. In general, it is a period in which the society seems to be changing very little, and most people seem to have fairly stable status situations in the social structure. But, under the surface, much of importance is taking place and, above all, the process of investment and invention that will make possible the following period of expansion is taking place.

The Stage of Expansion is marked by four kinds of expansion: (*a*) increased production of goods, eventually reflected in rising standards of living; (*b*) increase in population of the society, generally because of a declining death rate; (*c*) an increase in the geographic extent of the civilization, for this is a period of exploration and colonization; and (*d*) an increase in knowledge. There are intimate interrelationships among these four. Increase in production is aided by expanding knowledge; the growth of population helps to increase production as well as to extend the geographic area of the society; the exploration and colonization associated with this extension of the society's geographic area is made possible by the growth of production and the growth of population, both of which permit people to be released for what are, at the beginning at least, nonproductive activities such as exploration; the same factors allow people to be released to seek knowledge of various kinds or to engage in nonmaterial activities such as artistic or philosophic activities, while the geographic expansion in itself leads to substantial increases in knowledge. This period of expansion is frequently a period of democracy, of scientific advance, and of revolutionary political change (as the various levels of society become adapted to an expanding mode of life from the more static mode of life prevalent in Stage 2). As a result of the geographic expansion of the society, it comes to be divided into two areas: the core area, which the civilization occupied at the end of Stage 2, and the peripheral area into which it expanded during Stage 3. The core area of Mesopotamian civilization was the lower valley of the Tigris and Euphrates rivers; the peripheral area was the highlands surrounding this valley and more remote areas like Iran, Syria, and Anatolia. The core area of Minoan civilization was the island of Crete; its peripheral area included the

Aegean Islands and the Balkan coast. The core area of Classical civilization was the shores of the Aegean Sea; its peripheral areas were the whole Mediterranean seacoast and ultimately Spain, North Africa, and Gaul. The core area of Western civilization covered northern Italy, most of France, the Low Countries, England, and extreme western Germany; its peripheral areas included the rest of Europe to eastern Poland, North and South America, and Australia.

When expansion begins to slow up in the core areas, as a result of the instrument of expansion becoming institutionalized, and the core area becomes increasingly static and legalistic, the peripheral areas continue to expand (by what is essentially a process of geographic circumvention) and frequently shortcut many of the developments experienced by the core area. As a result, by the latter half of Stage 3, the peripheral areas are tending to become wealthier and more powerful than the core areas. Another way of saying this is that the core area tends to pass from Stage 3 to Stage 4 earlier than do the peripheral areas. In time the instrument of expansion becomes an institution throughout the society, investment begins to decrease, and *the rate of expansion* (although not expansion itself) begins to decline.

As soon as the rate of expansion in a civilization begins to decline noticeably, it enters Stage 4, the Age of Conflict. This is probably the most complex, most interesting, and most critical of all the seven stages. It is marked by four chief characteristics: (*a*) it is a period of declining rate of expansion; (*b*) it is a period of growing tension of evolution and increasing class conflicts, especially in the core area; (*c*) it is a period of increasingly frequent and increasingly violent imperialist wars; and (*d*) it is a period of growing irrationality, pessimism, superstitions, and otherworldliness. The declining rate of expansion is caused by the institutionalization of the instrument of expansion. The growing class conflicts arise from the increasing tension of evolution, from the obvious conflict of interests between a society adapted to expansion and the vested interests controlling the uninvested surpluses of the institution of expansion who fear social change more than anything else. Usually there is a majority of the frustrated struggling against the minority of vested interests, although usually neither side has any clear idea of the real issues at stake or what would give a workable solution to the crisis. All programs for sharing the surplus of the few among the discontented many are worse than useless, since expansion can be resumed only if the three necessary elements of an instrument of expansion are provided, and the dissipation of surpluses among a large mass of consumers will not provide any one of these three necessary elements. On the contrary most revolutionary programs, aroused by the failure of the third element (investment), will merely make the crisis more acute by destroying the second element (accumulation of surplus). The only sensible or workable solution to the crisis of the civilization would be to reform or circumvent the old institution of expansion by establishing again the three basic elements of any instrument of expansion. Since the disgruntled masses know nothing about such things, and since the vested interests do not know much more and are usually concentrating their energies on an effort to defend their vested interests, a new instrument of expansion, if it appears, usually does so by accident and through the path of circumvention rather than by reform. If a new instrument of expansion does come into existence, the civilization begins to expand again, the tension of evolution and the crisis subside, and the civilization is once again in Stage 3.

The Age of Conflict (Stage 4) is a period of imperialist

wars and of irrationality supported for reasons that are usually different in the different social classes. The masses of the people (who have no vested interest in the existing institution of expansion) engage in imperialist wars because it seems the only way to overcome the slowing down of expansion. Unable to get ahead by other means (such as economic means), they seek to get ahead by political action, above all by taking wealth from their political neighbors. At the same time they turn to irrationality to compensate for the growing insecurity of life, for the chronic economic depression, for the growing bitterness and dangers of class struggles, for the growing social disruption and insecurity from imperialist wars. This is generally a period of gambling, use of narcotics or intoxicants, obsession with sex (frequently as perversion), increasing crime, growing numbers of neurotics and psychotics, growing obsession with death and with the Hereafter.

The vested interests encourage the growth of imperialist wars and irrationality because both serve to divert the discontent of the masses away from their vested interests (the uninvested surplus). Accordingly, some of the defenders of vested interests divert a certain part of their surplus to create instruments of class oppression, instruments of imperialist wars, and instruments of irrationality. Once these instruments are created and begin to become institutions of class oppression, of imperialist wars, and of irrationality, the chances of the institution of expansion being reformed into an instrument of expansion become almost nil. These three new vested interests in combination with the older vested institution of expansion are in a position to prevent all reform. The last of these three, the old institution of expansion, now begins to lose its privileges and advantages to the three institutions it has financed. Of these three, the institution of class oppression controls much of the political power of the society; the institution of imperialist wars controls much of the military power of the society; and the institution of irrationality controls much of the intellectual life of the society. These three (which may be combined into only two or one) become dominant, and the group that formerly controlled the institution of expansion falls back into a secondary role, its surpluses largely absorbed by its own creations. In this way, in Mesopotamian civilization, the Sumerian priesthood, which had been the original instrument of expansion, fell into a secondary role behind the secular kings it had set up to command its armies in the imperialist wars of its Age of Conflict. In the same way in Classical civilization the slaveowning landlords who had been the original instrument of expansion were largely eclipsed by the mercenary army that had been created to carry on the imperialist wars of the Age of Conflict but took on life and purposes of its own and came to dominate Classical civilization completely. So too the Nazi party, which had been financed by some of the German monopoly capitalists as an instrument of class oppression, of imperialist war, and of irrationality, took on purposes of its own and began to dominate the monopoly capitalists for its own ends.

As a result of the imperialist wars of the Age of Conflict, the number of political units in the civilization is reduced. Eventually one unit emerges triumphant. When this occurs we are in Stage 5, the Stage of Universal Empire. Just as the core area passes from Stage 3 to Stage 4 earlier than the peripheral area does, so the core area comes to be conquered by a single state before the whole civilization is conquered by the universal empire. In Mesopotamia the core area was conquered by Babylonia as early as 1700 B.C., but the whole civilization was not conquered by a universal empire until Assyria about 725 B.C. (replaced by Persia about 525 B.C.). In Classical civilization the core area was conquered by Macedonia about 330 B.C.; the whole civilization was conquered by Rome about 146 B.C. Western civilization has gone from Stage 3 to Stage 4 three different times. The three Ages of Conflict are: (a) the period of the Hundred Years' War, say 1300–1430; (b) the period of the Second Hundred Years' War, say 1650–1815; and (c) the period of war crisis that began about 1900 and still continues. In each case the core was conquered by an imperialist state: by England under Henry V about 1420, by France under Napoleon about 1810, and by Germany under Hitler about 1942. In the first two cases the old institution of expansion (chivalry and mercantilism) was circumvented by a new instrument of expansion (commercial capitalism and industrial capitalism), and a new period of expansion commenced. In the third case it is too early to see what has happened. We may be getting a new instrument of expansion that will circumvent monopoly capitalism and bring our civilization once again into a period of expansion. Or we may continue in the Age of Conflict until the whole of our civilization comes to be dominated by a single state (probably the United States).

In the imperialist wars of Stage 4 of a civilization the more peripheral states are consistently victorious over less peripheral states. In Mesopotamian civilization the core states like Uruk, Kish, Ur, Nippur, and Lagash were conquered by more peripheral states like Agade and Babylon. These in turn were conquered by peripheral Assyria, and the whole of western Asia was ultimately conquered by fully peripheral Persia. In Minoan civilization the core area of

Crete itself seems to have been conquered by peripheral Mycenae. In Classical civilization the core area Ionian states led by Athens were conquered by the semiperipheral Dorian states Sparta and Thebes, and the whole Greek-speaking world was then conquered by more peripheral Macedonia. Ultimately the whole of Classical civilization was conquered by fully peripheral Rome. In the New World the two isolated maize civilizations seem to provide a similar pattern. In Mesoamerica the core Mayan cities of Yucatan and Guatemala seem to have been overcome by the semiperipheral Toltecs and these, in turn, by the fully peripheral Aztecs of highland Mexico. In the Andes region the core area seems to have been along the coast and in the northern highlands of Peru. These cultures were submerged by a number of more peripheral cultures of which the most successful was the Tiahuanaco from the southern highlands of Peru. And finally, at a late date, not a century before Pizarro, the whole Andean civilization was conquered by the fully peripheral Incas from the forbidding central highlands.

In the Far East and Middle East the same sequence can be discerned. The core area of Sinic civilization was in the Huang Ho Valley. This area was conquered by Chou about 1000 B.C. and by semiperipheral Ch'in from the mountains of Shensi eight centuries later (221 B.C.). The whole of Sinic society was then brought into a single universal empire by the Han dynasty from its southern periphery (202 B.C.– A.D. 220). The Sinic civilization was destroyed by Hunnish nomad invaders before A.D. 400, and a new civilization, which we call Chinese, began to rise from the wreckage along its southern frontier. The core of this society seems to have been south of the Yangtze River. This core came under a single political rule as early as 700 under the T'ang dynasty. Wider areas were added by successive dynasties of which the Yuan or Mongols were so remote that they can be regarded neither as peripheral nor even as Chinese (1260–1368); the Ming (1368–1644) were of southern Chinese (and thus peripheral) origin; and the final universal empire of the Manchu (1644–1912) was from the peripheral north, Manchuria, with its original seat of power at Mukden.

The history of the Middle East provides similar evidence. We cannot speak with any assurance about the Indic civilization, but it seems likely that its earliest origins were in the lower valley (Sind) and are to be seen in the excavations at Chandu-Daro, while later it moved northward into the Punjab (upper valley) and found its universal empire in the originally peripheral Harappa area. After the destruction of this culture by the Aryan invaders from the northwest, the successor Hindu civilization began to arise (late second millennium B.C.) in the Ganges Valley. The core area of this new civilization fell under the political control of the local Maurya (ca. 540–184 B.C.) and Gupta (ca. 320–535) dynasties. Then, as Hindu culture spread over the whole Indian subcontinent, political dominance shifted to peripheral powers such as the Gurjara-Prathihara dynasty (ca. 740–1036), originating from Central Asiatic pastoral invaders, and a series of Moslem dynasties, mostly Turkish, at Delhi (after 1266), culminating in the universal empire of the Moguls (1526–1857).

In the Islamic civilization a similar pattern seems to have occurred. The core area of this civilization is to be found in western Arabia. As its culture spread over most of western Asia and northern Africa, political domination fell to increasingly peripheral dynasties: the Ommiad Caliphate, of Arabic origin, ruled from Damascus during much of its period (661–750), while its successor, the Abbaside Caliphate, ruled from Bagdad (750–ca. 930). The Seljuk Turks ruled briefly (1050–1110) from Persia and were ultimately succeeded by the universal empire of the Ottoman Turks with its center in Anatolia (1300–1922).

The victory of more peripheral states over less peripheral states during Stage 4 of any civilization seems so well established that it is worthwhile to seek the reasons for it. A number of these can be mentioned. In the first place, as a general rule, material culture diffuses more easily than non-material culture, so that peripheral areas tend to become more materialistic than less peripheral areas; while the latter spend much of their time, wealth, energy, and attention on religion, philosophy, art, or literature, the former spend a much greater proportion of these resources on military, political, and economic matters. Therefore, peripheral areas are more likely to win victories. This contrast is quite clear between, let us say, Sumerians and Assyrians, between Ionians and Dorians, between Greeks and Latins, between Mayas and Aztecs, or even between Europeans and Americans.

A second reason for the victories of more peripheral states arises from the fact that the process of evolution is slightly earlier in more central areas than in peripheral ones. Thus the central areas have already passed on to Stage 4 and may even have achieved a premature dress rehearsal of Stage 5 (with the achievement of a single core empire) while peripheral areas are still in a relatively vigorous Stage 3. Generally speaking, military victory is more likely to go to an area or state in Stage 3 than to one in any later stage, because the later stages (and the more central areas) are more harassed by class conflicts and are more paralyzed by the inertia and obstruction of institutions. Core areas generally have been ravaged for a longer period of imperialist wars. The combination of these obstacles gives the inhabitants of a core area a kind of world-weariness (sometimes called a "failure of nerve") that is in sharp contrast to their own earlier attitudes or to those of their more peripheral rivals. Accordingly, the task of creating a universal empire is likely to be left to such rivals.

It should be noted that in some cases, such as Egypt, Crete, or Russia, a single political unit has ruled over the civilization from its early history. This generally arises in civilizations whose instrument of expansion is a socialist state. In such a case imperialist wars are not so prevalent a characteristic of Stage 4, and the achievement of a single political unit (universal empire) is not one of the chief characteristics of that stage. As a result the stage may last a shorter time and cannot be so easily demarcated from earlier and later stages as can be done in civilizations where imperialist war and achievement of a universal empire are two of the most prominent marks of the stage. Absence of these items does not indicate absence of the stage, which is marked by its other, less easily observed, characteristics, such as decreasing rate of expansion, growing class conflicts, declining democracy, dying science, decreasing inventiveness, and growing irrationality.

These characteristics and the commonly observed achievement of political domination by a single (peripheral) state bring the civilization to Stage 5, the Stage of Universal Empire.

When a universal empire is established in a civilization, the society enters upon a "golden age." At least this is what it seems to the periods that follow it. Such a golden age is a period of peace and of relative prosperity. Peace arises from the absence of any competing political units within the area of the civilization itself, and from the remoteness or even absence of struggles with other societies outside. Prosperity arises from the ending of internal belligerent destruction, the reduction of internal trade barriers, the establishment of a common system of weights, measures, and coinage, and from the extensive government spending associated with the establishment of a universal empire. But this appearance of prosperity is deceptive. Little real economic expansion is possible because no real instrument of expansion exists. New inventions are rare, and real economic investment is lacking. The vested interests have triumphed and are living off their capital, building unproductive and blatant monuments like the Pyramids, the "Hanging Gardens of Babylon," the Colosseum, or (as premature examples) Hitler's Chancellery and the Victor Emmanuel Memorial. The masses of the people in such an empire live from the waste of these nonproductive expenditures. The golden age is really the glow of overripeness, and soon decline begins. When it becomes evident, we pass from Stage 5 (Universal Empire) to Stage 6 (Decay).

The Stage of Decay is a period of acute economic depression, declining standards of living, civil wars between the various vested interests, and growing illiteracy. The society grows weaker and weaker. Vain efforts are made to stop the wastage by legislation. But the decline continues. The religious, intellectual, social, and political levels of the society begin to lose the allegiance of the masses of the people on a large scale. New religious movements begin to sweep over the society. There is a growing reluctance to fight for the society or even to support it by paying taxes.

This period of decay may last for a long time, but eventually the civilization can no longer defend itself, as Mesopotamia could not after 400 B.C., as Egypt could not about the same time, as Crete could not after 1400 B.C., as Rome could not after A.D. 350, as the Incas and Aztecs could not after 1500, as India could not after 1700, as China could not after 1830, and as Islam could not after 1850.

Stage 7 is the Stage of Invasion, when the civilization, no longer *able* to defend itself because it is no longer *willing* to defend itself, lies wide open to "barbarian invaders." These invaders are "barbarians" only in the sense that they are "outsiders." Frequently these outsiders are another, younger, and more powerful civilization. The following list of universal empires shows the barbarian invader that destroyed the civilization in question:

CIVILIZATION	UNIVERSAL EMPIRE	INVADER	DATE
Mesopotamian	Persian	Greeks	334–300 B.C.
Egyptian	Egyptian	Greeks	334–300 B.C.
Cretan	Minoan	Greek Tribes	1400–1100 B.C.
Canaanite	Punic	Romans	264–146 B.C.
Classical	Roman	Germanic Tribes	350–550
Andean	Inca	Spaniards	1534–1550
Mesoamerican	Aztec	Spaniards	1519–1550
Chinese	Manchu	Europeans	1800–1930
Hindu	Mogul	Europeans	1500–1945
Islamic	Ottoman	Europeans	1770–1920

As a result of these invasions by an outside society, the civilization is destroyed and ceases to exist. This Stage of Invasion is also a period of mixture. As such, it may be, but does not need to be, Stage 1 of a new civilization. This condition was true of several of the invasions listed above. The invasions of the Greek tribes, which ended Minoan civilization, marked Stage 1 of Classical civilization; the invasions of the Germanic tribes, which ended Classical civilization, marked Stage 1 of Western civilization.

The seven stages are merely a convenient way of dividing a complex historical process. This process is not relentlessly deterministic at all points but merely at some points, in the sense that men have power and free will but their actions have consequences nevertheless. In general, if cultural mixture produces a new producing society with an instrument of expansion we have Stage 1 of a civilization. Stages 2, 3, and 4 will follow inevitably. This means that, if a producing society has an instrument of expansion, saving and investment will lead to expansion, and this expansion will eventually slow up as the instrument becomes an institution. At this point, in the early part of Stage 4 there is considerable freedom since the institutionalized instrument of expansion may be reformed or circumvented. If it is, expansion will be resumed, and the civilization will again be in Stage 3. If it is not reformed or circumvented, reaction will triumph, and the crisis will become worse. The choice between reform and reaction is not, however, a rigid one. The last part of Stage 3 may be a continual series of minor reforms and circumventions to the point where the creation of new instruments just about balances the institutionalization of old instruments and expansion continues at a fair rate for a considerable time. Circumvention, especially geographic circumvention, may force institutions that would not otherwise have reformed to do so in order to compete. Thus, for example, as the textile industry of New England became institutionalized, new, more modern plants grew up in the

South; the existence of these southern plants (a case of geographic circumvention) forced the textile mills of New England either to modernize or to perish. On a more dramatic scale the whole industrial system of England, in recent times, has been in an institutionalized condition and has been faced with the choice of reforming, thus creating new economic activities and new economic organizations, or perishing from the competition of peripheral areas, like the United States, or semiperipheral areas, like Germany (or even other civilizations, like Japan or India).

Because of such conditions as these, the whole first part of the Age of Conflict (Stage 4) is a period of crisis and of hope. Only when the vested interests create new instruments of class oppression, of imperialist wars, and of irrationality, and when these new instruments, in turn, begin to become institutions, does hope fade. Crisis becomes endemic in the civilization, and continues until the universal empire with its golden age is established. In those civilizations that had a single political unit from an earlier stage, like Egyptian, Minoan, or Orthodox civilization, the Age of Conflict is frequently of briefer duration because imperialist wars are of limited extent. The fact that these one-state civilizations frequently have a socialist state as their instrument of expansion also serves to obscure the duration of the Age of Conflict because such a civilization has weak incentives to invent in its Age of Expansion and less dramatic class conflicts in its Age of Conflict, thus serving to obscure the transition from one of these stages to the other.

In theory there is nothing rigid about Stage 5. So far as observations of past civilizations indicate, every civilization passes from the Age of Conflict to the Age of Universal Empire. That means that one state, probably a peripheral one, emerges triumphant over the whole area of the civilization. But in theory it is at least conceivable that the competing states of Stage 4 might just fight each other down and down to lower and lower levels of prosperity and public order without one emerging triumphant over all the others. In such a case, Stage 5 might be omitted, and the civilization would pass directly from Stage 4 to Stage 6 (Conflict to Decay) without achieving any universal empire. Something like this may have been true of Mesoamerican civilization. In a similar way, it is conceivable, in theory, that a civilization could continue for a very long time in the Stage of Decay without passing on to Stage 7. For there can be no invasion to end the civilization unless there are invaders to come in. Egypt, for example, was so well protected by seas and deserts against invaders that its Stage of Decay lasted for more than a thousand years. It is also, in theory, conceivable that some universal empire some day might cover the whole globe, leaving no external "barbarians" to serve as invaders.

This point leads to one final consideration, namely, the relationship of outside societies to any civilization. In theory again, it would seem that an outside society that was stronger than a given civilization might at any time come in and smash it. In practice, however, it seems that civilizations are in little danger of such an experience except early or late in their careers. In general, a civilization is in no danger from any society except another civilization from Stage 2 to Stage 6. In Stage 6, however, it is in danger from any society, even a parasitic one, as is clear from the destruction of Cretan, Classical, Hittite, and Sinic civilizations by non-civilized invaders. When two civilizations collide we may use the tentative rule that the victory will go to the one that is closer to Stage 3 (Expansion) but that neither one will be destroyed unless it is in Stage 6. In 492–479 B.C. Classical civilization, in Stage 3, and Mesopotamian civilization, in the last part of Stage 5, collided, and the former won; in 336–323 they collided again, with Classical in Stage 4 and Mesopotamian in Stage 6, and the latter was destroyed. In 264–146 B.C. Classical civilization in Stage 4 met Canaanite civilization in Stage 6, and destroyed it. In 711–814 Western civilization in Stage 2 was able to preserve itself against Islamic civilization in Stage 3; three hundred years later, in what we call the Crusades, Western civilization in Stage 3 returned the visit to Islamic civilization, then in Stage 4, but could not destroy it. However, in 1850–1920, Western civilization, just reaching the end of Stage 3, again collided with Islamic civilization, now in Stage 6, and destroyed its universal empire, the Ottoman Empire, and probably liquidated the whole civilization, a process that is still going on. This was only one of several civilizations that were in a similar stage and that have met, or appear to be now meeting, a similar fate. The other universal empires in Stage 6 that have been destroyed by Western civilization while in Stage 3 are the Inca, the Aztec, the Manchu, the Mogul (in India), and perhaps the Tokugawa (in Japan). At the present time India seems to be in Stage 2 of a new civilization; China may be in Stage 1 of a new civilization; while the situation in Japan and in the Near East is still too chaotic to make any judgments about what is happening. Russian civilization, which began about A.D. 500 and had its period of expansion about 1500–1900, had the state as its instrument of expansion and was just entering upon Stage 4 in 1917 when the reform of this institution gave it a new instrument of expansion. As a result, Russian civilization has been

Civilization	Mesopotamian	Minoan	Classical	Western	Russian
1. Mixture	6000–5000 B.C.	3500–3000 B.C	1200–900 B.C.	A.D. 300–750	A.D. 500–1300
2. Gestation	5000–4500	3000–2500	900–800	750–970	1300–1500
3. Expansion	4500–2500	2500–1700	800–450 in East 600–250 in West	970–1300 1420–1650 1770–1929	1500–1900 1917–
4. Conflict	2500–800	1700–1600	450–330 in East 250–146 in West	1300–1430 1650–1815 1900–	1900–1917
5. Universal Empire *a.* Core	1700–1650		330–A.D. 150	1420; 1810; 1942	
b. Whole Civilization	725–450	1600–1450	146–A.D. 150		
6. Decay	450–350	1450–1250	A.D. 150–300		
7. Invasion	350–200	1250–1100	A.D. 300–600		

in Stage 3 for the second time in recent years, but it remains a relatively weak civilization because of its weak incentives to invention. A collision between this civilization, which is early in Stage 3, and Western civilization, which has just begun Stage 4, would probably be indecisive in its outcome. If Western civilization reforms and again passes into Stage 3, it will be far too powerful to be defeated by Russian civilization; if Western civilization does not reform, but continues through the Stage of Conflict into the Stage of Universal Empire, the threat from Russian civilization will be much greater. However, by that time the new Indian civilization or the new Chinese civilization may be in Stage 3 and will present greater threats to both Western and Russian civilizations than either of these will present to the other. The possible, but by no means inevitable, relationships of these four civilizations in terms of the relevant stages can be seen from the following chart.

CIVILIZATION	PRESENT TIME	FUTURE	REMOTE FUTURE
Western	Stage 4	Stage 5	Stage 6
Russian	Stage 3	Stage 4	Stage 5
Indian II	Stage 2	Stage 3	
Chinese II	Stage 1 or 2	Stage 3	

This chart is purely guesswork, because if Western civilization reforms in the Present Time (as appears highly likely), or if any revolutionary new technological discovery (such as the conquest of photosynthesis) is made in the near future, this whole relationship will be modified.

Returning from the unknown future to the partially known past, we can conclude this chapter by a chart that gives, in a rough fashion, the chronology of the seven stages for the civilizations with which we shall be most concerned.

6

The Matrix of Early Civilizations

We have already said that civilizations are like crystals, which are frequently distorted by efforts to share the same crystalline material. They are also distorted by the noncrystalline material or "matrix" in which they are embedded. The matrix source from which diamonds are derived is great cylindrical pipes of friable blue clay that rise vertically from the remote depths of the earth to just below the surface. In this clay the diamonds are found embedded like currants in a fruitcake. Of course the diamonds in a "pipe" of blue clay are much less frequent than the currants in any acceptable piece of cake. In this they are like civilizations, which are very infrequent occurrences in a matrix of time, space, and noncivilized cultures.

The matrix in which civilizations occur is five-dimensional just as culture is. These include the same three dimensions of space, the fourth dimension of time, and the fifth dimension of abstraction. Before we make any serious attempt to apply the seven stages of civilization, we should have a somewhat clearer idea of this matrix in order to understand the distorting influences it may exercise on the seven stages of normal evolution in a civilization.

The three dimensions of space in which a civilization is found include its geographic environment. Since we are primarily interested in our own Western civilization and its direct predecessors rather than in the New World or the Far Eastern civilizations, we shall speak here only of the geographic matrix in which Western civilization arose. This area, including Europe, northern Africa, and western Asia, was aptly called the "Northwest Quadrant" by the historian James Henry Breasted. Bounded on the south by the Sahara Desert along the line of latitude 20°N. and on the east by the northeast-running line of the Pamir, Tien Shan, and Altai Mountains, its western and northern frontiers are formed by the great arc of the Atlantic and Arctic Oceans.

Within this great quadrant the land mass of Afro-Eurasia has the form of a letter "L" which has been rotated in a clockwise direction a quarter turn. The apex of this figure lies in the northwest, in Europe, while one limb runs eastward into Asia and the other limb runs southward into Africa. Europe's position at the apex of these two lines has made it a mixing area, with the African influences more important in the prehistoric period and the Asiatic influences more important in the historic period. This mixing role of Europe has been modified also by the extreme diversity of Europe's terrain, which has given it a very convoluted coast line, creating numerous inland seas and semiisolated valleys that give onto the sea. The result of these two geographic influences has been to give Europe great diversity of both geographic conditions and cultural influences in a small area.

The Northwest Quadrant falls into three zones, flatlands in the north and south being separated by the east-west spine of the Highland Zone. The Highland Zone is a broken sequence of mountains and plateaus from the Pyrenees through the Alps, Apennines, Balkan highlands, Carpathian Mountains, Anatolian Plateau, Caucasus, and Iranian Plateau to the Himalayas and the line of highlands that form the eastern boundary of the Northwest Quadrant. North of this Highland Zone lie the Northern Flatlands, which begin as a narrow wedge in the Netherlands and run eastward across the Northwest Quadrant, widening steadily as they move eastward so that they are only a couple of hundred miles wide in western Europe but broaden to almost two thousand miles wide in Asia.

The Southern Flatlands are opposite in pattern to the Northern Flatlands since they are broadest in the extreme west and are narrower in northeastern Africa and Arabia, finally falling below sea level in the extreme east to form the bottoms of the Arabian Sea and Indian Ocean.

This simple, and oversimplified, three zone pattern of the Northwest Quadrant is complicated by a number of other features of which the most obvious are the inland seas, rivers, and mountain passes. One of the chief of these features is the Mediterranean Sea, which runs east and west just south of the Highland Zone. The geographic significance of the Mediterranean Sea, of course, is that it divides Europe from Africa, but its cultural significance is distinctly different because it has served to link its shores together rather than to divide them. This binding influence of the Mediterranean in the cultural sphere lasted for over 4,000 years, from the first establishment of distant maritime travel about 3500 B.C. to the Arab conquest of North Africa and the Near East about A.D. 700. During this period the techniques of water transportation were far more efficient and cheaper than the techniques of land travel. This superiority of movement by water continued for more than a thousand years after the Arab conquest, the technological lag of land travel beginning to close only with the invention of the macadam road, the coàch, and the railroad after 1750. In the thousand or more years after 700, the linking influence of superior maritime communication in the Mediterranean was counterweighed by the cultural division between Moslem culture on its southern and eastern shores and Christian culture on its northern and western shores; but in the four thousand years before the Arabic conquest the technological factor was not counteracted by any profound cultural differences, and the shores tended to be drawn together by marine communication into a single cultural system. At that time the cultural division was not along the Mediterranean Sea but on the mountain barrier running parallel to it to the north. Classical civilization, especially as it grew into the Roman Empire, was the culmination of these influences. They were reflected in the term "Our Sea" (*Mare nostrum*), applied by the Romans to the Mediterranean, while the peoples north of the mountains (who were biologically closer relatives but culturally remote) were called "barbarians" for most of the Classical period.

Less obvious than the Mediterranean were other geographical features of the Northwest Quadrant, especially those serving as interregional connections. Of these links two of the more significant were the "Syrian Saddle" and the "Vardar-Morava route." The Syrian Saddle is the low pass across the Lebanon and Anti-Lebanon Mountains around the northern edge of the Syrian Desert just at the point where the Euphrates River approaches closest to the Mediterranean Sea. The mountains and deserts surrounding this

Major geographic features of the Northwest Quadrant (bounded by 20° N. latitude, 80° E. longitude, the Atlantic Ocean, and the Arctic Ocean)

"saddle" make it the only feasible route connecting the Aegean, the Mediterranean, and Egypt to the west with Mesopotamia and the Persian Gulf to the east. In a similar fashion the Vardar-Morava river valleys provide a route that joins the Aegean Sea near Salonika with the middle Danube. The importance of these two links can be seen in the fact that such significant innovations as metallurgy, alphabetic writing, and Christianity came to Europe by way of the Syrian Saddle and the Mediterranean, while the knowledge of agriculture first came to Europe north of the mountains by way of the Vardar-Morava valley.

We have already said that the first civilization began in Mesopotamia before 5000 B.C. when people of the Neolithic Garden cultures moved from the Highland Zone down into the alluvial valley and were able to create permanent settlements because of the refertilizing function of the annual floods. These people are known as Sumerians. They were distinguished by two significant features. Physically they were a rather stocky, roundheaded people who seem to have worn closely clipped hair and no beards. And linguistically they spoke an agglutinative language related to Elamite, Hurrian, and other Highland Zone languages but not related either to the inflected Indo-European languages then forming on the Northern Flatlands or to the inflected Semite languages already formed on the Southern Flatlands (Arabia). This difference in language between the Highland Zone peoples and their neighbors in the Flatlands to the north and the south(at least in western Asia) was also reflected in a difference of physical type. The peoples of both Flatlands tended to be longheaded, wore long hair and beards, and were less stocky in bone structure. The peoples of the Southern Flatlands (the Semite speakers) were less tall, and

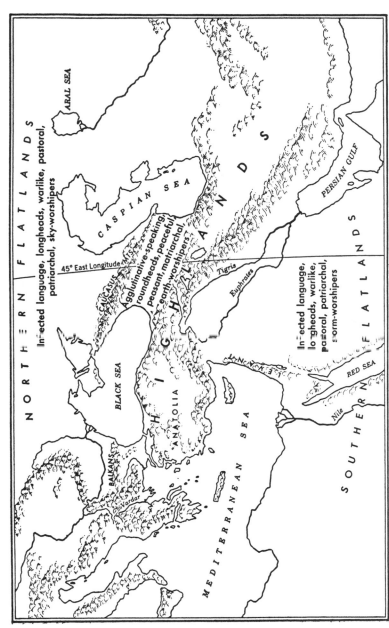

Sandwich distribution of peoples, languages, and cultures along 45th meridian East about 3000 B.C.

The labels visible within the map include:

NORTHERN FLATLANDS
Inflected language, longheads, warlike, pastoral, patriarchal, sky-worshipers

Agglutinative-speaking, roundheads, peaceful, peasant, matriarchal, earth-worshipers

SOUTHERN FLATLANDS
Inflected language, longheads, warlike, pastoral, patriarchal, storm-worshipers

HIGHLANDS

45° East Longitude

ARAL SEA

CASPIAN SEA

PERSIAN GULF

BLACK SEA

CAUCASUS MTS.

Tigris

Euphrates

RED SEA

Nile

LEVANT

ANATOLIA

BALKANS

Vardar

MEDITERRANEAN SEA

darker in eye, hair color, and complexion than the peoples of the Northern Flatlands (the proto-Indo-European speakers).

This sandwichlike arrangement of peoples on the triple-zoned terrain of western Asia seems to have existed when Mesopotamian civilization was first beginning in the centuries before 5000 B.C. and was still in existence two thousand years later (say 3300 B.C.) when the invention of writing and of bronze making marked the shift, at almost the same time, from the prehistoric to the historic period and from the Chalcolithic (or Copper-Stone Age) to the Bronze Age. In fact, the sandwichlike appearance of western Asia was, if anything, increased by 3300 B.C., because by that later date the Highland Zone peoples remained agriculturalists in the double sense we have indicated, while both the Semites to the south and the proto-Indo-Europeans to the north had adopted the care of domestic animals (but not the planting of crops) and had become pastoral peoples. There were other, less dramatic, evidences of this sandwich arrangement. For example, both Flatland dwellers tended to be warlike and patriarchal, and, in religion, emphasized the power of masculine sky gods, while the Highland dwellers tended to be more peaceful, more matriarchal, and had as their chief deity a goddess of fertility and sex who resided in the earth.

This triple pattern of language, physical type, and social customs must not, of course, be made too rigid. A certain amount of mixture and confusion of the pattern must have existed at all times. But there can be no doubt that some such pattern as this did exist on the three-zoned terrain of western Asia along the line of longitude 45° East at the moment when the invention of writing in Mesopotamia marked the advent of the historic period in human history and the clear establishment of the first civilization.

One of the principal tasks of Old World history is to find some explanation of this sandwich pattern of human society at the dawn of history. This can be done to some extent by the triple pattern of geographic terrain, but, while such explanation may be helpful in respect to social customs, it is not completely satisfactory there, and is completely inadequate in explaining the distribution of languages or of physical types of men. Accordingly, explanation based on geographic factors must be supplemented by inferences regarding the events of the prehistoric period before 3000 B.C. In making such inferences we have the evidence supplied by archaeology, but this in turn must be interpreted in terms of the sandwich pattern to be found in the later, historic period. Unfortunately, the areal and chronological specialization of most archaeologists and ancient historians has hampered them in making such inferences or even in realizing the need for them.

Before we present our own inferences on this matter, we should be quite clear what it is that we are seeking to do. We are trying to explain the distribution of languages, physical types, and social customs of western Asia as the matrix in which the earliest, and later, civilizations of that area appeared. Specifically, we wish to explain the pattern of these along the line of 45° East longitude just before 3000 B.C. This pattern can be summed up in the table on page 165.

Some of this pattern can be explained in terms of fairly obvious geographic and social factors. The archaeological record shows that the earliest agriculturalists were Highland Zone peoples who had both domestic animals (goats, sheep, and cattle) and crop planting, at a time when the dwellers in both Flatlands were still hunters. The earliest peasants were peaceful because there was a supply of adequately watered land available for occupation by the limited numbers of peasants, without any need to fight for it. Moreover these earliest gardeners engaged in hoe culture (without plows), which was originally a female activity at a time

NORTHERN FLATLANDS	Inflected languages
	Longheads
	Long-boned
	Pastoral
	Warlike
	Patriarchal
	Sky worshipers
HIGHLAND ZONE	Agglutinative languages
	Roundheads
	Stocky-boned
	Gardeners
	Peaceful
	Matriarchal
	Fertility worshipers
SOUTHERN FLATLANDS	Inflected languages
	Longheads
	Slight-boned
	Pastoral
	Warlike
	Patriarchal
	Weather worshipers

when males continued to hunt. Later, as the development of sedentary life made hunting dwindle in significance, men became animal tenders, but the food for both the men and their animals was a female product. Furthermore, the shift from hunting to agriculture provided a rising and more secure standard of living that made possible, as well as desirable, an increase in population. This was also produced by females. The upshot of all this was that the two chief desires of men, that the earth should produce crops and that women should produce offspring, became intellectually confused into a single mystery best summed up in the word "fertility." The reverence and desire for fertility led to a higher social and economic status for women and to the growth of new religious ideas quite different from the animistic religious conceptions of earlier hunting peoples. These new ideas are usually associated with a belief in an earth mother goddess whose confused powers of sexual and agrarian fertility were revered for thousands of years afterward.

The Neolithic Garden cultures were well adapted to the adequately watered hills, parklands, and valleys of the Highland Zone and, with certain modifications, were able to move into alluvial river valleys and across the loess and other semiopen areas of Europe and Asia, but they were not able to penetrate the grassy flatlands, both North and South. In many places these flatlands were too arid for neolithic cultures; in more humid regions the grassy sod was too thick to yield to hoe culture; but, above all, most grasslands were inhabited by savage, warlike, hunting peoples struggling for the right to live from the grass-eating herds of the flatlands. In the north these herds were mostly horses and cattle; in the south they were mostly antelope, camels, and asses. In both cases crop planting and the peasant way of life were excluded.

But the domestication of animals and, later, the use of metals were not excluded. In the period before 3000 B.C., both of these diffused from the Highland Zone to the flatlands of Arabia and of the trans-Caspian steppes. Thus, at the dawn of history the peoples of those areas had made the shift from Stone Age hunting peoples to Bronze Age pastoral peoples, while retaining and even intensifying their warlike, patriarchal social system. And, naturally, their linguistic and physical characteristics remained as before.

In order to explain these linguistic and physical characteristics of the three-zoned sandwich of western Asia, we must go much more deeply into the prehistory of the peoples involved. This will require some speculations about the origins of these peoples before they arrived in their respective areas of western Asia. In order to handle these problems, we must have a chronological system that will permit us to organize the population movements that brought these peoples to the places they occupied at the dawn of history. Such a chronology can be established in terms of climate changes.

Once again we must begin with the better-known present and work backward into the less-known past. On the oversimplified picture of the Northwest Quadrant as a three-zoned geographic pattern, we should like to superimpose an equally simplified climate picture of a six-zoned pattern. This pattern is most clear on the western, oceanic border of the Northwest Quadrant, and is modified considerably farther east by the influence of high altitudes and continental land masses. From north to south the six zones are:

1. arctic
2. cyclonic rainfall
3. Mediterranean

4. desert
5. subequatorial
6. equatorial (or tropical)

The nature of these six zones is well known, but the influences that they have exercised throughout history on the matrix of civilizations is not generally recognized. The arctic, or polar, climate is one of almost permanent frost. South of it the zone of cyclonic storms has adequate rainfall, coming from the west and equally distributed throughout the year. The third zone with Mediterranean climate and the fifth zone with subequatorial climate are both transition zones and have rain in half of the year and drought in the other half. They have the significant difference that the Mediterranean zone gets rainfall in the winter with drought in the summer, while the subequatorial has the opposite experience with rain during the summer and drought in the winter. The fourth zone between these two is a region of permanent desert, while the sixth, or southernmost, zone of tropical climate has excessive rainfall throughout the year.

The zone of equatorial rainfall is the area of low atmospheric pressure directly below the vertical rays of the sun. Because of the seasonal tipping of the earth on its axis, this area of vertical rays and of rainfall moves northward as far as the Tropic of Cancer in June and southward as far as the Tropic of Capricorn in December. It is this northward extension of the tropical area that creates the subequatorial zone of summer rains in latitudes otherwise desert. The northern belt of adequate rainfall, associated with the eastward moving cyclonic storms, also moves northward and southward with the sun, forcing the arctic zone northward in the summer and forcing the desert zone southward in the winter. This desert zone, holding a position between the cyclonic-rainfall zone of the north and the equatorial-rainfall zone of the south, is the area that is never reached by either of these rainy belts, while its northern and southern edges are reached by one or the other, in opposite seasons of the year, to create the two transition zones (Mediterranean and sub-equatorial) that we have mentioned.

Since the rainfall of the Northwest Quadrant comes generally from the Atlantic in the west, the eastern portions of the quadrant have much less moisture even in the cyclonic and equatorial zones, and it is frequently quite inadequate in the two transition zones between these. This really means that the desert zone in the middle widens considerably as it stretches eastward and that the eastern portions of both the Southern Flatlands (Arabia) and the Northern Flatlands (Kirghiz Steppes) are generally desert.

The seasonal changes with which we are familiar are caused by the annual tipping of the earth on its axis. As a result of this, the arctic and cyclonic-rainfall zones move southward and then return northward, giving us winter followed by summer conditions in the Northern Hemisphere. For reasons we do not yet understand, this movement southward of the first two zones was greatly exaggerated and long maintained on four separate occasions during the last 900,000 years. By "greatly exaggerated" we mean that arctic conditions extended southward as far as the Highland Zone, while the cyclonic storms followed tracks across the Southern Flatlands over what is today the Sahara Desert. By "long maintained" we mean that these exaggerated winter conditions continued for tens of thousands of years, probably for as long as 75,000 years at a time. These periods of extreme cold are known as the glacial ages.

There have been four of these glacial ages of Europe in the vicinity of the Alps, although probably fewer in some other areas. In southern Germany, where they have been most studied, the four glaciers have been given Alpine names: Günz, Mindel, Riss, and Würm. These names are sometimes applied to the glacial periods in other areas, although it will be just as convenient to speak of them by numbers from one to four. The periods between the glaciers, when there were temperate or even semitropical conditions in Europe, are called interglacial periods and are also numbered. The period in which we live, following the fourth glacier, is known as the postglacial period, or, more technically, as the Holocene. If we were to assume that a fifth glacial period might occur in the future, it would probably be more accurate to call the Holocene, in which we live, the fourth interglacial period.

Each glacial period lasted for about 75,000 years. The interglacial periods were not of uniform length, the first and third lasting for about 150,000 years, while the second, or "Great Interglacial," lasted almost twice as long. If we add together the lengths of the four glacials, the three interglacials, and the postglacial, we obtain a total of about 920,000 years. This period of something less than a million years happens also to be the period in which man in a biological form somewhat like our own has been on this earth. The whole million-year epoch is called the Quaternary Age, while the major portion of it, during which the glaciers were advancing and retreating, is known as the Pleistocene.

During the glacial periods when Europe was under arctic

conditions and the Sahara was under pluvial conditions, the former was an undesirable place for human residence, while the latter was well adapted to man. In the interglacial periods when the pluvial zone had moved northward and the Sahara had become desert, Europe was a desirable place for human habitation, while the African flatlands became almost uninhabitable. For this reason the pluvial and interpluvial periods of African history are even more significant than the contemporary glacial and interglacial periods of European history. In effect, man followed the pluvial zone north into Europe and south into Africa four times during the Pleistocene era. Of course, the movement of people was considerably less than this implies. In reality, relatively few persons followed the rain belt north and south, and these moved so slowly that they were probably unaware that they were moving. As Africa became drier with the approach of an interglacial period, the grass became scantier and grass-eating game animals fewer. The human population, which had increased substantially there in the preceding, more lush, pluvial period, dwindled in numbers and moved both northward and southward in search of more adequate hunting grounds. The majority, unsuccessful in this search, perished, either from lack of food or in combat with other tribesmen for control of the diminishing hunting grounds. Those who moved south mostly died in an effort to deal with the inhospitable tropical jungles. Those who moved northward had a similar fate along the southern shores of the Mediterranean seas, except for the comparatively small number who could find a way northward across Sinai and the Levant to the Highland Zone and the Northern Flatlands beyond. It has been suggested that the glacial age tied up so much water in the form of ice on the northern land sur-

ZONES IN JULY --- ZONES IN JANUARY

North Latitude

South Latitude

North Latitudes 40° 30° 15° 0° 10° 25° 33° 65° South Latitudes

65°N · 35°N · 25°N · 10°N · 0° · 15°S · 30°S · 40°S · 70°S

CONDITIONS IN FROM WESTERN COAST OF AFRICA AND EUROPE

ATMOSPHERIC PRESSURE ZONES	PREVAILING WINDS	RAINFALL	VEGETATION	
Polar highs	Polar winds		Tundra	90° / 65°
Cyclonic lows	Prevailing westerlies	Rain in all seasons	Forest	40° / 35°
High pressure	Subtropical calms	Winter rain	Scrub and grass	30° / 25°
	Northeast trade winds	No rain	Desert	20°
Equatorial low pressure	Doldrums (calms)	Summer rain	Grasslands	10°
		Rain in all seasons	Tropical forest	0° / 5°
	Southeast trade winds	Summer rain	Grasslands	15°
High pressure	Subtropical calms	No rain	Desert	30° / 35°
Cyclonic lows	Prevailing westerlies	Winter rain	Scrub and grass	40°
Polar highs	Polar winds	Rain in all seasons	Forest	70°
			Tundra	90°

Simplified diagram of the world globe showing the shift north and south of the zones of atmospheric pressure and prevailing winds caused by the annual inclination of the globe between July and January. The two columns on the right show the resulting distribution under present conditions of rainfall and vegetation at various latitudes along the western edges of Europe and Africa. In the glacial ages the northern polar area moved southward to about 45° N. latitude forcing the cyclonic rain belt and the winter rain belt southward about 10°, so that the two grasslands converged and the desert now found at 25° N. latitude was almost eliminated.

faces that the level of the ocean fell sufficiently to create land bridges between Europe and Africa at Gibraltar and Sicily. It is quite true that sea levels were considerably lower during the glacial periods, but it is doubtful that this was ever sufficient to open trans-Mediterranean land bridges, at least for any very long time.

This whole process of population growth and movement was reversed at the onset of a glacial period. In the preceding interglacial age the population of Europe, especially on the grassy Northern Flatlands, must have reached a maximum because of the adequate supply of herding game animals, while in the Southern Flatlands desert conditions must have reduced grass, animals, and men to a minimum. As the advancing glacier moved southward, preceded by the pluvial zone, living conditions in Europe worsened and population became reduced, either by emigration or by death, while the population of the Southern Flatlands, largely from more successful biological reproduction, increased.

It should be clearly understood that all these great changes took thousands of years and occurred so slowly that the individual persons involved could have had no realization that they were concerned with the processes we have described. They knew nothing of moving glaciers or rain belts and had no glimmering conception that they were one generation in a family line that was migrating successfully or was perishing locally. This is clearly one case where the historical events we describe were occurring to statistical masses rather than to isolated individual persons.

Although migration was only a minor portion of the population changes of the Pleistocene, we may picture the glaciers as a great piston that advanced and withdrew four times, expelling population from Europe as it advanced and sucking it back again from Africa as it withdrew northward. This fundamental but oversimplified picture must now be modified by two other considerations. The first of these arises from the fact that glacial advance came down altitudes as well as latitudes, while the second arises from the fact that such glacial movements were not steady but fluctuating.

When we say that glaciers advanced down the altitudes as well as down the latitudes, we mean that glacial advance not only consisted of a southward advance of the polar ice-cap; it also consisted of a downward extension of the snow line on mountain peaks. The latter movement, on the northern side of mountain ranges like the Alps, Caucasus, or Himalayas, appeared as a northward advance of ice. More significant for human history is the fact that the lowering of the snow line closed mountain passes while the lower altitudes to the north were still habitable, thus trapping groups of people north of the mountain barriers in the face of the advancing Ice Age. These trapped peoples were able to survive only if they could adapt their social customs to living under glacial conditions. This would have required, as a minimum, the acquisition of fire and the use of clothing. Since these people would have been separated from the main stock of mankind in Africa for a long period, at least 100,-000 years, it is almost inevitable that they would have become changed in physical features and that these changes would be those such as shorter neck and limbs, chunkier body, thicker hair, narrower nostrils, protected eye sockets, and other modifications helpful in living under arctic conditions.

The development of such a distinctive type of man did

occur, at least once, probably in eastern Asia north of the Himalayas, during the second or third glacial age. This type is called Neanderthal man.

Neanderthal man was so different in appearance from most modern men that no observer would be likely to confuse them. His bodily proportions were quite different, since he had shorter legs and almost no neck. There were other, more technical, differences. His rib bones were rounder, rather than flattened as ours are; he had no real chin or forehead; his eyes were protected by bony eye ridges along the brows; and his head was attached to the front rather than to the top of the last vertebra.

Because of these differences, Neanderthal man is frequently regarded as a different species from modern man, or Homo sapiens. But he is more correctly regarded as a variety, since the critical mark of species difference, inability to interbreed to produce fertile offspring, was not true of the Neanderthal and Homo sapiens types. It is now generally recognized that these two were able to interbreed and leave descendants on those rare occasions when they encountered each other along the margins of their customary habitats.

Such encounters were on the margins of their ranges because Homo sapiens lived under temperate conditions, while Neanderthal man lived under semiglacial conditions. They both lived in Europe but at different times. Homo sapiens retreated to Africa when Europe was glacial, thus abandoning Europe to Neanderthal man, while the latter retreated northeastward toward Asia, where he had originated, as the interglacial period commenced. Just as we associated the movements of Homo sapiens with the movements of a glacial piston that ejected him from Europe or sucked him back from Africa, so we could associate the movements of the same piston with Neanderthal man, who came into

Europe with the glacier and retreated with it toward northern Asia when it departed.

Because of the conceit of normal egotism, it is customary to regard Homo sapiens as of higher intellectual capacity than Neanderthal man. This is a matter on which real evidence is scanty, but the evidence that is available would clearly indicate that Neanderthal man was at least as intelligent as Homo sapiens. This evidence includes the following: Neanderthal man possessed both fire and clothing, necessities for glacial living, before Homo sapiens did. He seems to have buried his dead, leaving with the body equipment needed in some future life, at an earlier period, thus giving evidence of an earlier recognition of spiritual values. His tools were frequently made in greater variety and with somewhat greater skill, and include the earliest compound tools (in which the blade and handle were separate pieces). But these achievements, which might be interpreted to indicate a fairly high level of brain power, apparently do not indicate sufficient mental flexibility to permit Neanderthal man to survive the ending of glacial conditions. By adapting his way of life so successfully to glacial conditions and to the pursuit of the great glacial mammals such as mammoths, Neanderthal man made his way of life too rigid to permit him to exist under postglacial conditions when such mammals became extinct.

We have suggested that Neanderthal man developed as an offshoot from the main line of human evolution by being trapped by a glacial age north of the mountains in Asia. We do not know whether the glacier that did this was the second (Mindel) or the third (Riss), but it is clear that Neanderthal man was alone in Europe during the early portion of the fourth, Würm, glacier.

The fourth glacier had two icy peaks known as Würm I

and Würm II. The interval between them, known as Achen, occurred when the glacier withdrew part way and then returned with full intensity in the phase called Würm II (or Bühl). The withdrawal of Würm I gave rise to the usual population movements that we have posited of a glacial retreat, Neanderthal man withdrawing toward Asia while Homo sapiens began to move to Europe from Africa. With the return of Würm II, this process was reversed; but this time, probably for the first time, some Homo sapiens groups were able to remain in Europe under glacial conditions by adopting the techniques of fire, fur clothing, and cave dwelling that had been developed by Neanderthal man. Thus, for the first time, especially during the early stages of the withdrawal of Würm II, Homo sapiens and Neanderthal man came into close biological contact, with consequent interbreeding. This occurred on the fringes of Asia and Europe, north and east of the Mediterranean Sea, and may have occurred south of the sea in parts of North Africa. As a consequence, the early postglacial period found three human types in the Northwest Quadrant, Neanderthal in northern Europe retreating toward Asia, Homo sapiens in the Southern Flatlands moving toward Asia and Europe (largely by way of the Levant), and a mixed group in between, chiefly in the Highland Zone of the Caucasus and Iran. It is probable that we owe the later existence of a stocky, roundheaded, agglutinative-speaking people in the Highland Zone to the existence of this mixed group.

This does not mean that the mixed group stayed in the Highland Zone. They undoubtedly moved along it, both east and west, even before the final glacial withdrawal began. Then, as this withdrawal became definite, this mixed group moved northward and eastward, hunting reindeer and cold-loving animals. They were following on the heels of the pure Neanderthal, who was moving in the same direction, closer to the glacier's edge, and still hunting mammoths, mastodons, and other glacial fauna soon to become extinct.

At the same time, other mixed persons remained in the Highland Zone and its adjacent parklands, hunting such temperate animals as deer, elk, and the great European wild cattle. This last group we may call by the name Alpine men, a term which refers to their physical type. They spoke agglutinative languages of which the only surviving remnants are Basque and certain archaic languages of the Caucasus. The other mixed group that followed the reindeer northeastward were of a similar physical type, but may be called by the linguistic term proto-Finnish. These were the linguistic ancestors of the Ural-Altaic languages such as Finnish, Turkish, Magyar, Mongolian, and probably Chinese (now greatly modified by new vocabulary and the isolation of the meaningful syllables whose gluing together is one of the chief features of agglutinative languages). These languages are frequently called Ural-Altaic because they were centered, in historic times, in the area between the Ural and Altai mountains just east of the center from which the Indo-European (inflected) languages dispersed.

The early postglacial dispersal of agglutinative-speaking roundheads on the heels of the departing Neanderthal was soon disrupted by the arrival of a new wave from Africa. During Würm II the Sahara grasslands had built up a fairly numerous population of the familiar Mediterranean physical type: longheaded, slim-boned, rather dark-skinned, with dark eyes and hair. The appearance of postglacial arid conditions in the central Sahara split this group, pushing some southward toward the southern grasslands of the subequatorial climate zone and driving the rest northward toward the retreating belt of cyclonic storms. The group that moved southward mixed with earlier travelers in that direction, became darker-skinned and taller, while remaining longheaded, giving rise to negroid groups. The group that moved northward eventually crossed the Sinai Peninsula and the Levant. Those who remained in Arabia became the ancestors of the longheaded, slim speakers of inflected languages whom we call Semites. Those who continued northward, across the Caucasus into the Northern Flatlands, became the ancestors of the longheaded, slim speakers of inflected languages whom we call Indo-Europeans.

The latter group, the proto-Indo-Europeans, moved slowly northwestward, becoming taller and paler-skinned as they moved. They drove a wedge of tall, inflected-language longheads between the agglutinative-speaking proto-Finnish to the northeast and the agglutinative-speaking Alpines in the Highland Zone to the south and southwest. At a fairly recent date, in the northwestern extremity of their range, these intrusive Indo-European speakers became very tall, blond, fair-skinned, and blue-eyed in that Scandinavian type known as Nordic. Their ancestors remaining on the southeastern steppes stayed much less Nordic in physical type, since that type is an extreme aberrant probably caused by the lessened amounts of ultraviolet radiations in the cloud-shrouded northwestern sunlight.

Thus in the immediate postglacial period, during a rather dry and cold climate, the Northwest Quadrant had seven different types of peoples distributed in rough bands from the extreme northeast in Asia to the extreme southwest in Africa. These bands were the following: (1) Neanderthal, moving to extinction on the shores of the Arctic Ocean; (2) a mixed group of agglutinative-speaking roundheads

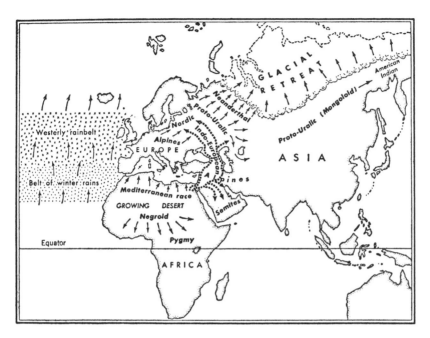

Population movements (10,000–6000 B.C.) following northward re treat of glacier and rain belts with the consequent appearance and growth of the Sahara

moving eastward across Asia at a rather high latitude and leaving behind the ancestors of the Ural-Altaic peoples as well as those of the Mongols, Eskimos, and American Indians; (3) the longheaded, inflective-speaking proto-Indo-European group moving northwestward from the Kirghiz Steppes toward Scandinavia where it would develop into the Nordic type; (4) the Highland Zone Alpine, an agglutinative-speaking roundhead; (5) the Mediterranean type, an inflective-language longhead, on the northern fringes of the Southern Flatlands; (6) the negroid, a tall longhead, resident in the subequatorial grasslands and the edges of the equatorial forests; and (7) the pygmy, a very short, yellow-skinned roundhead, living in the equatorial forest itself. Of these groups the oldest by far is the last, since the pygmy goes back to a very early period, considerably before the six other types had developed, and probably shares, in that remote period, a common ancestry with the group from which the glacial-entrapped Neanderthals emerged.

If we leave aside the pygmy as an ancient aberrant created by isolation in a sunless hot climate, and widen our field of geographic concern, for a moment, to include the whole Old World hemisphere, we might make three observations. In the first place, the Old World linguistic pattern, in the terms we are using, is fairly simple. At the center, as a recent emergent from the Southern Flatlands, we find a great core of inflected languages divided into two main groups of Semite and Indo-European. Around this core, as an earlier emergent from the same prolific Southern Flatlands, is a band of agglutinative-speaking languages, also divided into two groups, the Ural-Altaic of central Asia and the Bantu of grassland Africa. And last, at the two extremes, in the Far East of Asia and in the west of grassland Africa, are two blocs of isolating languages that probably arose from the syllabic disintegration of the oldest agglutinative languages. It might be added that at the dawn of history (about 3000 B.C.) this pattern was further complicated by the Highland Zone block of agglutinative speakers separating the two inflective groups, the Semites and Indo-Europeans. One of the great events of the historic period has been the linguistic submergence of these Alpine agglutinatives by the longheaded inflective speakers, especially by Indo-Europeans, as a consequence of population movements engendered by two acute dry spells of the historic period.

Our second observation is concerned with Africa. The earliest postglacial climate period, called the Boreal (about 14,000 to 6000 B.C.), was dry and cool. Its dryness resulted in the depopulation of the African Flatlands, already mentioned. In the subsequent wetter period known as the period of Atlantic climate (6000 B.C. to 3000 B.C.), there was a movement of population back into the area, chiefly from Arabia. The people who moved westward across Africa under these influences are called Hamites. Later, in the subsequent drier period after 3000 B.C., a second and larger movement from Arabia into Africa was made by Semite peoples. Both of these peoples had profound influences on the negroid peoples of the African grasslands and on the complex mixed peoples of Egypt and Ethopia.

Our third observation is concerned with a group that is now linguistically extinct and may appear to many as of little historic significance. These are the agglutinative-speaking Alpine peoples of the Highland Zone. This group, which usually receives only passing references in most histories, are, in fact, the most important group of humans who ever existed. They were the inventors of agriculture as we know it, using the same crops and domestic animals we have today. They were also the inventors of metallurgy (copper, bronze, and possibly iron) and were the founders of the first civilization, in the valley of Mesopotamia.

From these last remarks it must be clear that climate change continued to determine the chronological pattern of events even in the postglacial period. This is correct. Following the Boreal period (14,000–6000 B.C.) we find great cultural significance in a period of warmer and drier climate from about 2500 to about 1000 B.C. This period, called the Sub-Boreal, was preceded and followed by periods of more adequate rainfall. The earlier of these, known as Atlantic climate, lasted from about 6000 B.C. to 2500 B.C., while the later, known as the Sub-Atlantic, lasted from about 1000 B.C. to about A.D. 200. In these two periods of more plentiful rainfall, the Northern and Southern Flatlands, especially in Arabia and on the Kirghiz Steppes, had a more plentiful supply of grass and thus supported more numerous herds of grazing animals and larger numbers of men. In the intervening Sub-Boreal period, as well as during the drier period after A.D. 200 (for about a thousand years), the increased drought reduced the grass and the grazing herds and forced the tribesmen who lived off these to migrate out of these Flatlands toward the Highland Zone and the Mediterranean. One of the master patterns of the chronology of postglacial human history in the Northwest Quadrant was this four-stage sequence of climate change that saw each of two periods of adequate rainfall and relatively sedentary populations followed by a period of inadequate rainfall and devastating tribal migrations. The explosive qualities of the two drier periods following 2500 B.C. and A.D. 200 were intensified by the fact that the earlier periods of adequate rainfall, following 6000 B.C. and 1000 B.C., had greatly increased the density of population in the Flatlands and thus intensified the movement of peoples when the climate finally became drier.

It should be noted that the dates given for these climate changes are those that apply to the Northern Flatlands (and thus to Eurasia) and that the corresponding changes in the Southern Flatlands of Sahara-Arabia occurred a little earlier.

The most notable consequence of the Sub-Boreal dry period following 2500 B.C. and of the post-Classical dry period following A.D. 200 has been the outpouring of peoples from Arabia and from the areas around and to the east of the Kirghiz Steppes. During both dry periods the peoples who moved out of Arabia are called Semites. In the earlier dry period the peoples who moved out of the Northern Flatlands were Indo-Europeans, while those who moved out of this area during the later dry period were Ural-Altaic speakers.

The Semites who moved out of Arabia because of the Sub-Boreal and post-Classical dry periods did not emerge in any constant or steady stream but rather came in waves. These waves went in three chief directions: (1) southwestward into Africa; (2) westward into the Levant (Palestine and Syria); and (3) eastward into Mesopotamia (Iraq). We shall say nothing more about the ones who went into Africa, but those who went into the Levant and Mesopotamia are too significant to be neglected even in the most cursory examination of Old World history. These two areas together form a semicircle, open to the south, around the Arabian Desert, and called by Breasted "the Fertile Crescent." This crescent, like a great horseshoe curving northward, has its western leg resting on the head of the Red Sea near Aqaba, while its eastern leg rests on the head of the Persian Gulf. Any movement of peoples out of Arabia by land would be into the Fertile Crescent.

There have been four such waves bringing newcomers either into the Levant on the west or into Mesopotamia on the east. Although these emigrants were quite closely related to one another, they are usually known by different names in the two halves of the Fertile Crescent even in the same outward movement.

The first wave of emigrants into the Levant, just before

3000 B.C., are simply called Semites, while their brothers who moved eastward are called Akkadians in the middle valley and Assyrians in the northern valley. The second wave, just before 2000 B.C., are known as Canaanites in the Levant and as Amorites in Mesopotamia. In the course of the second millennium B.C., various branches of these two groups became distinguished in different areas so that some of the Canaanites came to be known as Ugarites, Phoenicians, and Hebrews, while some of the Amorites came to be called Babylonians. The third wave out of Arabia brought people known as Arameans in the Levant and as Chaldeans in Mesopotamia. The fourth wave, which began about A.D. 600, were known as Arabs in both areas.

The chronological relationships among these various groups of Semites can be seen in the following tabulation:

	LEVANT	MESOPOTAMIA
3000 B.C.	Semites	Assyrians (N)
		Akkadians (S)
2000 B.C.	Canaanites	Amorites
1000 B.C.	Arameans	Chaldeans
A.D. 600	Arabs	Arabs

Naturally movements of these Semite peoples outward from Arabia had profound effects upon the history of civilizations. The Canaanites became the chief element in a civilization of their own, known as Canaanite civilization, which lasted for almost 2000 years, ending with the destruction of Punic culture by the Romans about 100 B.C. The Arabs also came to form a distinct civilization, called Islamic, which lasted about 1400 years and ended with the destruction of the Ottoman Empire in the twentieth century. The other peoples named (Akkadians, Amorites, Arameans, Chaldeans, and Assyrians) played varied roles in that most venerable of civilizations, Mesopotamian, which originated in the activities of a non-Semite people, the Sumerians, and ended with the imperial achievements of another non-Semite people, the Persians.

While the Semite peoples were emerging from the Arabian desert to play the roles we have mentioned, even greater activities were being performed by the Indo-European peoples who were emerging from the drying Northern Flatlands. These peoples pushed out from the Flatlands in two waves, of which the earlier are called the Bronze Age invaders, while the others, 800 years or so later, are known as the Iron Age invaders. These two waves, shortly after 2000 B.C. and again shortly before 1000 B.C., were both results of Sub-Boreal climate changes, and consisted of Indo-European-speaking peoples. A third wave, after A.D. 200, contained a considerable number of other Indo-European speakers, notably the Germans, but the original impetus came from the pressure of Ural-Altaic speakers. Of these Ural-Altaic speakers who pushed out of the Asiatic Flatlands after A.D. 200, the earliest were the Huns. These were followed, during the next thousand years, by other Ural-Altaic-speaking peoples such as the Avars, Bulgars, Magyars (Hungarians), Mongols (or Tartars), and Turks.

A chronological table showing the movements of the Indo-European peoples in the two earlier waves originating from the Sub-Boreal climate is by no means as simple as it might be because these movements sent peoples into many geographic areas, in each of which they are known by a different name. The earlier, or Bronze Age, invaders, about 1800 B.C., originated in the Flatlands north of the Caspian Sea and sent peoples into areas extending from central or western Europe to India. The later, or Iron Age, invaders, about 1100 B.C., originated northwest of the Black Sea and sent peoples into areas from central Europe to Palestine, but not farther east. As a result we must include in our table nine different regions, as follows:

Locality	Bronze Age Invaders	Iron Age Invaders
1. Central Europe	Battle-ax peoples (2000)	Celts (1400)
2. Italy	Terremare (1700)	Villanovans (1100)
3. Greece	Achaeans (1800)	Dorians (1200)
4. Anatolia	Hittites (1900)	Lydians, Phrygians (1200)
5. Egypt	Hyksos (1600)	Peoples of the Sea (1194)
6. Levant	Mitanni (1900)	Philistines (1190)
7. Mesopotamia	Kassites (1650)	
8. Iran	Persians (1900)	
9. India	Aryans (1700)	

In Europe itself the third millennium B.C., especially the latter half of it, saw the most important changes in all Europe's history. The preceding period of warm, moist climate had continued for over three thousand years, and led to the growth of thick forests that broke up the human inhabitants into small isolated bands dwelling in the rare open sites on the banks of rivers or on the shores of lakes and seas. The herds of grass-eating animals almost disappeared, and the highly successful paleolithic way of life in which man was a hunter of big game was replaced by a sedentary way of life in which man was a gleaner, a fisherman, or a hunter of small game in wooded terrain. This new way of life, known as the mesolithic, lasted about three thousand years (6000–3000 B.C.) and was also found on the western fringes of Asia and the northern fringes of Africa where the increase in rainfall was also evident. This mesolithic culture is re-

Bronze Age invasions from the Flatlands (3000–1000 B.C.)

garded by most writers as a retrogression from the much more dramatic big-game hunting of an earlier period, but it seems to me that this is a mistaken point of view. It is also generally considered to be a local, European, development, which seems to be equally wrong.

My own opinion on the mesolithic is that it was a period of progress to a higher culture, in terms of technology and human productivity, and that it was not a local invention but rather came in from the tropical forest zone where a somewhat similar way of life must have existed for a considerable period. There is no space here for the rather technical arguments that would support this theory of mesolithic diffusion from a tropical forest area, but it is possible to mention the kind of evidence that would be used.

In Pin Hole Cave in England, just at the level where the mesolithic evidence begins, was found an Indian Ocean cowrie shell. Obviously, if a shell could come that distance, some of the new techniques of mesolithic culture could come the same route. Or again, Europe's first domestic animal, the dog, whose origins seem to go back to southeast Asia, arrived just at the beginning of the mesolithic period. This animal, well adapted to small-game forest hunting and to the sedentary, trash-accumulating life of the mesolithic, could have come by the same route as the cowrie shell. Moreover, in the very late mesolithic period in Europe there appeared two other domestic animals, the fowl and swine. Both of these are of Asiatic tropical forest origin and thus have quite a distinct source from the later Highland Zone domestic animals associated with early peasant agriculture. These later animals, such as sheep, goats, and cattle, are grass-eating Highland Zone herd animals, and are not tropical forest gleaners as are the chicken and pig.

Mesolithic technology had a much reduced concern with stone tools and a greatly increased concern with fiber cords and wickerwork. It included fish lines and fishhooks, nets and weirs, snares, bows and arrows, permanent huts of wicker and mud (or, as the English say, "wattle-and-daub"), basketry, canoes and paddles and, toward the end of the period (4000 B.C.), crude pottery and even some crop planting. The evidence for this new mesolithic technology, which has recently been described by J. G. D. Clark of

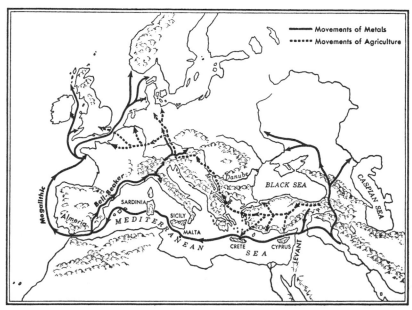

Movements of metals (solid line) and of agriculture (broken line) to Europe 4000–2000 B.C.

Cambridge University, is often to be found in shell heaps and trash mounds ("kitchen midden") associated with the mesolithic's sedentary settlements.

At the end of the third millennium B.C., this mesolithic way of life was disrupted by a series of events that pushed European societies forward to new economic levels. About 2700 B.C., a cultural movement from the Levant or southern Anatolia had arrived in southeastern Spain by way of the Mediterranean. This movement, sometimes called the megalithic movement, brought to Europe a number of cultural innovations, of which the chief was the use of metal (copper and bronze). From southwestern Spain, near Almería, these innovations spread to Europe by two subsidiary routes. While the megalithic movement went on to western

Europe by sea, crossing the Atlantic waters and the Bay of Biscay to Britanny (2500 B.C.) and the narrow seas to Britain and Denmark (2200 B.C.), groups of Spanish origin, called the Bell-Beaker people, moved northward, across the Pyrenees and southern France, to northern Italy, Switzerland, and central Europe by land.

At the very time that the megalithic and Bell-Beaker movements were bringing metals to Europe from the west, the Neolithic Garden cultures were bringing Highland Zone peasant agriculture to Europe from the east. This innovation first appeared, according to the available evidence, in the Western Asiatic Highland Zone, possibly near Armenia, in the seventh millennium B.C. As we have already indicated, the search for fertile plots of semiopen parklands resulted in a steady diffusion of this culture and its peoples. Crossing Anatolia and the Aegean Sea, they were in northeastern Greece by 3500 and then proceeded, by way of the Vardar-Morava route, to the middle Danube. While some descended the river to Romania and Bessarabia, where further passage was blocked by the warlike hunters of the steppes, others moved upstream across the loess lands of Hungary to Austria, the shores of Swiss lakes, and the Upper Rhine. Down the Rhine they proceeded to the lower valley whence they fanned out, going eastward across southern Germany and westward across northern France. By 2200 the latter branch had crossed into England, and within a few generations the central European branch was moving into Denmark from the south.

In this way both agriculture and metals had penetrated to western and central Europe before the onset of Sub-Boreal climate brought in the Bronze Age horse-using Indo-European warrior peoples from the eastern steppes. The arrival of these new people and of drier Sub-Boreal climate led to a drastic reorganization of Europe's societies. The climate change, by 2000 B.C., opened the forests of Europe, so that megalithic traders abandoned the seaways of the west in all of southwestern Europe as far east as the Adriatic and as far north as Britanny and, instead, crossed Europe by boat on the rivers, bringing Irish gold, Cornish tin, and Danish amber across Bohemia and southern Germany to the Danube. Down this river they went to the mouth of the Morava where they split, some continuing down the Danube, while others turned south to the Isthmus of Corinth and the Gulf of Argos beyond. In Argos, the new commercial cities of Mycenae and Tiryns welcomed the northern traders and grew rich from their commerce, which continued on, by sea, to Crete, to Egypt, or to the Syrian Saddle. Those traders who had continued down the Danube crossed Thrace to receive an equally warm welcome in Troy, whence the trade routes continued across Hittite Anatolia and the Assyrian outposts in Cilicia to the Syrian Saddle and Mesopotamia.

These European trade routes of the Sub-Boreal period were not disrupted, but were rather developed, by the arrival of the Indo-European warrior peoples in central Europe about 2000 B.C. From the neolithic peasant peoples these conquerors extracted food, and from the megalithic traders they extracted tribute, using the surplus accumulated to exploit the bronze-making resources of Bohemia in forest forges. From this system emerged a prosperous, barbaric (but not civilized) culture known as the Great Central European Bronze Age. This culture reached its peak about 1400 B.C., with northern and western connections to megalithic Ireland, England (Stonehenge), and Denmark, and even more significant connections to Terremare Italy, Mycenaean Greece, and Hittite Anatolia. These southern and eastern connections were with similar Indo-European Bronze Age invaders in other areas. The whole system was destroyed by the onslaught of Indo-European Iron Age invaders about 1200 B.C. These later peoples exploded out of the northern Balkans with devastating force, and established in various areas the Celtic speakers of central and western Europe, the Dorian speakers of Greece, and a variety of Anatolian peoples, such as Phrygians and Carians. In the Aegean and Balkans these Iron Age invaders ended Cretan civilization forever and established a Dark Age that lasted for several centuries. This Dark Age, centering on the period 1000 B.C., marks the transition between Cretan civilization and its descendant Classical Mediterranean civilization, performing a double role as the period of invasion of the former (Stage 7) and as the period of mixture of the other (Stage 1).

Farther east the same Indo-European population movements performed different roles in other civilizations. In Anatolia the Bronze Age Hittite invaders who came in over the Caucasus across Armenia acted as Stage 1 of Hittite civilization (1900 B.C.), while the Iron Age invaders from Thrace destroyed and ended this civilization a short eight hundred years later, providing the limits to the briefest and least known of all major civilizations.

The Iron Age invaders of the Aegean area, whom we have called by different names in the Balkans and in western Anatolia, drove fleeing before them a mixed group of earlier inhabitants of those shores, including Achaeans, Etruscans (Trojans), Cretans, some Dorians, and various dimly known peoples of the Anatolian shore. This mixed group

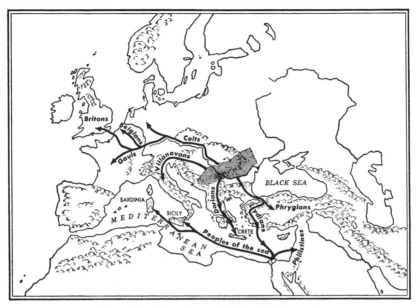

Iron Age invasions (1200–1000 B.C.)

crossed the Mediterranean and became the unsuccessful Iron Age invaders of Egypt. In two amphibious assaults on the Nile Delta, one about 1221 and the second about 1194, they were thrown back by Egyptian forces under the leadership of the Pharaoh, Ramses III. Thus repulsed, they scattered on the Mediterranean shores to seek new homes. Egyptian pictures, which show their Viking-like ships, and accompanying inscriptions give us the most specific evidence we have of these tumultuous events. The written evidence tells us the names of some of the frustrated invaders, including in the enumeration such intriguing terms as Sarda, Sicani, and others. It has been suggested that subsequent settlements of these refugees in the western Mediterranean gave Sardinia and Sicily their names and may have brought the Etruscans from an original home near Troy to Tuscany on the shores of the Tyrrhenian Sea.

More significant for civilized history, however, was the fate of those Iron Age invaders who fell back from the unsuccessful assault on Egypt and turned eastward to land on the more weakly defended coasts of Canaanite Levant. This group, known to us from biblical records as Philistines, gave their name permanently to the area we call Palestine.

Eight centuries before the Philistines came into the Levant from the west by sea, Bronze Age invaders had come down into the Levant from the north by land. This was part of the great flood of Indo-European pastoral peoples who broke over the Caucasus from the Northern Flatlands about 1900 B.C. As this flood crossed Armenia to enter Kurdistan, it split into three branches. The branch that turned sharply west into Anatolia became the Hittites. The branch that continued south underwent complicated changes. Originally Indo-European, it pushed ahead of it a large mass of Highland Zone roundheaded agglutinative speakers who are frequently called Hurrians, and these, as the flood continued southward, began to push before them a mass of Semite-speaking peoples. Of these peoples, the advance guard, largely Semite, invaded Egypt, where they are known as Hyksos. The middle mass, chiefly Hurrian, spread over much of the Levant, and are frequently mentioned in the Old Testament as Hurri, Hivites, or even "Hittites." The driving rearguard of this movement, mostly Indo-European, settled on the Syrian Saddle as exploitative tribute gatherers and breeders of horses for much of the Near East. They are known as Mitanni. An offshoot of this migration, more Hurrian than Indo-European, moved down into Mesopotamia and set up numerous local kingships known as Kassites (1650–1300). These peoples were gradually absorbed into the basically Semitic population of the river valley over the next few centuries.

East of Mesopotamia, where the later Iron Age invasions did not reach, the influence of the earlier Bronze Age invasions are well known. In the first three centuries of the second millennium these peoples moved southward and eastward from the Caspian Steppes. Those who settled in Iran were known later as Medes and Persians, but played no great role in history until the sixth century B.C. when they took over political domination of Mesopotamian civilization from the Chaldeans in the last stages of that civilization. Further east the Bronze Age invaders of India, known as Aryans, destroyed the Indus civilization and instigated a period of turmoil that was Stage 7 of Indic civilization and Stage 1 of Hindu civilization

The events described in this chapter, performed on the three-zoned Northwest Quadrant within a chronology based on climate changes, form the matrix in which the earliest civilizations evolved. These events, examined in detail with careful attention to brief periods or to small areas, probably seem very confused. But organized in terms of the whole history of the Quadrant during the Quaternary Age, as we have tried to do, these events begin to assume relatively simple patterns. During the Pleistocene period there came into existence the triple-layered linguistic and physical pattern that we have described. During the Holocene this pattern was somewhat complicated, but the chief event was the invention of agriculture, metallurgy, and civilized living by the Highland Zone peoples and the subsequent linguistic and cultural submergence of these peoples by inflective-speaking longheaded pastoralists pushed in waves from the Flatlands by the two postglacial dry periods. One of the chief results of this process, a result seen perhaps most clearly in Europe, was to create a political and social structure in which patriarchal, warlike, horse-loving, sky-worshiping, honor-seeking Indo-Europeans were established as a ruling class over peaceful, earth-loving, fertility-dominated, female-oriented peasant peoples. This pattern, first established in central Europe almost four thousand years ago, was not destroyed, in spite of Rome, Christianity, and later migrations, until the appearance of industrialized urban society in the last four generations.

7

Mesopotamian Civilization

The degree to which civilizations conform to the seven-stage pattern, and the distortions made in these stages by the matrix in which each civilization is embedded, can be seen by examining the historical evolution of various civilizations. In this chapter we shall try to do this for the first civilization that ever existed, the one founded by the Sumerians in the valley of the Tigris and Euphrates rivers.

We have pointed out that the peasants of the Neolithic Garden cultures practiced shifting cultivation, tilling the soil in an area for seven or eight years until the fertility of their fields was reduced sufficiently to curtail their crop yields and make it advantageous to abandon their huts and move on a short distance to more productive fields. In general these peasant peoples followed the hilly edges of the Highland Zone, avoiding heavily forested areas or the steeper slopes, and clinging rather to the lower valleys, parklands, or loess lands. Although they could cut down forest trees, it was easier to use more open areas; above all, it was necessary to settle near water, either from springs or from local streams.

Eventually some of these peoples came into the alluvial river valleys, including that of the Tigris-Euphrates system.

Here conditions were quite different from what they were on the flanks of the hills above these streams. The annual flood, whose sediment replaced the nutritive elements taken from the soil by cropping, made possible, for the first time, permanent settlements and thus the foundation of city life and civilized living. But the same flood that made the valley fertile made living in it dangerous and precarious. It takes an imaginative effort on our part to picture the minds of these early peasants who were ignorant of what we take to be self-evident. They had no calendars or other methods for keeping track of time; in fact they hardly recognized the existence of time as we know it. They knew nothing of the year or of the movements of the earth that determine it; they had no knowledge of the causes of the flood and, at the beginning, may not even have recognized that it was periodic. Above all, they could not have imagined any connection between the movements of the sun and the arrival of the flood.

Undoubtedly, as can be seen in the archaeological evidence, the flood struck unexpectedly and brought destruction, death, and fear, along with its fertilizing sediment. At Ur, in the lower valley, Sir Leonard Woolley found evidence of human residence both below and above a layer of flood-deposited clay, from eight to fourteen feet thick, laid down by a great prehistoric inundation which had covered about 40,000 square miles of valley. Sir Leonard believed that this might have been the Deluge of the Bible, about 3600 B.C., but this view has not been generally accepted. There is no need to accept it, for similar, if perhaps less devastating, floods must have been a frequent occurrence in these valleys.

We have no knowledge of how the early peasant residents of Mesopotamia dealt with this problem or with another, similar, one. The excess of water in the valley at one season was balanced by a deficiency of water during much of the growing season, so that irrigation was almost as urgent as flood control. For projects such as these the early peasant peoples lacked both knowledge and capital. No individuals, families, or small groups of families could find the economic surplus or the social organization that would permit them to construct such projects.

Undoubtedly, for a long time, the peasant inhabitants of the valley must have lived a precarious life, perhaps keeping their homes on the higher sites that were less frequently flooded, while their fields were down in the flood plain itself. But eventually, possibly before 5000 B.C., a social organization capable of accumulating an economic surplus and able to direct its application to productive projects came into existence. The nature of this organization in the prehistoric period must be inferred from the evidence available about such an organization in the earliest historic period. At that later time, about 3000 B.C., in each city-state of Mesopotamia, the accumulation of economic surplus was in the hands of a distinctive social group, the Sumerian priesthood; it arose from their control, in the name of the gods they served, of a considerable part of the land of the community and of tributes levied, usually in kind, upon the produce of lands owned by others. The chief tasks of the priesthoods, at the later date, beyond their obvious religious functions, were the study of the stars and the keeping of the records of celestial observations.

From this evidence we might infer that, at some remote date, some unsung genius or, better, some observant family, saw a connection between the advent of the flood and the movements of the sun—two events that had not previously seemed connected. This individual or family noted that the rising sun appeared at a slightly different point on the horizon each morning, finally reaching a limit where it hesitated for a few days before it began to return. We would say that the position at which the sun rose moves 47 degrees of the full circle of the horizon over a period of some 180 days or more. Thus was born a rudimentary idea of the solar year, the full duration of the sun's movement back to its starting point. In time these observers noticed that the flood always came about the same number of days after the sun reached its most southern rising point. With this information the observer was able to estimate roughly the day on which the flood would arrive each year. This calculation the discoverers kept secret, for their own profit, using the knowledge to work on the fears and superstitions of their neighbors, trying to convince others that they possessed magical powers enabling them to foretell the arrival of the flood, or even the power to make it arrive. The original discoverers of this information could hardly have told the arrival of the flood within a span of time much less than ten days. However, the fear engendered by the flood was so great, increased by the realization that the crops would fail if it did not arrive, that some, at least, accepted the discoverers' claims and yielded to their demands for tribute. The discoverers probably offered to reveal the time of the flood in advance to those who would contribute a share of their crops, or perhaps they even threatened to bring the flood or to keep it away if they failed to obtain promises of tithes from the crops of their neighbors. However skeptical these neighbors might be of such claims the first year, no more than one lucky forecast was needed for most of them to become willing givers. After all, in such an important matter, it is safer to be on the right side. The ignorance of the majority made it easy for the possessors of this specialized knowledge to use it as proof that they had supernatural powers. Moreover, it was not necessary to convince a majority or even many of the neighbors. If any small number contributed, a surplus would accumulate which could be used, in the form of flood-protection embankments or irrigation ditches, to provide very concrete evidence that it was worthwhile to belong to the new organization. Thus came into existence the central institution of ancient Mesopotamia—the Sumerian priest-hood.

This priesthood became a closed group, able to control enormous wealth and incomes, and concerned very largely with the study of the solar and astronomical periodicities on which their influence was orginally based. With the surplus thus created, the priesthood was able to command human labor in large amounts and to direct this labor from the simple tillage of the peasant peoples to the diversified and specialized activities that constitute civilized living. Above all, this centralized direction provided the system of flood control and irrigation on which all subsequent progress was founded. Similarly, these priest-controlled surpluses provided the capital for the many inventions of the age of expansion of Mesopotamian civilization.

1. Mixture

Mesopotamian civilization began with a period of mix-ture, although this occurred at such an early date that we must, once again, work from inference. We have already mentioned the fact that the sexagesimal number system of

Mesopotamia in the historic period must have arisen from a fusion of a decimal system and a duodecimal system, and possibly of a third element based on twenty. The widespread evidence for the very early duodecimal system, especially in the diffusion of the practice of dividing into twelve parts the wide band of fixed stars through which the sun passes in its annual revolution (the zodiac), and the association of this feature with painted pottery gardening would indicate that the duodecimal system was a characteristic of the Highland Zone neolithic peasant cultures. The decimal usage probably came from the Semite peoples within the Fertile Crescent. If a vigesimal system also entered into the mixture, it might have come from the south or southeast, for there seem to be, in the substrata of Mesopotamian culture, elements of tropical forest origin from this direction. Of course, these tropical forest elements, including the use of the dugout canoe and of certain vegetally reproduced plants (especially the date palm), may have come into Mesopotamia somewhat earlier with the diffusion of those forest-dwelling traits that went to make up the European mesolithic cultures. The chief reason for attributing these elements to the period of mixture of Mesopotamian civilization is the very powerful one that no archaeological evidence for these elements or for any human habitation of the lower valley earlier than the Neolithic Garden occupation of the upper valley has been found. Yet the fact that Mesopotamia received tropical livestock like fowl and swine about the same time that it received the Highland Zone herd animals, as well as the fact that neither came from the Semites, makes it necessary to postulate a third element, of southern origin, in the Mesopotamian mixture. This element may have come by way of the mysterious civilization recently discovered by Danish archaeologists on Bahrein Island.

Additional evidence for early cultural mixture can be found in the confusion that existed, in the early historic period, between solar and lunar deities. Sometimes the sun was regarded as a male god, less frequently as a female goddess; it was usually symbolized by a disk or a many-pointed sunburst (star). Usually the moon was regarded as a female deity, but occasionally it was considered to be male; the usual moon symbol was a crescent, but sometimes it seems to have been symbolized as a complete circle (thus leading to confusion with the solar disk). This ambivalence of ideas on these two heavenly bodies seems to have arisen from a mixture of ideas from neolithic peasant and from pastoral Semite sources. It seems evident that early hunting people were patriarchal, regarded the male as more important than the female, and similarly considered the moon as more significant than the sun. The changes of the moon were more easily observed than any changes in the sun's position would be to hunting people (especially at low latitudes), and the use of the moon, rather than the sun, for hunting or fishing made it a much more significant object in their lives. Accordingly, almost all early hunting people told time by the moon, and many of them considered it to be a male, if not a deity; the sun would obviously be the moon's consort, and thus female.

When people passed from a hunting existence to pastoralism without any intervening stage of peasant agriculture, as the Semites did, these ideas were retained, since moon changes were very significant to livestock tenders. It is therefore not surprising that the early Semite pastoralists knew the moon as a male deity, sometimes called Sin, and knew the sun as a goddess, frequently called Shapash. These ideas, like the Semites themselves, came into Mesopotamia.

The Highland Garden peoples, as we have indicated, had

quite different ideas, since they regarded the female as more important than the male in economic and social life, and had as their chief deity the earth mother goddess. The sun, which was of secondary importance to the earth, was male, if it was regarded as a deity at all.

When the neolithic peasant peoples developed civilizations in the alluvial river valleys, males became more significant in their social, economic, and political life, and the sun became much more significant in their economic activities. In religion this served to reduce the earth goddess to a secondary role and make a male solar deity of primary significance. But this whole development was much confused by the persistent intrusion of Semite religious ideas in which the moon was male and of more importance. The rather chaotic ideas on these matters to be found in Mesopotamia in the historic period were thus a consequence of cultural mixtures, and not a reflection of incapacity to think clearly.

2. Gestation

Since the Stage of Gestation is, by definition, a period in which nothing sensational happens, it is not an easy period to discern in the prehistoric evidence. If we assume that the first agriculturalists came into Mesopotamia about 6000 B.C., we might postulate a period of mixture for about a thousand years and a period of gestation about half as long. In this period a new way of life different from the Neolithic Garden culture existed. Sedentary existence for centuries in one area would have reduced game and made hunting of little importance. On the other hand, especially in the more humid southern valley where there was abundance of grass and reeds, the care of domestic animals would have increased in importance. As long as hoe culture continued as the normal method of tillage, this probably remained a largely feminine occupation. Thus the neolithic society where women generally tilled the soil and men hunted, or did little, was superseded by a new culture where men became active contributors to economic life, caring for domestic animals. As a consequence dairying became of great significance, eventually with powerful religious overtones, and the social superiority of women was reduced. This rise in the position of men was increased by the appearance of the Sumerian priesthood, which must have been a predominantly masculine organization, since idly looking at the heavenly bodies or speculating on the relationships between their movements and earthly events is not something busy females would be likely to do. It would be much more likely to be found among watchers of herds than among those whose eyes are directed downward in daylight hoeing of the soil.

The growth in importance of animal care may also have resulted in clearer recognition of the male role in reproduction. Where the neolithic culture had regarded women as productive, both of crops and of children, the new Mesopotamian culture came to recognize the male role in production of both. This, in time, led to a shift in religious emphasis from fertility to virility. The symbol of the former had been the earth mother, represented by a female figurine, or simple torso, of clay, usually shown as pregnant and always shown as excessively female; the symbol of virility now came to be symbolized by the bull. This does not mean that the older ideas of fertility and the earth mother were abandoned, but that they were supplemented, and, to some extent, eclipsed by newer ideas. The earth mother was given a son, who was also her lover, a heavenly bull, who was associated with the periodicity of the year and thus with the sun. As the sun came and went, and the crops died and were reborn, so this new male god of growing things and of life's vigor died and was reborn annually. His mother, like all women, was associated with the moon in a monthly cycle. In time the symbol of the dying god became the sun's disk, while that of the earth mother became the moon, either as circle or as crescent. These two gave rise to a large number of paired symbols that together stood for the productiveness of natural processes of birth and decay. The sun bull became equivalent to the high-flying eagle or falcon, while the earth cow became equivalent to the crescent ship or to the earth's intimate, the snake. The life-giving subterranean waters of the earth mother were given symbolic fertility by representing the dying god as a fish in these waters. Or, by a similar juxtaposition, the swelling mound of earth that stood for the productive female principle was made fertile by inserting in it a rod, or a pole, a pillar or a tree. In Egypt, where the mound of earth became a pyramid, the pillar became an obelisk. The pubic triangle, sharply marked on the torso figurines of the earth mother, was made into a more powerful symbol of productive force by attaching to the triangle a rod representing the male principle. This combination of triangle and rod came to be regarded as an ax symbol, one of the most pervasive archaic representations of natural productiveness and power.

These new religious ideas, in their generalized forms, were widely diffused. They included the belief that death was an essential preliminary to resurrection, both for men and for crops, and the idea that reproduction, of children through sex and of crops from planting, were but two aspects of the fruitful relationship of two pervasive principles of fertility and virility. The deities associated with these ideas are known, in general terms, as the earth mother goddess and the dying god.

Babylonian Ishtar had a consort, Tammuz; Egyptian Isis had Osiris; Syrian Astarte had her son Adon; Anatolian Cybele had a son Attis; the Cretan Rhea had a son Zeus (who became confused, in character and name, with the pastoral sky god of the Northern Flatlands). In Greece and Rome, where Indo-European ideas were powerful, there was considerable confusion of these ideas: the sexual aspect became separated from the vegetation aspect, one being associated with Aphrodite, or Venus, and her lover, Adonis, while the other was associated with Demeter, or Ceres. In Greece the old oriental legend of the dying god became the familiar story of Demeter and her daughter Persephone, whose annual visit to Hades caused the death of vegetation in the summer season.

Changes such as these are not easy to document from the archaeological record since they are not material, but they clearly must be inferred to explain the evidence of the later period, when the invention of writing makes it possible to obtain clearer records of ideological developments.

These changes, which we can postulate for the Ages of Mixture and Gestation, were greatly influenced by the development of the Sumerian priesthood. It is extremely likely that the importance of this priesthood was organizational rather than religious or ideological at first. By 4500 this organizational significance was fully established: a new, separate group had emerged in Mesopotamian society, and this group was accumulating control of wealth beyond its own immediate consumption needs, and using this surplus to command the resources of production into capital projects. It is not clear to us how this development took place, nor why it occurred at numerous different sites in Mesopotamia, but the consequences of it are quite evident: society was launched into an Age of Expansion.

3. Expansion

The Age of Expansion of Mesopotamian civilization lasted about two thousand years, say from just before 4500 to just before 2500. In this period some of the most significant advances in human history were either made or adapted to large-scale use. These include the plow, wheeled carts and draft animals, bricks, the arch, city life, industrialized manufacture of pottery on the potter's wheel, copper and bronze smelting, a great extension of distant trade, sailboats, writing, an elaborate number system, including positional notation; remarkable advances in astronomy and to a lesser extent in medicine, and fundamental changes in religious and social life.

It is not certain that the plow is a Sumerian invention, although it was clearly used in the prehistoric period before 3000 B.C. It may have been invented by the Painted Pottery Peoples, since large stones which might have been plowshares (but are more likely to be carpentry tools) have been found in their sites in Europe before 2000 B.C. But this is a thousand years after the plow was used in Mesopotamia or in Egypt.

The early plows of the alluvial valleys were shaped to dig into the soil to break up the sunbaked flood crust rather than to turn over sod. They were simply enlarged and reinforced neolithic grubbing hoes drawn by draft animals. The use of animals, usually oxen, was one of the factors that transformed agriculture from a female to a male activity, since control of oxen was no easy task. From the economic point of view the significant result of this change was a considerable increase in production, since a much larger area of more fertile ground could be prepared for planting by a plow than by a neolithic hoe.

The wheel is almost certainly a Mesopotamian invention, being found there before 4000 B.C., more than two thousand years before it was known in Egypt. It was, of course, better adapted to the broad flat alluvial plain of Mesopotamia than it was to the narrow rocky land of Egypt, especially as the latter's transport needs were much more adequately served by river traffic, and draft animals were more conveniently available to the valley of the Two Rivers.

It is usually assumed that the earliest wheels must have been solid (rather than spoked) and were simply cross sections of tree trunks previously used as rollers. This is weakened by the fact that large tree trunks were very scarce in Mesopotamia, and the earliest representations we have of wheels are spoked. The first of these representations is from Level VI at Hassuna, about 4000 B.C., and shows a spoked wheel on a piece of pottery. It seems very likely that this was intended to be a symbol of the sun rather than a wheel and that the idea of a wheel arose from recognition that sun disks, either solid or rayed (spoked), would roll. From a very early period, symbols of the gods were displayed as emblems on the walls of temples or were exposed before the temples or carried in processions mounted on standards. One of the most common of these emblems was the rayed sun disk. Once it was recognized that such disks would roll, it is very likely that they were first used as wheels on ceremonial carts kept in the temple, as the Juggernaut car was in India. In fact the Juggernaut procession as a necessary ceremony for agrarian fertility, ensured by soaking the earth with blood under the wheels of a solar car, is closely related to some of the earliest religious ideas of Mesopotamia.

Once the wheeled cart was invented as a religious ceremonial object, its utilitarian use soon became established, probably to carry tribute to the god's storehouses. In a short time it was being used as a war vehicle drawn by more speedy asses or onagers. By 2500 B.C. priestly tombs at Ur contained four-wheel ox-drawn carts of advanced design.

The surplus controlled by the priesthood had to be stored, and the priests themselves needed residences and administrative centers for their many activities. In Mesopotamia, which lacked both stone and wood, a solution to this problem was found in the invention of sun-dried bricks about 5000 B.C. From this came the invention of the arch, the construction of temple platforms (ziggurats), and eventually the creation of the debris mounds (tells) found throughout southwestern Asia. The arch is a very difficult invention, made only once in human history, and accordingly unknown to the Incas or Aztecs. Used in Mesopotamia by the fourth millennium, the arch was probably invented in the form of the dome, of which it is a cross section. Early Sumerian huts were circular in ground plan, constructed of rushes and wicker wands stuck upright in the earth and tied together at their upper ends. It would soon be noticed that this structure would enclose a wider, more spherical space if a heavy weight were suspended from the center of the roof where the wickers came together. In this way the whole shape became less of a cone and more of a dome. If an effort were made to face this structure with brick, it would soon appear that the weight hanging from the upper center was an essential feature of the structure and must be retained in the form of a keystone. The arch itself could easily develop from efforts to make a more elongated building from this dome-like structure, just as happened with Eskimo igloos.

The arch, which did not diffuse to Egypt until very late, diffused across Syria and Anatolia, and was carried from northwestern Anatolia to northwestern Italy by the Etruscans after 1000 B.C. Adopted by the Romans, it was spread by them throughout western Europe and back to the Near East to Greece and Egypt, becoming the chief feature of ecclesiastical architecture in the medieval period both in Western cathedrals and in Byzantine churches. An alternative method for roofing large spaces, by supporting a lintel across the tops of columns, is so simple that it has been invented independently by every child who has played with blocks in his nursery. This was the method that was used regularly by the Egyptians, Minoans, Greeks, and the civilized peoples of America. In this structure the distance between columns is determined by the breaking point of the lintel under stress from its own weight. This point was so low with the materials available to ancient man that any room of normal width had to be supported by rows of columns down the middle.

The temples and priestly palaces of the Mesopotamians were built on the summits of flat-topped stepped pyramids on mounds, made of mud or clay and faced with sun-dried or oven-baked bricks or by pottery jars. These ziggurats, as they were called, are taken as evidence for the Highland origin of the Sumerians, since they evidently believed that their gods would feel at home on a high spot, and the word "ziggurat" meant "peak" in their language. The earliest temple, found at Tepe Gawra in northern Iraq, goes back to about 4500 B.C., on a site that was occupied, seven hundred years later, by an elaborate ziggurat surmounted by three large temples. Later, more impressive ziggurats were built at other places, notably further down the valley at Uruk, Ur, and Babylon. The one at Uruk, built about 3200 B.C., was oriented to the four points of the compass and measured 140 by 150 feet and was 30 feet high. It supported the oldest stone construction in the valley and a temple measuring 50 by 65 feet. The most famous of these structures was the biblical "Tower of Babel" built at Babylon about 2000 B.C. and rebuilt by Nebuchadrezzar about 600 B.C.

At a very early date, long before 4000 B.C., metal began to be used in the form of natural nuggets of gold and copper. These materials were so valuable and so soft that they could not be used for tools, which continued to be, as previously, of stone. Ornaments, however, were made by hammering and later (probably after the discovery of smelting from ores) by casting. Soon weapons, probably ceremonial, were made of copper. Eventually, possibly by natural contamination, it was found that the addition of a small percentage of tin or other metal to copper lowered the melting point and gave a much stronger alloy. By 3000 B.C. the correct proportions of tin and copper (one to ten) to give strong bronze had been found. As a result the use of bronze for weapons or tools spread rapidly, and the use of stone decreased.

The metallurgical discoveries we have mentioned were not made in Mesopotamia or in any other alluvial valley, since these lacked the necessary raw materials. They were rather products of the Highland Zone, probably on its southern fringe and fairly close to Lake Van. But the rapidly rising standards of living in the river valleys created a demand able to suck ores and metal products from great distances into the civilized areas. Thus there arose lines of distant trade converging on the Mesopotamian cities. The chief of these lines pobably went northward toward Afghanistan, Iran, Armenia, and the Caucasus, but these lines have not been explored in any adequate fashion by archaeologists. Other, better known, routes, which are of greater significance to our story, went westward across the Syrian Saddle toward Anatolia and the seaports of the Levant.

The demand for metals from remote areas was supported by the surpluses accumulated in priestly hands in Mesopotamia. As a result of such demand, small quantities of metal had a great value in terms of agricultural produce, and it was worthwhile to carry metallic products great distances. By 2000 B.C., as we have indicated, intermediaries, who were originally Semites but were later more mixed in origin, were bringing Spanish copper, Irish gold, Cornish tin, Bohemian copper, as well as Danish amber, to both Mesopotamia and Egypt. Such distant trade would not have been possible without sailing vessels that were developed somewhere in the Near East (probably on the Persian Gulf) before 3000 B.C.

The introduction of writing and of a system of numbers was undoubtedly made in Mesopotamia, as a consequence of their highly developed sense of private property. Seals with incised designs were being used to indicate ownership by impression on clay labels in the fifth millennium. The agglutinative character of the Sumerian language probably assisted the growth of writing, since symbolic marks could readily come to stand for syllables, and its full development was undoubtedly aided by the needs of large-scale priestly administration of temple wealth. Since tribute was contributed to the god in hope of a favorable flood and good crops, and payment was made for water from the god's irrigation channels, records had to be kept. Long before 3000 B.C. this was being done by scratching on pieces of clay with marsh reeds. Soon this was done by stamp seals and later still by cylinder seals that could inscribe a continuous record of ownership by being rolled across wet clay. Slowly an arbitrary system of symbols came to stand for numbers, amounts, and commodities. Later other symbols came to stand for ideas and thus for syllables. Such ideographic or syllabic writings were not completely satisfactory because ideas and syllables are so numerous that a large number of distinct symbols was needed to express even quite simple messages. None of the river-valley civilizations ever made the next step to a system of writing in which a small number of symbols represented the relatively few basic sounds used in any language. The Egyptians came close to this achievement because they did have twenty-four symbols that stood for monosyllabic words consisting of a consonant and a vowel, and were used to represent the consonant alone. But the Egyptians continued to use hundreds of other symbols for ideas, syllables, or words, and thus never acquired the true alphabet. This great achievement, as we shall see, was made by the Canaanite civilization in the course of the second millennium B.C.

The number system of Mesopotamian civilization, fully worked out by 2000 B.C., was much more efficient than their method of writing. At first they used a system based on ten, but by the historic period they had added one based on sixty for scientific work. This was much more convenient to use because it eliminated most fractions. The base 10 is divisible only by itself and 1, 2, and 5; the base 60 is divisible by itself and 1, 2, 3, 4, 5, 6, 10, 15, 20, and 30. Fractions were difficult for these archaic peoples because they could not conceive of fractions except with numerators of 1; thus ¾ was written as ½ plus ¼.

A great advance was made about 2100 B.C. when the Babylonians adopted positional notation, such as we use. In our decimal system each place from right to left represents a higher power of ten, the figure in each column indicating how many times that power of ten is to be taken. For example, the number 256 represents the sum of 2 times 10^2, 5 times 10^1, and 6 times 10^0. In the Babylonian system, where each column represented similar powers of sixty, the symbol 256 would refer to the sum of 2 times 60^2, 5 times 60^1, and 6 times 60^0, or 7,506 in our decimal system.

Positional notation for numbers, even without a symbol for zero (which the Sumerians lacked), is one of the fundamental inventions on which our Western civilization is based. Strangely enough it was not known to Classical antiquity, which used the cumbersome method familiar to us in Roman numerals. With this system calculations directly with numbers were not possible and had to be performed by some kind of calculating machine such as pebbles in boxes or by the use of the abacus.

As a result of studies based on religious motives, great progress was made in the field of astronomy. Originally this interest came from the Sumerian priesthood's concern with the seasons, the solar year, and the date of the flood. It undoubtedly continued because of tradition, from a superstitious interest in astrology, and from the hope that knowledge of astral behavior would help the priests in controlling the credulous masses of the population.

At no time was the Mesopotamian approach to astronomy scientific in our sense, and it became less so as time went on. Rather it was empirical. In our scientific approach we have an idealized picture of the interrelations of the heavenly bodies, and we try to forecast astronomical events by projecting the relationships of the heavenly bodies into the future from our knowledge of their present positions and future motions. The Mesopotamians made no use of such a picture. Instead they kept accurate records over long periods of the occurrence of certain events and tried to forecast future occurrences by adding the average period between all past observances of the event to the date of the last observation of it. Since each observation gave them one more period to use in calculating the average period, their estimates became increasingly accurate right to the end of Mesopotamian civilization. This increasing accuracy, for example in foretelling eclipses, must not be taken to indicate a continued advance of science, since the whole system was empirical rather than scientific.

But the results are impressive. The work of the late Chaldean astronomers, such as Naburimanni (alive in 490 B.C.) or Kidinnu (alive in 379), is almost unbelievable. Naburimanni gave lists of eclipses of the sun, including ones he knew would not be visible in Babylon; he gave the times on which these eclipses would begin, with errors of only a few minutes; he gave the positions of the planets far into the future with similar small errors. His successor Kidinnu gave the length of the sidereal year as 365 days 6 hours, 13 minutes, 43.4 seconds, which is only 4 minutes, 32.65 seconds too long. He gave the length of the earth's movement from its closest distance to the sun, away, and back again as 365 days, 6 hours, 25 minutes, 46 seconds—the still accepted figure. He gave many other calculations with an accuracy that was not exceeded until the nineteenth century or is still accepted today.

In spite of such observations Mesopotamia never achieved a 365-day calendar as accurate as the Egyptian. All the alluvial civilizations were troubled by efforts to combine the old paleolithic month based on changes of the moon with the new agrarian year based on movements of the sun. Since the phases of the moon take about 29½ days, while the shifts of the sun take approximately 365¼ days, it is not possible to fit a round number of lunar months into a solar year. Originally both civilizations did this by making the year 360 days or 12 lunar months of 30 days each. In such a system, both the year and the month were incorrect. The Egyptians remedied the error in the length of the year by adding five days which belonged to no month; the Mesopotamians tried to remedy the error in the length of the month by alternating months of 29 and 30 days. This difference arose because the Egyptian economy was largely agricultural, and thus emphasized the sun and the year, while the Mesopotamians were constantly under pressure from Semitic pastoral peoples to whom the moon was more important than the sun. As a result, the length of the Semitic year came to be only 354 days long, and the seasons (which require 365¼ days to pass in review) moved slowly through the various months. To remedy this a nineteen-year cycle was established in 747 B.C. by inserting seven months in every nineteen-year period, just as we insert a day in leap year. The older unreformed Babylonian calendar of 354 days was adopted by the Semites, and came through the Phoenicians to the Greeks.

This chaotic calendar continued to be used at Athens, although Democritus learned of the nineteen-year cycle on a visit to Babylon about 448, and Meton, in 433, tried to introduce it but could not win Athenian approval. The 354-day calendar of Mesopotamia is known to the Arabs to this day.

The attempt to fit the lunar month into the solar year was continued until the time of Julius Caesar (45 B.C.). The Romans used a modified version of an Anatolian calendar which they had obtained from the Etruscans, but they mismanaged it so completely that by the time of Caesar the civic year was about three months ahead of the solar year. Caesar adopted the Egyptian calendar of 365¼ days by inserting two months before March and rearranging the number of days in the months as we have them today. This calendar was made even more accurate when Pope Gregory XIII provided in 1582 that full century years (like 1800, 1900, 2000, and so on) would not be leap years except when they could be divided by 400.

The obsession of the archaic civilizations with astronomy and calendars had, originally, a rational and practical explanation and undoubtedly it was pursued with this end in view in the period 5000–2500 B.C. By the third millennium, however, both in Mesopotamia and in Egypt, the rate of expansion was beginning to slow down, the priestly or royal surpluses were increasingly being used for nonproductive purposes, and social discontents were rising. These priestly surpluses were controlled by such a small group that they could be applied to utilize new and better methods of production only by extending the benefits of such increased production to wider and wider circles of society. The priestly groups already had more of the necessities of life than they

could possibly consume, but they were, perhaps uncon-
sciously, reluctant to extend these benefits to such a wide
group as to make their clique's existence meaningless or
even impossible. Instead of using their surpluses for increased production, which would involve a drastic redistribution of the society's income, they began to apply this
income to nonproductive purposes. As a result the age of
expansion began to draw to its close about the middle of the
third millennium B.C.

We have said that an Age of Expansion shows geographic
extension of the area of the society's culture, increase in its
population, increase in its economic production, growth of
factual knowledge, and, probably, certain elements of science and of democracy. The existence of all these seems well
established in the period of expansion of Mesopotamian
society. Its area filled the Tigris-Euphrates Valley and
pushed up into the surrounding highlands and across the
Syrian Saddle into the Levant and Anatolia; it even spread
down the Persian Gulf to its lower shores. The growth of
population is evident from the great number of tells across
the plain and from the debris of thousands of residential
houses in the ruined strata of these mounds. The rise in
production and in standards of living is clearly established
by the same evidence, while the growth of knowledge is
recorded in the hundreds of thousands of inscribed clay
tablets in these ruins. The advance of science has been
mentioned already and is beyond doubt, but the existence
of primitive democratic elements in Sumerian life must be
based on inference. The arguments to support the existence
of democratic influences in the prehistoric period have been
given by Thorkild Jacobsen of the University of Chicago.
They have not won universal acceptance by other scholars

because of differences of opinion on how much democracy is necessary to make a society "democratic"; there seems no doubt about the existence of democratic elements in the earlier period.

The position held by at least some members of the ruling groups in Mesopotamia at the very end of the age of expansion can be seen in the famous "Royal" graves at Ur about 2500 B.C. By that time the people believed that their priestly ruler (called *ensi*) was the god's representative on earth and that his intercession was necessary to obtain the god's support for all the orderly periodicities necessary to human life on earth. Since they believed in a life after death similar to the life on this earth, these priestly leaders were, in some cases, buried with food, furniture, treasures, and even servants to assist their life in the hereafter. At Ur the tombs, buried in the earth, were full-size rooms constructed of brick and stone, the latter brought from the hills thirty miles distant. When the body of the *ensi* was placed in the tomb, his servants and wives were killed at his side, several four-wheeled oxcarts were driven in and the oxen and drivers killed, and he was surrounded with rich furnishings. One *ensi*'s tomb contained the bodies of sixty persons killed with him; another contained the remains of six men and sixty-eight women; in another, twenty-five persons were buried with the wife of the *ensi*. Although many of these tombs have been plundered by grave robbers, we possess numerous magnificent objects that were left with the dead. Among these were a twenty-five-inch model ship made of silver, an elaborate headdress containing more than twenty-five feet of gold band, a helmet of sheet gold hammered to resemble locks of hair and even individual hairs, numerous cups, vases, and bowls of gold and silver, daggers of gold with lapis-lazuli handles, magnificently decorated harps, and many statues of animals in precious metals.

The increased concentration of wealth, the increased diversion of this wealth from productive to unproductive purposes, and the great growth in superstition, magic, and irrational practices were soon followed, in the late third millennium B.C., by a rapid increase in the frequency and intensity of imperialist war. All of these changes mark the shift from the Age of Expansion to an Age of Conflict.

4. The Age of Conflict

We have defined the Age of Conflict as extending from the date when the rate of expansion begins to decline to the period when one political unit establishes a universal empire by conquering the entire area of the civilization. In the earlier part of this period the whole core of the civilization may be conquered by one or more preliminary empires. In Mesopotamian society we may fix the dates of the Age of Conflict from about 2700 B.C. to the Assyrian Conquest about 700 B.C. The preliminary universal empires would be found in the Akkadian period about 2350 B.C. and again in the Babylonian period about 1700 B.C.

We have already listed the chief characteristics of an Age of Conflict to be (1) decreasing rate of expansion, (2) imperialist wars, (3) class conflicts, and (4) irrationality. These qualities were generally prevalent in the two thousand years that we have called Mesopotamia's Age of Conflict. Of these the second is most obvious. By the latter half of the third millennium, war became the dominant activity of the society, and secular military leaders of the armies rose to a social position so high that they were able to dominate, without ever completely replacing, the religious leaders who had previously dominated the society. War became, in the minds of many people, the only way in which adequate supplies of slaves and metals could be obtained and by which some compensation could be obtained for the slowing up of economic and technical progress. The slowing up of such advance is clearly visible after 2500 B.C., although the dissipation of the priestly surplus gave, for a while, a more equitable distribution of the social income and the appearance of a rise in standards of living. This slowing up can be seen by comparing the technical advances of the two millennia 4700–2700 with those of the equally long period 2700–700. In the earlier interval we find dozens of significant inventions and discoveries; in the later one we find, according to V. Gordon Childe, only two. These two are positional notation of numbers, in Babylon, about 2000, and the invention of aqueducts by the Assyrians at the end of the eighth century B.C. There were a few other minor advances, chiefly in military tactics and governmental administration, but progress, in the old nineteenth century meaning of that abused word, never again moved Mesopotamian civilization at such a high rate as it did around 3000 B.C.

Instead of progress, the whole period of 2,000 years was filled with wars. In the first part of the period, during the third millennium, these wars were local struggles within the river valleys themselves. For the later and longer portion of the period, covering most of the second and first millennia B.C., these wars developed into violent struggles between civilizations. The chief aim of these later conflicts was to control the Syrian Saddle and thus to win, at one stroke, an important source of timber, control of the link between the eastern and western areas of civilization, and the right to impose tribute—in succession to the Mitanni—on a major part of the commercial activities of the Near East. In these struggles the chief contenders were the Egyptian Empire, the Hittite Empire in Anatolia, and whatever empire was dominant in Mesopotamia.

We say "whatever empire was dominant in Mesopotamia" because there was a sequence of empires in the valley of the two rivers, roughly corresponding to the sequence of dynasties in Egypt. Ultimately the Hittites and Egyptians, who had been struggling violently for Syria in the thirteenth century, were both eclipsed, and the final victory in the whole Near East, including rule over all these areas, went to the universal empire of Mesopotamia. The Hittite civilization was ended by the Iron Age invaders of the twelfth century B.C., while Egypt, which had a shorter Age of Conquest but a much longer Age of Decay than Mesopotamia, suffered the consequence of this phasing by being conquered by Mesopotamian society.

If we examine the history of Mesopotamia and Egypt from this point of view, we find an extraordinary parallel. This parallel was distorted by two, relatively minor, differences. Mesopotamia was older than Egypt and thus entered upon its Age of Conflict somewhat earlier (2500 B.C., as compared to 2200 B.C.), but, being politically disunited and in an exposed geographic position, had a much longer Age of Conflict and a very much shorter Age of Decay. Egypt's protected geographic position, which allowed it to decay without much outside interference for a long time, fell to the Greeks without even a token resistance in 334 B.C., while Mesopotamia, which had reached its Age of Universal

Empire so much later, had only a brief Age of Decay and accordingly still had sufficient vitality to put up a vigorous resistance to Alexander's invasion before it also succumbed in 333 B.C.

The parallelism of the two civilizations may be seen in the following table:

Period	Egypt	Mesopotamia
1. Mixture	5500–4000	6000–5000
2. Gestation	4000–3500	5000–4500
3. Expansion	3500–2200	4500–2500
4. Conflict	2200–1550	2500–750
5. Universal Empire	1550–1100	750–450
6. Decay	1100–350	450–350
7. Invasion	350–300	350–300

In both societies the Age of Conflict was punctuated by the intrusion of pastoral intruders, the Hyksos in Egypt and the Kassites in Mesopotamia, both shortly after 1700 B.C. In Egypt the Hyksos remained a people apart, with their center outside Egypt itself (at Avaris in Sinai) and occupying only a portion of the Delta for exploitative purposes; they were more easily expelled, about 1567, and Egypt resumed its autonomous evolution, achieving its full universal empire in what we call the New Kingdom (1570–1166).

In Mesopotamia the process was more prolonged. The preliminary core empire of the Akkadians (2250–2150) was overthrown to be followed by another Semitic intrusion (the Amorites), and a second preliminary core empire of Semitic domination centered at Babylon. This latter state, whose best known ruler was the famous Hammurabi (1728–1686), was never firmly established, and the intrusion of the Kassites, a generation later, broke Mesopotamia up into conflicting political units once more. Only after centuries of interminable struggles did a real universal empire emerge under the Assyrians. Armed with iron weapons and employing a policy of ruthless militarism, peripheral Assyria emerged from the hill country north of the river valley in the ninth century B.C. Under Tiglath-Pileser I (1114–1076) and Ashurnasirpal II (883–859) they conquered the area between Armenia, the Tigris, and Syria. The methods they used have been recorded by Ashurnasirpal himself in the following inscriptions:

"I stormed the mountain peaks and took them. In the midst of the mighty mountain I slaughtered them, and, with their blood, dyed the mountain red like wool. . . . I carried off their spoil and their possessions. The heads of their warriors I cut off, and I formed them into a pillar over against their city. Their young men and maidens I burned in the fire. . . . I flayed all the chief men who had revolted and I covered the pillar with their skins; some I walled up within the pillar; some I impaled upon the pillar on stakes. . . . Many within the border of my own land I flayed, and I spread their skins upon the walls, and I cut off the limbs of the royal officers who had rebelled."

With methods such as these, Assyria conquered most of the Near East and even conquered Egypt for a brief period (668–652), but was replaced by Chaldea, a state of Aramean Semites, in 612 B.C. Chaldea, in turn, yielded to the last Mesopotamian universal empire, Persia, in 538.

The sequence of universal empires in Mesopotamia helped to keep the society stronger than it would otherwise have been. This is equivalent to saying that its period of decay was postponed. Each state yielded to its successor because its own instruments of governing had become institutionalized, but the arrival of new instruments of government at the succession of a new state in supreme control served to revitalize the society. This was especially true of the last of these universal empires, that of the Persians, which assumed control in 538 B.C. and provided a very vigorous government for so late in the career of a civilization. By 350, of course, the Stage of Decay had been reached, but even then Mesopotamia, unlike Egypt, was not deep in decay, as Egypt was.

From these rather cursory remarks it would seem that both Mesopotamian and Egyptian civilizations followed the pattern of the seven stages of civilization with only minor distortions. The word "minor" can, however, hardly be applied to the next civilization we wish to examine, that of the Canaanites (2200 B.C.–100 B.C.).

8

Canaanite and Minoan Civilizations

Two civilizations, utterly dissimilar in character, serve as connecting links between Sumerian culture and Classical civilization. Of these, Minoan civilization is considerably the older, beginning to form before 3000 B.C. and dissolving to death about 1000 B.C. The younger, Canaanite civilization, followed along at least a millennium later, in the period 2200 B.C.–50 B.C. The difference in character of the two is almost as great as could be, the younger one being violent and bloodthirsty, especially in its religious ceremonies, to a degree exceeded by no other society, except perhaps the Mesoamerican during the Aztec period, while Minoan society was gentle and peaceful, without temples or any known religious ceremonies.

Chronologically Minoan civilization should be discussed first, but logically it is better to reverse the order because of the close cultural relations between Minoan society and Classical civilization to be discussed in the chapter to follow.

A. *Canaanite Civilization*

Because of its exposed geographic position, at the crossroads between Egyptian, Mesopotamian, and Hittite civilizations and the frequent incursions of these powerful cultures into its core area, Canaanite society has the most distorted sequence of stages of any civilization we shall discuss. Of its importance there can be no doubt, since it contributed much to later peoples, including the alphabet and two great religions. But its basic unity as a single society is frequently missed because of emphasis placed on geographic areas, linguistic groupings, political units, or religious groups. The situation is further complicated by the fact that its universal empire (Carthage) was so distant as to justify to many students a completely isolated treatment from the core area (the Levant) whence it arose.

The instrument of expansion of Canaanite society is also a source of difficulty because it is a type of economic organization so familiar to us that it is taken as a matter of course without the emphasis which is placed, for example, on Mesopotamian temple administration or the domination of Egyptian economic life by the Pharaonic state. The Canaanite instrument of expansion seems to have been commercial capitalism. Thus it is similar to the instrument of expansion that gave our Western civilization its second age of expansion in 1440–1690.

Capitalism might be defined, if we wish to be scientific, as a form of economic organization motivated by the pursuit of profit within a price structure. Thus defined, it should be evident that there can be more than one kind of capitalism and that any kind can perform as an instrument or perform with decreasing effectiveness by becoming institutionalized.

When profits are pursued by geographic interchange of goods, so that commerce for profit becomes the central mechanism of the system, we usually call it "commercial capitalism." In such a system goods are conveyed from areas where they are more common (and therefore cheaper) to areas where they are less common (and therefore less cheap). This process leads to regional specialization and to division of labor, both in agricultural production and in handicrafts. Both of these, as well as the interlinking commercial groups, become specialized activities within a market nexus.

It is extremely likely that Canaanite society developed commercial capitalism as its instrument of expansion because its core area, the Levant, was on the western approaches to the Syrian Saddle at the point where these approaches shifted from waterborne to land transportation. This point was the juncture between the demand for raw materials, especially metals, created by the high standard of living of Mesopotamian civilization to the east and the sources of such raw materials, accessible by water, to the west. These created a powerful mutual attraction that could hardly fail to turn the incipient Canaanite society toward trading for profit. In fact, this attraction was operating even before the Canaanites settled on the western approaches to the Syrian Saddle about 2200 B.C.; it drew into this activity the proto-Assyrian peoples on the eastern approaches of the Syrian Saddle, on the upper Tigris drainage, so that these Assyrian speakers were settled as far west as southern Anatolia (Cappadocia), if not farther, in defended trading posts, even before 2200 B.C.

Commercial capitalism, as an instrument of expansion, has powerful tendencies to become institutionalized, to the

injury of continued economic advance. Such institutionalization arises when pursuit of profit becomes dominant over
the real, if remote, goals of any economic system. These real
goals include high enjoyment of wealth, and can be analyzed into high production, high distribution, and high
consumption of goods. As long as the pursuit of profits
serves to assist these goals, any profit organization of the
economic system remains an instrument, but this is likely to
continue only as long as the trading system is a competitive
one. As long as the competitive aspect of the organization
continues, each entrepreneur seeks to obtain a larger share
of the total trade for himself, and invests his savings, as in
ships, wharves, or warehouses, in order to do so. Such investment increases the total volume of trade, which, in turn,
increases the total volume of production on one side, and
the total volume of consumption on the other side. This
increase in wealth has, eventually, an adverse effect on the
volume of profits, since profits (meaning a surplus over the
total of the costs of production and of distribution) require
a scarcity system. Increase in volume, by making goods
less scarce, reduces the margin by which retail selling prices
exceed costs and thus, in general terms, jeopardizes profits.
When this occurs, and the commercial traders are in a position to reduce their mutual competition, they seek to man-
age the market, by reducing volume in order to raise profits.
In this way profits become dominant over wealth as an
economic goal, to the jeopardy of volume and high living
standards. Means have become ends—or, as we put it, an
instrument has become an institution. This process took place
in our own Western civilization about the seventeenth century, and of that process we generally say that commercial
capitalism (or the "commercial revolution," in the older

books) was transformed into mercantilism. In Canaanite society we speak of the rise of a "commercial oligarchy" in the later days of Phoenicia or of Carthage. When this occurred, the society ceased to expand by economic means (that is, by increasing volume of wealth, or by intensification of economic activities) and tried to expand by political means (that is, to increase profits by extensification of economic activities by bringing wider geographic areas under the institutionalized economic organization). Thus, the economic imperialism and wars typical of Stage 4 of any civilization replaced the earlier economic expansion (which also involved geographic expansion, but by exploration and colonization rather than by imperialist wars).

1. Mixture

The period of mixture in Canaanite society is clear enough. About 2200 B.C., and for several centuries after that, the Amurru were pushing out of the Syrian Desert into the Fertile Crescent. Those who moved eastward into Mesopotamia we call Amorites (Babylonians), while those who moved westward into the Levant are generally called Canaanites. Many of these intruders were pastoral peoples with herds of sheep or asses, but it is possible that some of them were tillers of the soil. In any case, they were Semite peoples, warlike and patriarchal, with a multiplicity of gods. Some of these deities were simply animistic spirits found in rocks, trees, or springs. Others were spirits of nature, including deities of storms, the sky, fertility, fire, water, and such. Others were gods of more abstract ideas representing the creator, justice, mercy, or crafts. This variety of deities in itself reflects a mixed culture coming into a situation where further mixture was inevitable. These other peoples came chiefly from Mesopotamia to the east and from Egypt to the south, but the Indo-European people from the north, known as Mitanni, and the Alpine peoples from the same direction, whom we call Hurrians, helped to contribute to what must have been a very complex mixture. And finally, during the middle centuries of the second millennium B.C., there were pervasive cultural elements from the seaways to the west, especially from Crete. These included Minoan and later Mycenaean influences. Thus it would seem that the period of mixture could be stretched to cover almost a whole millennium, from about 2300 to about 1300 B.C.

In spite of this great mixture of different elements, Canaanite society developed its own distinctive outlook and character. Vigorous, practical, almost crude; grasping, unesthetic, yet with powerful spiritual impulses; filled with sensual desires and crass superstitions, yet with basic intelligence the equal of any other people in history—such was the complex nature of these Canaanite peoples, a nature which leaves them, to this day, a constant puzzle and source of interest to students.

Whatever may have been the social organization of the Canaanites before they migrated, they came into the Fertile Crescent organized on the basis of blood groupings, either as families or tribes. Almost at once the more successful of these groups began to hack out areas of influence and create principalities organized on a somewhat different basis, since they claimed powers over peoples who were not related to the family of the prince. Thus, the idea of the state, coming perhaps from the city civilizations not far off, began to replace the older ideas of tribal loyalty and blood vengeance.

The second millennium was still in its early centuries when a series of Amurru princes ruled the whole Fertile Crescent from the Persian Gulf to the Nile and, as "Hyksos," were beginning to force their way into Egypt. Amorite names like Abram, Jacob, and Benjamin were recorded in cuneiform writing for the whole area. Tribal or family influence was still so powerful in most places that individual rights were very weak, and a strong family group was a better guarantee of personal safety or of individual rights than either personal prowess or princely power.

In this rapidly developing society there were scattered persons whom the documents called "Habiru" or some similar term. They are recorded from Mesopotamia, Asia Minor, Egypt, and the Levant. The meaning of the term Habiru is disputed, but it seems to apply to persons whose social position did not provide them with the protection of blood relatives and of the threat of retaliatory feuding by their families. They were, what Maitland called in the early Middle Ages in England, "landless and kin-shattered men." The cause of this "kin-shattered" condition which left the Habiru in a precarious social condition is fairly clear. Any individual who had killed a member of his own family obviously lost the protection of that family and became socially isolated. Or again, any person who had made a formal agreement to become the bondsman of another had voluntarily renounced the protection of his blood relatives. Similarly, men who bound themselves to fight for money could not expect their families to stand by prepared to avenge any injuries they might suffer in their combats. Such persons, without family to protect them or to force the prince to extend his protection, needed some other protector. This was found by seeking the favor of Yahveh, the God of mercy, one of the lesser deities in the numerous Canaanite pantheon. Such allegiance to Yahveh by bondsmen, murderers, or other "kin-shattered" persons did not originally imply any renunciation of the other deities in the Canaanite pantheon, and the Habiru continued to worship, as seemed fit, the other Canaanite Baals, working downward from the greatest, El, God of justice and Creator of the world.

The economic activities of these Habiru were probably not much different from those of other Canaanites. But two comments might be made. As persons with weak or no kinship ties they probably wandered about from place to place more readily than other Canaanites. And there clearly seems to be, among the Habiru, a large proportion of wandering metalworkers and musicmakers. Some of these metalworkers were known as Kenites, a name traditionally derived from Cain, the son of Adam. It is worth noting that the mark the Lord put upon Cain was not a mark of damnation, as some believe, but a mark of protection: "the Lord put a mark on Cain, lest any who came upon him should kill him."

It would appear thus that the Habiru who became the worshipers of Yahveh and later strict monotheists began as a legal or social group, later (at the time of Moses) became a religious group, and still later (at the time of Joshua) began to develop into a political group. Much later, after the Assyrian destruction of the Hebrew state, they became, once more, primarily a religious group, although there always were tendencies to become a political group (by establishing Hebrew rule in some area) or to become a biological group (by insisting on endogamy). At any rate the Hebrews always were a group within Canaanite society and never became a society of their own.

2. Gestation

Because the process of mixture continued so long in Canaanite civilization, probably because of the very exposed geographic position of the Levant, we cannot fix any rigid date when mixture ended and gestation began. There was rather a series of advances and relapses not only in regard to these two stages but possibly in regard to the next as well. Moreover, the instrument of expansion we have posited for this society, commercial capitalism, is one in which there is no great interval between accumulation of surplus, plowing of this surplus back into the business, and increase of output arising from such investment. This process undoubtedly existed among the Canaanites at an early date in the second millennium, but it seems clear that the Levant was too closely dominated by Egyptian and Hittite influences for us to attribute much of its social dynamics to Canaanite organization until fairly well along in that second millennium. By 1300 Egyptian power was in full retreat from the Levant, and a century later the Hittite Empire was breaking up under the blows of the Iron Age invaders. At that point, about 1200, the period of expansion of Canaanite society was beginning.

3. Expansion

The period of expansion of Canaanite society began as the withdrawal of Egyptian and Hittite influence and the absorption of Hurrian and Mitanni peoples allowed this new commercial society to emerge. At that time we find a three-fold situation: the Canaanite pagans in control of the southern Levant were being squeezed between the Philistines coming in from the sea to the west and the Hebrews coming in from the desert to the east.

The Canaanite pagans in this period were to be found not only in Palestine but also in Syria, where they were already engaged in the Levantine trading activities we associate with the Phoenicians. In fact they were early Phoenicians, although historians usually call them by the names of their respective cities. Of these cities the best known are probably Ras Shamra and Alalakh in northern Syria. The archaeological evidence from these, especially from Ras Shamra (the ancient Ugarit), shows a flourishing trade going on between Mesopotamia and the Mediterranean peoples, particularly the Mycenaeans from 1700 to 1200. It is clear that the period of expansion, in this area at least, was in full swing before the fourteenth century B.C. By the end of that century pressure from the Hittites and the damage caused by the great earthquake of about 1365 B.C., had hampered these more northern seaports and provided an opportunity for more southern seaports such as Byblos, Sidon, and Tyre to break into the western trade. It was these Phoenician cities that took Canaanite commerce through the Age of Expansion.

While these developments were occurring in the north the Hebrew peoples were forming in the south. Some Habiru had accompanied the Hyksos into Egypt in the eighteenth century B.C. When these "Shepherd Peoples" were expelled from Egypt by Ahmose I about 1567, many of the Habiru remained, working as copper miners and coppersmiths in Sinai or as bondsmen and mercenary soldiers in Egypt itself. In time, Egyptian rule over these peoples became increasingly oppressive. About 1300 a man with the Egyptian name of Moses killed an Egyptian and had to flee into the eastern deserts beyond Sinai. There he became acquainted with Yahveh, married the daughter of the Midianite priest of Yahveh, and returned to Egypt to lead the Habiru to safety. Instead of following the regular coast road from Egypt to Canaan, Moses led his followers eastward into the desert. After the revelation on Mount Sinai and the death of Moses, the new leader, Joshua, led the Hebrews into Canaan by making a wide swing into the desert to the east. The invaders sacked the Canaanite city of Jericho, which guarded the approach road from the east (about 1230) but were unable to cross the hills down into the western plains where the Canaanite war chariots were still undefeated. The new invention of lime-plastered cisterns for catching rain made it possible for the Israelites to expand along the hitherto unoccupied hills above the Canaanite-controlled springs and streams. Eventually the Canaanites were absorbed between the Hebrew pressure from the eastern hills and the seaborne invasions of the Philistines from the west (1200–1000), but the basic character of Canaanite culture was not greatly changed. There was a good deal of mutual assimilation and agricultural resettlement, but the chief changes were the acquisition by the Hebrews of agriculture with iron tools and weapons. By 1000 B.C. the chief distinction between Hebrews and Canaanites was religious, the former slowly abandoning the old, bloodthirsty Canaanite gods in favor of a supreme God of mercy and justice as a result of Moses' covenant from Mount Sinai. Even this was a slow process, and for many centuries persons who called themselves Hebrews, including the well-known kings of Israel, lapsed into polytheistic acts.

In Canaan the Hebrews built up two kingdoms in the interior of the country. *Judah* extended from the northern end of the Dead Sea at Jericho to the northern end of the Red Sea at the Gulf of Aqaba, and *Israel* extended from Jericho northward to Mount Hermon. Except for a short stretch from the latitude of Jericho north to Mount Carmel, the Hebrews did not control the Mediterranean seacoast, the southern section remaining in the hands of the Philistines while the northern section (Syria) rested in the hands of the Canaanites (Phoenicians).

Under David and Solomon (ca. 1010–930) the priestly democracy of the earlier Hebrews, known as the "period of the Judges," was replaced by an autocratic, militaristic monarchy, patterned after other oriental kingdoms, with a standing army, a governmental bureaucracy, and annual taxes. Israel and Judah were united into the Kingdom of Israel with its capital at Jerusalem. With the help of Canaanite artisans and architects, a great temple and palace were built at Jersulaem, and a stone stable capable of accommodating over four hundred horses was built at Megiddo. Although the Hebrews did not control the port cities of the Levant, they were able to finance this luxury by acting as middlemen in commercial relations between the Arabs of the Red Sea and the Canaanites of the Phoenician coast. Solomon built a great port city, Ezion-Geber, at the head of the Gulf of Aqaba and made a profitable alliance with Hiram of Tyre in Phoenicia. The Sabaean Arabs of the Red Sea brought spices, myrrh, incense, gold, silver, "ivory, apes, and peacocks" from India and other areas. The Phoenicians, for their part, began to push westward by 1000 B.C., and, within a couple of centuries, had colonies at Carthage, Sardinia, Malaga, and Gades (Cadiz), whence they brought copper, tin, and iron to their cities in the Levant. The overland route from Ezion-Geber to Phoenicia was controlled by Solomon, who added to the trade iron and copper from his extensive smelteries in the Jordan Valley and horses bred in his great stud farm at Megiddo.

In this way the Age of Expansion of Canaanite civilization continued for about five or more centuries. It had the typical characteristics of such a period: increased production, growing population, geographic exploration and colonization, and increased knowledge. The increasing availability of iron weapons and the spread of a money economy undoubtedly helped to advance democracy in this period although hardly enough to allow it to flourish. The Levant's exposed strategic position made any long-continued democracy unlikely. Nor is there much evidence for the existence of science. And finally, technological inventions, which are so often found in the Age of Expansion, were very rare.

The one invention that must be emphasized is the alphabet, certainly one of the most significant in all of human history. This seems to have started in several forms, among a number of Amurra groups, quite early in the growth of Canaanite society, possibly in its Age of Gestation. The original idea may well have been based on the twenty-four monosyllabic symbols in Egyptian hieroglyphics modified to fit the Canaanite tongue during the Hyksos period, or at least in the Sinai area.

One of the chief services performed by the Canaanites was the reestablishment of law and order on the high seas after the turmoil of the Iron Age invasions and the movements of the Peoples of the Sea. This greatly increased Mediterranean trade and introduced certain eastern factors into Classical civilization during its period of mixture.

The Evolution of Civilizations

4. Conflict and Empire

The flourishing situation that we have described began to
decline, shortly after 800 B.C. in the Levant, although not
until several generations later in the central and western
Mediterranean. There was growing social unrest in Palestine, a renewed split between the two Hebrew kingdoms,
democratic and puritanical agitations among certain religious leaders, generally inspired, it would seem, by those
closer to the pastoral desert peoples. There was also a considerable growth in religious animosities, chiefly because
of the survival of Canaanite fertility ideas among agricultural peoples and because of Phoenician influences (as
exercised through persons like Queen Jezebel). In addition
to these troubles there were growing external dangers, including renewed Egyptian invasions under Necho (608
B.C.), increasing Aramean pressures and, above all, the
continued savage assaults of the Assyrians. In a series of
brutal attacks the Levantine cities were looted, sacked, made
tributary, and their leading citizens deported. The northern
kingdom of Palestine (then called Samaria) was destroyed
in 722 and the southern one (Judaea) in 586. The more
prominent citizens, perhaps one-tenth of the population,
were deported to Babylon, the rest, mostly peasants, being
left in Palestine. As a result of their exile, the upper classes
became increasingly rigid in their religious orthodoxy. Accordingly, when some of these returned from their Babylonian captivity after the Persian conquest of Assyria in
538, controversy broke out between the more casual Pales-
tinian peasantry and the more rigid Babylonian exiles. The
chief disagreements were concerned with methods of sacri-

fice, use of images, and permission to marry non-Jews. All of these things added to the conflicts in the core area of Canaanite society, until that society had been almost torn to pieces by 500 B.C., although Tyre, situated on an island half a mile from the Levantine shore, continued to dominate the maritime commerce of the eastern Mediterranean until destroyed by Alexander the Great in 332 B.C.

In the meantime the periods of expansion and conflict were occurring at somewhat later dates in the more peripheral west. The Age of Expansion probably continued there until about 600 B.C., and was followed by a rather brief age of conflict. This was short, lasting little more than a century, because there was no other Canaanite state in the west in any position to challenge Carthage's claim to universal empire in that peripheral area and because the social triumph of the commercial oligarchy within Carthage made class struggles insignificant.

Carthage is to be regarded as the universal empire of Canaanite society despite its lack of political influence in the core areas in the Levant, since the strategically indefensible position of the Levant in the face of Assyrian power made it hopeless for Carthage to have any political ambitions there. A parallel situation could arise in our own Western civilization if Soviet domination of Europe left the United States as the only significant political force in the Western Hemisphere.

There can be no doubt that Carthage, as a political unit, was a part of Canaanite society. The inhabitants spoke a Canaanite tongue and called themselves Canaanites, although we usually speak of them by the name of the city and refer to their language by the Latin term "Punic." Their organization of expansion was the same institutionalized commercial capitalism. Their religion was clearly Canaanite, full of bloodthirsty superstitions concerned with various "baals," especially Moloch. This god, who was worshiped by throwing infants into his raging fires, was the principal deity of Carthage and Tyre and was not unknown in Palestine; there Solomon erected an altar to him, and other Israelites joined in his horrible sacrifices. This is only some of the evidence showing that Carthage, as a political unit, was in Canaanite culture.

5. Decay and Invasion

By 500 B.C. the period of decay was about to begin. Twenty years later (480), in both east and west, the Canaanite peoples suffered severe military defeats that serve as historical pointers to the downward way. In the east the Phoenician fleet in the service of Persia was destroyed by the Greeks at Salamis, while in the west Carthaginian forces were destroyed at Himera in Sicily by the forces of the western Greeks. These two events, which folk tales placed on the same day, marked a collision between declining Canaanite culture in its age of early decay and rising Classical civilization in its full flush of expansion. The final blow in this conflict did not fall until almost four centuries later. Canaanite culture slowly died in the east after Alexander destroyed Tyre in 332, and the same culture died more quickly in the west after Rome sacked Carthage in the Third Punic War (146 B.C.). By the time of Christ only a few remnants of this strange distorted civilization still survived.

B. *Minoan Civilization*

It is unfortunate that we know so little about the Cretan, or Minoan, civilization, for it has a number of distinctions of considerable significance. It was the first civilization that was not in an alluvial river valley, and, probably as a consequence, it retained its Neolithic Garden culture character more than any other. For one thing, it was peaceful, something that can hardly be said about other civilizations. It remained basically matriarchal, in the sense that women had at least social equality, if not social superiority; its chief deity was female; and women undoubtedly had greater political influence than in any other ancient civilization. Its religion was so unformalized that it had no temples and, so far as our evidence goes, no formal religious ceremonies. And to complete a rather paradoxical picture, its instrument of expansion seems to have been a socialistic state, yet its people, instead of being oppressed and regimented, had an outlook that was remarkably happy, optimistic, and carefree.

The statement that the instrument of expansion of Cretan civilization was a socialistic state is based on the fact that almost all handicraft production, commercial activities, and written records seem to be centered in large public buildings, such as the so-called palace at Cnossus in Crete. The ruins of this prehistoric Pentagon Building were excavated by Sir Arthur Evans after 1900. It is traditional among English archaeologists to call every large building that is excavated either a temple or a palace, and, since Sir Arthur found no evidence of religious ceremonies in this large building, it had to be a "palace" and its resident had to be a "king." This "king," according to Evans, was the legendary "Minos," a Cretan ruler well known in Greek traditions of the historic period. But these traditions seem to indicate that "Minos" was a title (like Pharaoh or President), not a personal name, and that the office was, at least in one period, an elective rather than a hereditary one. Homer tells us quite specifically that Minos served for nine years, so that he could have been a nonhereditary magistrate. This is supported by the evidence from the palace itself, since there is little trace of a personal ruler or of any effort to concentrate power, prestige, or honor about any single individual. Sir Arthur Evans called a small room containing a stone chair the "throne room," but the small size both of room and chair make it look rather like a place where someone might sit down in the morning to tie his shoelaces. There is a great deal of art in the palace, but none of it could be interpreted as "monarchial." In fact pictures of individuals, especially males, are rather rare. There are some representations of females dressed in what, even today, would be considered daring costumes, but most of the pictures are of nature in its most beautiful moods: the sea, shot through with sparkling sunlight and enlivened with fish, squid, and other forms of marine life; or lake shores with flowers and birds; or wild life in the countryside. Human figures appear occasionally, especially in connection with athletic events, notably with a rodeolike scene in which youths and maidens vault over the head of a bull by grasping its horns and somersaulting over its head, to land on its back—facing rearward—and hop off. This latter scene is frequently explained as a religious ceremony, and it may well be—but here, as elsewhere, there is no centralization of personality such as would almost inevitably appear in a monarchial regime and which is so obvious in other socialistic civilizations such as the Egyptian, the Andean, or the Russian.

1. Mixture

The period of mixture of Cretan society goes back almost to the first settlements on the island, and may continue as late as the third millennium. Rough dates could be set from before 3500 B.C. (perhaps as early as 4000) to after 3000. The elements that came together on this small island of Crete were (1) a mixed group from Anatolia who may have been in the mesolithic cultural stage, with a few early domestic animals and pottery made to look like leather bags; (2) a Neolithic Garden culture of the usual type, the major ingredient in the subsequent Cretan culture; (3) a significant Asiatic influence, possibly associated with the megalithic diffusion, bringing knowledge of metals; and (4) an Egyptian influence, which is sometimes attributed, without evidence, to refugees from the unification of Egypt by Menes, just before 3000 B.C. The last two of these influences continued to flow for much of the early portion of Minoan history, so that Cretan art, for example, continued to show Egyptian influences, while Minoan writing, like that of Mesopotamia, was made by impressions on clay tablets.

These civilizing influences did not change the basic Neolithic Garden foundation of Cretan culture except by building upon it, and the new society remained peaceful and cooperative. The most significant question, which to my knowledge has never been answered (or even asked), is how it was possible for a nonalluvial garden culture to adopt the fully sedentary life necessary for civilized existence. In a blunt sentence: Why did not the early Minoans exhaust the fertility of the soil and have to shift their fields as their neolithic ancestors did? The answer probably is that they developed a new diet which put less pressure on soil fertility. This diet was based on olive oil, grape wine, fish, and wheat, and proved so successful that it has remained the staple diet of the Mediterranean area to the present time. It is a very significant diet in a number of ways beyond its biologic adequacy for man: two of its elements were liquids, obtained from perennial plantings, while a third was derived from the sea. Oil and wine required sedentary farming and, at the same time, created a demand for pottery containers, which undoubtedly gave an impulse to craft specialization in this direction. In the palace at Cnossus was row after row of man-high pottery jars that had been filled with oil, wine, and wheat. The use of fish for the protein element in their diet served to tie the economy to the sea and provided the water-craft and maritime skills that allowed the Cretans to become the commercial middlemen of the Mediterranean basin when the need arose. And it is possible, although not clear from the evidence, that the grain fields could have been re-fertilized by products from the sea, such as burned seaweed. At any rate the Cretan people in their earliest centuries began to work out an economic system that moved them toward cooperation, specialized activities, and dependence on the sea without population pressure on the soil.

2. Gestation

As in so many civilizations, the period of gestation of Minoan society must rest on inference. The argument that the instrument of expansion was the public authority is itself based on inference, although a fairly obvious one, but we can hardly go behind this inference to any more remote ones about origins. All that we can say is that the cooperative elements of neolithic peasant agriculture were developed in the political security of an island existence and, probably under the influence of the sea, toward the development of a cooperative, nonmonarchical, nonmilitaristic, and nonecclesiastical public authority. We do not know if there was only a single such authority for the whole island or several of them. The archaeological evidence shows several centers in which urban centralized living developed on the island—at Cnossus and Mallia in the north and at Phaistos and Hagia Triada in the south. The existence of "palaces" in all of these does not necessarily indicate separate political units, especially if these buildings were administrative centers, as we have suggested. There is a basic pattern in them all, and the later ones may merely be decentralized administrative centers constructed by one political system. It has been suggested, largely because of the existence of a hard-surface road across the island from Phaistos to Cnossus, that these two were merely seasonal residences for the same ruler.

None of this kind of supposition gets us very far. The only established facts are that these various centers were unfortified and clearly lived in peaceful relationships and that the whole island, by the second millennium, was a single political unit. Since this political unity was achieved without clear evidence of warfare, it is possible that it grew up in the early periods of Minoan history. The lack of fortifications would also indicate that the island had a unified control of the sea and thus could protect itself against enemies from outside.

3. Expansion

By 2300 B.C., after a thousand years of existence, Cretan society was launched on a brilliant period of commercial expansion, cultural progress, and artistic accomplishment. It had a system of numbers and writing that is still beyond our ability to understand and may remain so, especially if the language used was an unknown Asian language, as seems possible. We know about a hundred words in the language, many of them place names or names of objects used by later Greeks, but these do not seem to be related to any known languages. Words ending in "-inth," like *Corinth, hyacinth, plinth,* and *labyrinth,* or words ending in "-assa," like the Greek word for sea, *thalassa,* were originally Minoan. The writing, which was probably originally ideographic and rather pictographic, became increasingly linear, changing by jumps rather than by gradual development, as might be expected under a centralized political system.

The commercial prosperity of Crete continued to grow in the first half of the second millennium and was benefited rather than harmed by the Bronze Age invasions. These intrusions did not reach Crete itself, and the disturbances of the Hurrians in the Levant and the Hyksos in Egypt made it possible for Crete to expand its economic life by adding craft activities to its commercial functions. Its products, including such objects as pottery, bronze weapons, engraved gems, and jewelry, were in great demand. The prosperity of the Bohemian Bronze Age and the growing trade of the Canaanite cities of Syria created new opportunities for Cretan traders. The "palaces" at various points were rebuilt on a more elaborate scale, especially at Cnossus and Phaistos. These two cities, forty miles apart, were joined by a highway of paved cobblestones provided with bridges. At the Cnossus end of this road stood an elaborate building, probably a hotel, offering all the conveniences necessary to the weary traveler, including baths and dinner in a beautiful large hall decorated with realistic frescoes of game birds.

At Cnossus itself the "palace" was a low, flat-topped structure covering about five acres. It had a system of baths and drains, flushed with water from rain tanks on the roofs. The naturalistic mural paintings were infused with nature, the open air, sunshine, and happiness; none showed warfare or death, religion, darkness, power, or majesty as were commonly shown on the paintings of the other early civilizations. The fertility goddess was still worshiped, but the idea of her was quite changed. Gone was the pregnant earth mother, replaced by a glamorous female, slim and straight, attired in a modish dress with a low-cut neckline, a tight bodice, and a long, full skirt with many flounces. Her hair, piled in curls on her head, was fastened by gold pins. Even serious French books call her "La Parisienne."

This Cretan goddess was associated with snakes, birds, pillars, sacred trees, and the symbols of a double ax. These symbols came from Asia but were given an additional lightness and elegance in Crete. The double-ax symbol was marked plentifully on the walls of the palace. The building itself was called "Labyrinth" in the Minoan language, an expression which meant "House of the Double Ax." With its numerous rooms and long corridors on various levels, this building seemed like a maze to the naive Greek-speaking barbarians when they first saw it, since they were probably familiar with no house of more than two rooms. They took the word "labyrinth" to mean a maze where one became lost. We still use the word in this sense today.

Beyond the "Labyrinth" was the city, a center of two- and three-story rectangular houses, providing every evidence of a prosperous, happy, secular free society. This society, in the course of the second millennium, found its growth arrested by the slowing up of its rate of expansion.

4. Conflict and Universal Empire

It is very difficult for us to distinguish with any confidence the middle stages in the evolution of Minoan civilization. Our natural ignorance of the history of a society unknown through written evidence is intensified by the ambiguities to be expected in a civilization whose instrument of expansion was a socialist state. Of the general characteristics of the Age of Conflict, such as decreasing expansion, imperialist wars, class conflicts, and irrationality, we know almost nothing. There may have been class disturbances or even interurban wars, but the evidence does not allow us to say so with any assurance. Just before the middle of the second millennium, layers of ashes indicate severe fires in most Cretan urban centers, but we cannot be sure if these resulted from class disturbances or war, or from foreign invasions or even from earthquakes. The possibility of these fires coming from earthquakes seems to be reduced by the fact that fortifications and a sharp rise in the occurrence of weapons seems to have appeared briefly in the Middle Minoan period. Moreover, a couple of centuries later, the style of writing made one of its periodic changes in Cnossus, adopting a form known as Lineal B, which we now know was used to write the Greek language. As Cnossus was not sacked at that time, although it was somewhat later, about 1430 B.C., we do not believe that these Greek speakers came in as invaders, but rather that they migrated in peacefully, perhaps by serving as workers or mercenary marines for the Cretan state.

A reconstruction of the history of the Aegean area during the second millennium from the archaeological evidence on the island of Crete and also on the mainland of Greece, especially in Argos, can be made with a certain degree of confidence. The Bronze Age invaders who came down into the Balkans from the north during the first half of the second millennium were the first Greek-speaking persons to enter the area. We call them the Achaeans. On the whole, they probably came in small bands or even as isolated warriors in a peaceful way, with no desire to destroy the growing trade over the routes from Crete to the Central European Bronze Age. By military prowess and by marriage with the daughters of the matrilineal natives and Cretan colonists, these Greeks gradually established control over the area and over the commercial routes. Although the trade continued, the Achaeans extorted tribute from it and were able to use this wealth to build a barbaric, semicivilized Cretan-Achaean society. This mixed culture is generally known as Mycenaean, after its chief city at the head of the Gulf of Argos. Elsewhere, as at Athens to the northeast, the Cretans either retained or reestablished control and were themselves in a position to demand tribute. In any case, for some time a *modus vivendi* existed in which both peoples could enjoy the expanding commerce.

In this process the Achaeans became Cretanized and are called Mycenaeans. They seem to have gradually adopted the Cretan diet by replacing meat and animal products with the fruit of the vine, the olive tree, and the sea; they adopted the use of stone buildings and more naturalistic paintings, but the buildings were fortresses and the pictures were of war, hunting, races, or other violent scenes. They largely shifted from cremation to burial of the dead, but they kept their beards, their patriarchal social patterns, and the loose, pinned clothing of Flatland pastoralists (rather than the fitted, buttoned clothing of Crete).

By 1450 this mixed Mycenaean culture covered much of Greece and had become, at least socially, the dominant element in Cnossus. The political structure seems to have been one of autonomous feudal princes surrounded by their war-loving retainers, the whole under the nominal overlordship of Mycenae and supporting a life of luxury, idleness, and warlike adventure by the tribute imposed on Cretan commerce. The political relationship of Mycenae with Crete and the role of Cnossus are ambiguous. The mainland city may have functioned as an undependable ally or it may have already taken over political power in Cnossus by peaceful means, either through slow immigration or by marriage into the commercial oligarchy of the country. By 1430 some Mycenaeans were no longer satisfied with their role. Taking advantage of political difficulties that Minos encountered in Sicily, and using their recently acquired knowledge of seafaring, some of the Greek speakers arose in revolt, sacked Cnossus, and permanently moved the center of Minoan civilization to the mainland. The next period is accordingly known as the Mycenaean age (1430–1150 B.C.), and represents the Age of Decay of Minoan society.

5. Decay and Invasion

The Mycenaean peoples could sack and destroy, but they could not organize or control the complicated Minoan economic structure. This structure, based on commerce, required security and order along its trade routes or it could not function. Such security had been provided on the sea by the Minoan fleet, but now the unruly Mycenaean warriors began to seize rather than to nurture commerce. As piracy rose, trade declined. On land the long trade route from Argos to central Europe had been maintained because of recognition of mutual benefits and, above all, by realization that small demands for tribute would provide income for an indefinite period, while total seizure of goods would kill the activities once for all.

Although Cretan craftsmen continued for a long time to turn out work of high quality, the themes of this art became increasingly violent, turning from sun-drenched nature to scenes of war and the hunt. In time, artistic techniques declined, realism being replaced by heraldic beasts and geometric designs. The system was increasingly supported by piracy, plunder, and imposed tribute. Having crippled one great trade route to the north by the destruction of Cnossus about 1430, the Mycenaeans could hardly permit the rival route to continue, and about 1184 they captured and sacked the second great commercial city of the Aegean, Troy. This city, of Anatolian rather than Aegean culture, existed from early in the third millennium, and its many levels of occupation give the archaeologist a dramatic picture of its tumultuous history. Its greatest city, the second on the site, had been destroyed by the Hittite invaders about 1900; its sixth city, a relatively prosperous town, was destroyed by an earthquake about 1365. It was rebuilt almost immediately but was sacked, as described in Homer's *Iliad*, by the Greeks in the twelfth century. This event marked the end of the great Bronze Age archaic cultures everywhere in the West. Shortly afterward the Iron Age invaders, the Dorians, Phrygians, Carians, and Lydians, poured out from the upper

Balkans and wiped out the Trojan, Hittite, and Mycenaean cultures together. A Dark Ages descended on the whole area west of the Levant for almost two centuries (1100–900 B.C.).

The process by which civilization, as an abstract entity distinct from the societies in which it is embodied, dies or is reborn is a very significant one. There are at least five steps in the process. Civilizations die as (1) decreasing political security and the ending of law and order make property precarious and make personal violence an increasingly significant element in life; accordingly (2) long-distance trade decreases; as a result (3) town life becomes precarious and there is a general exodus from the towns as people try to find a place in which they can be attached in some stable social and economic relationship to the food-producing earth; obviously (4) there is a decline and even a disappearance of the middle classes (the property-owning, commercial, literate, city-dwelling group); and (5) illiteracy rises rapidly. Civilization reappears through the same five steps, each in reverse: (1) law and order are reestablished; (2) commerce increases; (3) cities appear and grow; (4) a middle class, between soil tillers and fighting men, reappears; and (5) literacy reappears as a technique of record keeping and distant communication for the middle class.

This process has passed through these steps several times, two of them at the two extremities of the life of Classical civilization. This civilization, as is well known, had a "Dark Ages" at each end; the first, about 1100–900 B.C., marked the division between Cretan civilization and Classical culture, and the second, about A.D. 700 to 950, marked the division between Classical civilization and Western. Each "Dark Age" is the period between the five-step fall and the five-step rise of civilization of which we speak. In the earlier of the two, the political disorder that initiated the five-step sequence is associated with the Mycenaean exploitation and the Dorian invasions. Then, generations later, law and order were reestablished in the Mediterranean by the activities of the Phoenicians, and the five-stage sequence continued until Classical culture was established. The second "Dark Ages," at the end of Classical culture, was initiated by the political insecurity associated with the Germanic invasions and the fall of Roman political power in the West (A.D. 476); it was ended, and Western civilization begun, by the same five-step sequence beginning about A.D. 970.

The Iron Age invasions on both sides of the Aegean Sea established the basis on which the subsequent Classical civilization was to rise. In the Balkans itself the invaders (Dorians) came only a short distance from the north, but they came with such force and such destructive violence that the great mass of them ended up in southern Greece and in Crete itself. Thus in the Classical period these were Doric-speaking areas and still retained the crudities of their ancestors. The chief state and leader of this group came to be Sparta. On the other hand, the Dorians drove southward so rapidly that they did not turn eastward into the islands and peninsulas of eastern Greece, and large enclaves of Mycenaean (that is mixed Achaean-Cretan) culture persisted. In the Classical period these survivals are known as Ionian, and became the highest representatives of later Greek culture, undoubtedly because of the survival of elements of Cretan culture. Some Mycenaeans, driven from their homes in Greece by the Dorian advance, crossed the Aegean and settled on the middle shores of the western coast of Anatolia (Asia Minor). These are also called Ionians, and the shore

on which they settled is known as Ionia. Thus, closely related Ionian peoples, with a similar culture and a common
dialect, lived on both the eastern and western shores of the
middle Aegean Sea after 1000 B.C. It was among these
people, possessing strong elements of Minoan culture, that
the new Classical civilization was born. This culture was
passed on to the later society, not only by surviving vestiges
of social customs and personal outlook, but more explicitly
through the works of Homer. These works, written in Ionia
after the Dorian invasions, are based on memories of the
great deeds of the Cretanized Achaeans before the invasions.

9

Classical Civilization

Classical civilization, which occupied the shores of the Mediterranean Sea for almost a millennium and a half (950 B.C.–A.D. 550), follows the pattern of seven stages fairly closely, with no major distortions of the process. The only significant variation arises from the shape of the Mediterranean Sea itself, and this would not have given rise to a major distortion if it had not been reinforced by the fact that the Phoenicians (who provided the original impetus toward a revival of civilization in the Mediterranean basin) came from the extreme eastern end of the sea.

A glance at any map of the Mediterranean shows that it consists of two great basins divided by the line Calabria-Sicily-Tunis. This geographic schism was strengthened in the historic period by the fact that the eastern basin became Greek-speaking while the western basin became Latin. Most important of all, since Classical civilization originated near Phoenician influence in the eastern part of the eastern basin and spread along the west-running seaways, the core area and the peripheral areas of Mediterranean civilization became separated from each other by more than the usual chronological lag. Cultural distinctions as well as chronological ones are characteristic of these two portions of any civilization, but usually the periphery tends to surround the core, and such extreme geographic separation does not arise. This fact was, of course, also important in Canaanite civilization, where the core was in the Levant while the universal empire arose in the West. In Classical civilization the tendency for the society to split into eastern and western parts was always strong; it was counterbalanced, until the society was in its final stage, by the relative superiority of water transportation over land transportation. As a consequence of this, any part of the Mediterranean shore was likely to be more closely linked with any other part than it would be, by land communications, with its own hinterlands.

The instrument of expansion of Classical civilization was a social organization, slavery. This came into existence in the period of mixture as a consequence of the invasions of the Iron Age intruders. It remained an instrument so long as the slaveowners worked closely with their slaves, often in the fields themselves, as Cincinnatus was doing when appointed dictator, because then the surplus from the slave labor which accumulated to the owner from his legal rights over his slaves could be used for some productive use, since the owner's personal knowledge of the agricultural process permitted him to judge where such investment could best be made. But in the later period, when the slaves were operated in gangs in charge of a steward—usually a freed slave—with the owner absent from the estate for long periods, output suffered, investment decreased or was improperly applied, and expansion slowed up. After several centuries of this, the slave system became a highly inefficient method of agricultural production, with output, expressed either in terms of unit areas or in terms of labor expended, considerably below that of neighboring farms operated by their owners on a family basis. Pliny tells us that output per area was much greater on family farms than it was on latifundia. Slaveowners, whose prestige, economic independence, and leisure for political activity depended on their slaves, were determined to resist any efforts to free their slaves or to divide up their estates into family-size farms. The argument for greater production would have left them unmoved even if it had been made. Even if the landlords had obtained compensation for loss of their lands and slaves, there was no other practical way in which they could have invested their funds because of the great technological backwardness of the Classical economy. This excluded redistribution of land and freeing of slaves as practical large-scale alternatives to the latifundia system, and meant that the system could not be liquidated by any voluntary method but only by confiscation and violence, as finally occurred. But before it did occur Classical civilization had been destroyed by the struggles over this issue and especially by the vain efforts of the slaveowning group to prevent their own liquidation as a social and economic group. Moreover, replacement of the latifundia by peasant farms would have been no real solution because it would have resulted in a more equitable distribution of the society's income and ended most accumulation of capital. The only good solution was replacement of the slave institution by another instrument of expansion, but that meant the replacement of Classical civilization by another civilization.

It has sometimes been argued that slavery could not possibly have played the central role in Classical civilization which we are attributing to it, because the number of slaves in the society was relatively small and many of them were

well treated or were used in essentially nonproductive activities, such as household tasks. These objections are quite
beside the point, and are unconvincing even when they are
supported by elaborate statistical studies. Such statistical
studies are based on the available written evidence, mostly
Athenian, and do show that the slaves were only a minority
of the Athenian population (about one-quarter) and were
often household servants. Such studies overlook less specific
evidence tending to show that the percentage of slaves was
probably higher in many rural areas, especially in Dorian
states. In Sparta, for example, the number of Helots was
certainly several times the number of Spartan citizens, even
in the early period, and the proportion increased in the later
period as the number of Spartan citizens decreased. And
in Roman Italy there is good evidence that the countryside
lost much of its peasant population and increased its number
of slaves during several centuries following the end of the
Second Punic War (201 B.C.).

Moreover, even if the most moderate estimates produced
by the later-day apologists for Classical slavery are taken as
correct, this in no way would reduce the significance of
slavery as the instrument of expansion of Classical civilization. All that we require of such an instrument is that it
be an important (or perhaps the most important) mechanism in accumulating and investing savings in the society.
Such a role, I believe, cannot be withheld from Classical
slavery. Other organizations performed similar functions
in Mediterranean civilization, as they do in all societies, but
the important role played by slavery in the organizational
dynamics of Classical antiquity can hardly be denied.

The attempts to deny it, which are frequently quite emotional, even when they are made by classicists who pride

themselves on their objectivity, are but one class of examples of a notable weakness in Classical studies. This weakness arises from the failure, by the average classicist, to seek a complete and rounded view of Classical society. Instead it is usual to specialize one's attention on a few aspects of the subject, preferably on literature or philosophy or archaeology or even on only part of one of these: on Greek thought but not on Latin, on Plato but not on Virgil, on Aristotle but not on Theophrastus or Pythagoras or Archimedes, on Athenian excavations but not on Anatolian or on Etruscan ones.

And, of course, students who deal with these humanist areas have little time for other aspects of Classical society, such as science or mathematics or education, and are most unlikely to have any concern with such mundane matters as technology, economic organization, or the dynamics of social classes. Yet no adequate picture of Classical antiquity can be reconstructed without attention to all its aspects.

This is a weakness in Classical studies that has been remedied to some extent in recent years. But certainly not sufficiently remedied. We still hear a good deal of emotional talk about the "Greek miracle" or the "Greek genius." The "Greek miracle" is a term applied to the erroneous belief that Greek culture sprang up, fully formed, in no more than a couple of generations out of complete barbarism. This is based upon erroneous ideas about the nature of Greek culture, the speed with which it arose, and the background from which it emerged. To mention only one point: any culture that came from a mixture of Cretan, Phoenician, and Indo-European elements did not start from nothing, or from barbarism. As for "Greek genius," there can be no doubt that for a brief period, for a select social group, in a restricted area, there was a great opportunity for men to develop their higher capacities, but there is no need for awe-struck tones implying that some hereditary, biological burst of genius hit, like lightning, among the Greeks in Classical antiquity, without leaving any traces of its passage among their descendants over the next two thousand years.

The importance of the Minoan-Mycenaean contribution to Greek culture can hardly be overemphasized. From it came many later ideas about the gods and much mythology. Not only did the mythology provide the materials for later Greek art and literature, but Homer, who came from this earlier world, remained the inspiration and model of the Greeks throughout their history. This is of the greatest importance: Homer was not only the earliest figure in Greek literature; he was also the latest figure in an earlier literature. There is nothing primitive, experimental, or unsophisticated in Homer. His poems are not popular folk epics; they are aristocratic heroic sagas. Their chief figures are emancipated, free from social restraints, individualistic, far removed from any tribe or clan with its unexamined social customs or its clinging to the routine of static social life and equally free from any materialistic concerns and from the superstitions and social taboos of economic gain. Their gods are humanistic, and their society is secularized. These are barbarians who have taken over the wealth of the Minoan society and are breaking it up, just as their own tribal units have already broken up. They are enjoying their new, and unearned, wealth, power, and freedom. They have a "joy in life and pride in individual brilliance." They have freed themselves completely from the customs of their barbarian forebears; they have no understanding or sympathy for the customs of the submerged lower classes who support them.

They are completely unconcerned with problems of production, with the origin of the wealth they enjoy, with population pressures. Freed from such concerns, they occupy themselves with self-expression and the pursuit of honor and personal glory. This is an aristocratic outlook that ever after dominated Greek culture.

This outlook was, as we have said, Mycenaean. But beneath it was an older, more elegant yet more irrational tradition, closer to nature and thus both more concrete, more colorful, but at the same time less free and much closer to magic, superstition, and the fertility rites associated with the mysteries of agricultural production. This is the Minoan tradition. From this Minoan tradition comes much that we regard as typically Greek—love of nature, of the sun-drenched land and the mysterious sea—but it also provided the rural superstitions, the mystery rites of fertility, the orgies dimly associated with the intoxicants of Bacchus or the behavior excesses of Dionysius. The best of this tradition is found in Homer's literary expressions, figures of speech, and use of images. Artistic representation of these can be found in the art of the Minoan period and in the words of Homer. From the latter it passed on to the Greeks, so that when they, for example, thought of death and resurrection they thought of the poppy drooping with its seeds as the Minoans depicted it or as Homer described it.

Classical culture is a Greek creation—more accurately it is an Ionian creation and became Greek largely because the culture created by the Ionians was generally accepted by the literate and cultivated classes of all Greek-speaking peoples. This can be seen in the general admiration of Homer or Plato. Though this Greek culture was accepted by the Romans, it always remained for them an adopted culture, a garment that was put on and could be cast off without ever becoming an intimate or essential part of the wearer. Thus the history of the culture of the Romans (for example, in religion) is largely the history of how they found and adopted Greek culture. This history began only at a late date, about 200 B.C., when the Romans began to learn Greek; it reached its peak about 50 B.C. in Cicero, because Cicero fell in love with Greek culture and acquired a deep knowledge of Greek thought and the Greek language (without, it might be added, allowing these ever to become his own nature and outlook). Roman cultural history began to decline when Cicero died in a typically Roman way (murdered 43 B.C.), and it moved downward exactly in step with the decrease in Roman knowledge of Greek culture, with their decreasing interest in its message, and, most obviously, with the decrease in knowledge of the Greek language among educated Romans. This decrease in knowledge of Greek by Latin-speaking people marked not only a decline in Roman culture; it also marked the beginnings of the split between the Latin world and the Greek world which later appeared as a split between the Western Roman Empire (which disappeared in the fifth century) and the Eastern Roman, or Byzantine, Empire (which disappeared only in the fifteenth century), as well as the schism of the Christian church into Roman and Orthodox branches (that continues today).

The Ionian culture that was adopted as their own by the Greek-speaking world, and put on like a garment by the Latin-speaking world, was never the culture of the whole Mediterranean basin because it was the culture of the literate upper classes only. These were the slaveowning minority who knew how to read and write, who had leisure, and who used that leisure to read Homer, Plato, Cicero, and Virgil. The great mass of the inhabitants of the Mediterranean world did not share this culture; they were born, worked, had children, and died. This great mass included the rural inhabitants at all times and even the majority of city dwellers at most times. In other words, the Classical culture we so esteem was the culture of a small minority of city dwellers except for a brief period of a century and a half (480–330 B.C.) in Athens. In this brief period it may be that the majority of the inhabitants of that city had some idea of what we call Classical culture. Otherwise, in other cities generally, and in rural areas always, the masses of the people lived in a morass of ignorance and superstition that is difficult for us to imagine. To them life was an irrational chaos of conflicting powers and forces of which the chief were a myriad of local gods and spirits.

This substratum of irrationality and localism beneath the veneer of Classical culture must always be kept in mind if we are to appreciate properly the great achievement of the small minority that possessed this culture and if we are to understand how this culture was destroyed when this minority was crushed and finally submerged by the rising tide of militarism, ruralism, and irrationality.

Classical culture was a class culture and it was an urban culture. This was almost inevitable at a time when there was no general system of education (so that the majority was illiterate) and when all written material had to be copied by hand because of the lack of printing (so that it was too expensive for the majority to possess). Even for the minority most information came through conversation. Classical culture was also isolated from the economic activities of everyday life, because it was an urban culture at a time when the city had no real economic function, but was completely dependent for its economic support on the agricultural activities of the rural areas. The city did not pay for its agricultural imports by industrial exports or by commercial activities as a modern city does, except in a few cases of which the chief, once again, is Athens during the period 480–300 B.C. Otherwise, as a usual thing the city existed as an economic parasite on the country and was able to import food because of its political or legal position rather than because of its economic activities. This is merely another way of saying that Classical culture was a class culture, possessed by a small minority of city residents whose legal and political rights permitted them to make economic demands on the rural population and who were able to build up Classical culture because their legal rights gave them the leisure to do so. The key to this leisure and to their privileged position is to be found in slavery.

Many years ago I took an amazing course in which the whole history of German culture, its literature, music, art, and sculpture, was covered in a single semester from September to January. The most amazing thing about this course was not the amount that was attempted or the professor who taught it, but how successfully it was done. As we raced along, Goethe was covered in fifteen minutes, Schiller in ten, Fichte in five. Later I tried to analyze how this had been done, and realized that the professor had a profound understanding of much that he discussed and that he covered any topic simply by slicing it up into a small number of parts and giving a name to each part. The complex character and achievement of Goethe, for example, were divided into six portions, each was given a title, and, ever after, the whole of Goethe could be evoked merely by reciting six words.

The cultural synthesis that the Ionians created and handed on to the Greeks and that, however modified, remained very largely the culture of all of Classical antiquity is surely more complex than Goethe, but I should like to outdare even my former professor by dividing this greater complexity into only five parts. It seems to me that Classical culture was aristocratic; it was clarid; it was urban; it was balanced; and it was mundane. One of these words will not be found in any dictionary. When I say that Classical culture was "clarid," I mean that it was lucid, clear, rational, in some ways like the Mediterranean sunlight infusing the atmosphere to an astounding clarity.

When we say that Classical culture was *aristocratic,* we mean much more than that it was the possession of an upper-class minority. We mean that this culture refused to regard either profit or power as goals of life, but rather tended to regard honor and the esteem of one's equals as at least equally worthy goals. It was quite willing to accept a goal for life and an organization of life that functioned economically on a deficit basis, that could not be made available to all men or was not comprehensible to all men, but that had to be supported by many men who could neither share in it nor understand it. This point of view had an aversion to anything practical or vocational; it regarded its goal (honor) as one whose appeal is not (like wealth or power) automatically appreciated but one that is achieved by breeding and discipline. It regarded man as by nature close to the gods but very remote from the animals; it did not accept the equality of men, but did insist on a fraternity of equals within the select group of participants. It emphasized the dignity of the individual, at first only the individual within the chosen group; but later, as democratic influences spread, it tended to grant equality and individual dignity to all, not by bringing the outlook of ordinary men into the select group, but rather by spreading the outlook of the select group outward to ordinary men. To do this it was necessary, while allowing the select group to grow constantly larger, to continue to emphasize the superiority of the members of the group over outsiders. At first the group consisted only of those of noble birth; later it was the citizens of the city-state. As this group was expanded, emphasis continued on the distinction between free men and slaves, between Greek and barbarian, between those who had the political franchise and those who lacked it. Only when Classical culture was in its decline (after the time of Christ) did it begin to accept the equality of all men. Even then it insisted that all men had human dignity, had a kind of divinity, and were worthy of respect. Thus to the very end, Classical culture kept certain elements of its aristocratic outlook, and never, like the Hebrews, came to regard man as a helpless and cringing worm. One last characteristic of an aristocratic outlook that Classical culture maintained to the end was its belief in social retrogression rather than in social progress and its conviction that the golden age was to be found in the past rather than in the future. This gave the culture an underlying pessimism redeemed by the fact that man's fate, however hopeless, must be borne with dignity. This belief in a past golden age and the refusal to accept the idea of progress is to be found in Homer and Hesiod in a most explicit fashion and undoubtedly is the result of some dim social memory of the Cretan civilization or of Mycenaean culture.

In saying that Classical culture was *clarid,* we mean that it possessed the qualities of rationality, lucidity, and clarity.

This culture sought explanations rather than sensations. These explanations were regarded as satisfactory if they led to some concept that could be grasped by man's conscious mind. Thus, for example, the immortality of the gods was explained on the grounds that gods ate a special food, ambrosia, that would also give immortality to men, if they could obtain it.

When we say that this culture was *urban,* we mean that it was possessed by a city-dwelling group who knew one another personally, saw one another frequently, exchanged views by conversation or letter, rather than by media of mass communication, were remote from the productive system, either agriculture or commerce, and regarded loyalty to the state and to its gods as the chief duty and chief privilege of existence.

When we say that this culture was *balanced,* we mean that it held the golden mean in high esteem, that it regarded excess or extremes with distaste and felt that such excess could lead only to disaster and to retribution. The expression "golden mean," the motto "nothing too much," the idea that excess leads to retribution (nemesis): these are all derived from Classical culture. This ideal of balance appeared in their ethics as nemesis; in their politics in the idea that justice was a balance of different elements; in their art as the principle of proportion; in their literature, especially the drama, as the idea that *nemesis* is always the consequence of *hybris* (excess of personal pride and self-exaltation); in their social outlook in the belief that society was a balance of different groups or classes.

When we say that this culture was *mundane,* we mean that it was humanistic, anthropocentric, and thisworldly. It regarded man as the center of everything; it interpreted everything in terms of human aims; it had no real concern with life after death or with the gods, and had no real idea of eternity or of reward or punishment in the afterlife. It had no real idea of the nature of divinity until very late, and then achieved this idea as a consequence of an aristocratic pursuit of truth, a rationalistic pursuit by men with leisure and with no real regard for wealth or power. This mundane character of Classical culture meant that this culture, in extreme cases, was materialistic in its outlook; but it was able to escape the ordinary consequences of materialism because of its ideals of aristocracy and moderation.

The creation of this synthesis from past elements, some of which (like Minoan or Mesopotamian) had a long history, explains why there were so few primitive elements in Greek culture and why, when these elements did occasionally emerge from the submerged or rural masses (as in the mystery religions), they were immediately modified or rejected. This also explains why the oldest surviving Greek writer, Homer, was neither primitive nor unsophisticated, but had a simplicity, a gravity, a balance, a dignity, a subtlety, that made him appear as the culmination of a long epic tradition and the last example of a sophisticated culture. This indeed he was, a kind of post-mortem manifestation of the Mycenaean Age, looking back on it as a golden age, but nonetheless writing in Greek and thus capable of becoming, as he did become, the model for the future Classical culture.

1. Mixture

The period of mixture of Classical civilization covers the Iron Age invasions which destroyed Cretan civilization and continues onward into the period when the Phoenicians began to bring back the basic necessities of civilized living. In our usual arbitrary fashion we might say that the period of mixture lasted from 1200 to 900 and that the following Age of Gestation covered the next hundred years to about 800 B.C.

We have already said that Classical culture was Ionian. This means that the mixture that created it took place on the shores of the Aegean Sea, chiefly among people who spoke the Ionic dialect of Greek. This means that it was a synthesis from the activities of a relatively small number of persons in a relatively small area. It also means, as is generally true when one civilization descends from a predecessor, that the peripheral area of Cretan civilization became the core area of Classical civilization.

The elements that mixed to form Classical society were at least four: (1) Minoan; (2) Indo-European; (3) Mesopotamian; and (4) Semitic. None of these, except perhaps the last, was a direct influence; the others were indirect, filtered through intermediaries. The Minoan influence came through the Mycenaean Age, that is, in the Greek language and with heroic and warlike elements replacing the feminist and pacifist elements of Minoan. The Indo-European was also diluted by coming through the Mycenaean Age rather than as the direct influence of a warrior people such as we find in the Dorian Greeks. This means that the rationalist and individualist tendencies found in the Indo-Europeans were intensified by the weakening of the social and tribal beliefs usual among a more primitive people. This influence was passed on to the Greeks, largely through Homer. The Mesopotamian contribution came across Anatolia (where it picked up all kinds of dark superstitions and irrational

rites), as well as through the Phoenicians. The Semitic influence also came by way of the Phoenicians, which means
that it came through a practical, hardheaded, unimaginative,
and businesslike people.

It would be a difficult task to enumerate what Greek culture owed to each of these four; it would also be misleading,
because the Ionians took each element, modified it, and
merged it into a new synthesis. From the Mesopotamians
came much science and astronomy, weights and measures
(such as the twelve-hour day and night, and the use of sixty
for fractional parts), and considerable technology. From
the Indo-European came many pastoral elements, including
the religious dominance of a sky god (dyas = deus =
Zeus); a patriarchal and masculine-dominated social system; extreme emphasis on honor, competitiveness, heroism,
and war; and above all, rationalism. The last of these is so
important that it deserves more detailed consideration.

There can be little doubt that the rationalism of the
Greeks, which became one of the general qualities of
Classical culture, was derived from their Indo-European
heritage. The same quality is found among the early Persians
(for example, in the Zoroastrian religion) in an even more
definite way, and the Persians are the only Indo-European
group, on whom we have adequate information, that was
less culturally mixed than the Greeks. Of the other Indo-
European groups, the Mitanni were more purely Indo-
European, but we know very little about them; the Hittites
and Aryans were subjected to great cultural mixture, and we
have inadequate information on them. The early Romans
were much less clearly Indo-European than the Greeks,
were much less rational, and our information is much less
satisfactory. The correlation, so far as our knowledge goes,

between degree of Indo-European influence in a culture and the rationalism in the culture seems fairly close.

We may concede, then, that Greek rationalism was Indo-European in origin, but this does not explain why the Indo-Europeans had this tendency. A somewhat similar inclination is to be found among the Semites, and there too its degree seems to be correlated with the degree of purity of the Semite culture. The closer any Semite people were to their original Flatland pastoralism, the more pronounced the degree of rationalism in their culture. The Arabs, who were the most pastoral of all the Semites of which we have adequate knowledge, seem to have been the most rationalist of the Semite migrants out of the Arabian Flatland into the vision of history. Similarly the Hebrews, who were more pastoral than the other Canaanites, were considerably more rational than these others. In fact, the Canaanites of the Levant had a very nonrational culture, so that the emergence of the Hebrews as a separate social group among the Canaanites was, to a considerable extent, marked by the development of a more rational and more historical outlook, as well as by monotheism. The generally irrational character of Canaanite society probably arose from its extensive cultural mixture with local agricultural peoples and with immigrant Alpine peoples, such as the Hurrians.

The rationalism of the Indo-Europeans appears in their basic thinking habits. Its most notable feature, of course, is the effort to find explanations of events in terms understandable to our conscious mental processes. This leads to pervasive but less fundamental characteristics, such as the tendency to polarize continua that, in turn, leads to the use of two-valued logic in explanations. This last characteristic shows most clearly in the acceptance of the principle of contradiction (the essential feature of any system of two-valued logic) in the analysis of observations (in addition to the already mentioned inclination to analysis itself). The earlier civilizations, such as Mesopotamian and Egyptian, were not analytical and had no tendency to seek logical explanation. It would be incorrect to say that they were illogical, for this might indicate that they violated a logical system of which they were aware. Rather we should say that they were mythological. This means that they did not seek explanation by analysis in order to obtain logical sequence back to a "cause"; rather they found explanation in a story, as we still do in children's tales (like "How the Elephant Got His Trunk").

In our own development toward logical explanation, we find contributions from both the Hebrews and the Indo-Europeans. The Hebrews took the first great step toward the creation of our modern intellectual processes by turning from a mythological to a logical attitude toward the universe. They insisted on a rigid distinction between God and man, between past and future, between life and death, between male and female (especially in regard to deity), between man and nature, between the individual and the group, and between the righteous and the unrighteous. These logical distinctions were not made by earlier peoples, as they are not made, for example, by the Hindus. They were largely destroyed among the other Canaanites because of the powerful influences these received from the Mesopotamian, Hurrian, and Neolithic Garden cultures.

Similar rationalism is found among the Indo-Europeans. We might explain this quality as one of the attributes of Flatland pastoralism. Or we might attribute it to the grammatical structure of Indo-European languages and, in that way, trace it back to the common linguistic ancestor of Indo-European and Semite. For Indo-European grammar, with its categories of gender, its sharp distinction of person and number, and its great emphasis on chronological tense, must impress upon any child who learns it a certain amount of logical attitude toward experience. This would be quite different from the experience of the Japanese child, whose language emphasizes in its grammar relative class levels, or of the young Bantu speaker, who has little time emphasis (lacking any future tense), but divides everything in the universe into a score or so of basic qualitative classes.

Of course, we might abandon this rather Platonic effort to explain the logical quality of Greek thought by adopting, instead, the Sophist argument that there is nothing really logical about Greek thinking or Indo-European languages but that we simply call them logical because it is what we are used to in our own culture derived from them. If we do this, it will still be permissible to say that these qualities came into the Greek mixture from the Indo-European element in that mixture. It is obvious that the Indo-European element also contributed to Classical culture a large number of material traits. These included horses and war chariots, the use of flowing garments fastened by pins (the toga), iron weapons (from the Hittites by way of the Dorians), the wearing of beards, the megaron-style house, the social inferiority of women, and other features.

We have already indicated what the Minoan element contributed to this mixture. It included such very practical things as the Mediterranean diet, as well as less tangible traits such as much of the foundations of Greek esthetics: the sense of beauty and of proportion, the inclination toward naturalism in art, the love of nature, and the strong sense of community that was such a significant element in the Greek city-state. The development of naturalism out of earlier geometric art about the seventh century is usually regarded as a manifestation of the "Greek genius," but might better be regarded as a reemergence of Minoan tendencies after their submergence by Iron Age invaders.

The contributions of the Phoenicians to the period of mixture are well known. Coming late, they included the alphabet, many techniques in metalwork and other productive processes (including the goatskin bellows in ironwork), a considerable amount of mythology (such as Hephaestus, the god of craft skills), units of weight and measures (including money), and many musical instruments and techniques, generally attributed by the Greeks to Cinyras (the Canaanite Kinnor). In addition, of course, the Phoenicians contributed the basic conditions that led to a revival of civilized living in the West: law and order on the seas, extension of distant trade, reappearance of city life, the recreation of an urban class, and the revival of writing. On these foundations ancient society was able to rear a new civilization because it had an instrument of expansion. This instrument was slavery.

2. Gestation

Slavery arose originally from the Indo-European conquest of the archaic peoples of the Mediterranean basin. Some of this may have come with the Bronze Age invasions, but the greater part undoubtedly arose as a consequence of the Iron Age invasions. These events created a kind of domestic slavery used in agricultural activities rather than the kind of plantation slavery we generally think of because that is the kind we know from American history. This means that each family, except for the very greatest, had no more than a few or several slaves and that these lived with their owners' families under conditions of close personal relationships. In many cases the owner worked directly in the fields with his slaves, and he always supervised them, between intervals of military campaigns. Thus the owner had a personal knowledge of his lands, his slaves, and of agricultural techniques. If improvement in the use of these was needed, he was in a good position to know it. Moreover, he had an incentive to make such improvements, since any increased agricultural output would accrue to him. And, finally, he was in a position to mobilize capital to make such improvements, because he had the legal right and power to retain for his own use part of the output of each of his slaves. The slaveowner, especially in the earliest period, had very local interests, and the society in which he lived consisted very largely of small, almost self-sufficient economic units, largely agrarian in their activities. The earliest types of expansion were also local and agricultural—such things as clearing of wastelands for new fields, provision of a more adequate water supply, draining of swampy areas, the building of defensive stockades on neighboring hilltops, and terracing. The best known of such ancient works were the draining of Lake Copais in Boeotia and the many cuniculi of Etruscan Italy.

The accumulation of surpluses of the ordinary necessities of life in the control of slaveowners also contributed to expansion by creating a demand for luxury goods of remote origin. This demand, met by the activities of the Phoenicians, led to the beginnings of commerce and later to the rise of towns. At least three times in history a society organized in small self-sufficient agricultural units has shifted to an urbanized commercial society by the growth of a demand for luxury goods of remote origin because of the accumulation of surpluses of necessities of local origin within the self-sufficient agrarian units. This occurred about 4000 B.C. in western Asia; it occurred after 900 B.C. in Classical antiquity; and it occurred after A.D. 1000 in Western civilization. Without a little thought on the subject we might be tempted to believe that a tradeless society consisting of self-sufficient agricultural units would begin to develop trade by the growth of local trade in necessities, but history and logic demonstrate quite clearly that the earliest commerce to appear in a tradeless society is in luxury goods of remote origin. There would be no possibility of any local trade in necessities among units that were self-sufficient in necessities. Only later, when remote trade in luxuries has given rise to urban concentration of commercial people who lack necessities, does such local trade develop.

The growth of such commerce became a principal manifestation of expansion in Mediterranean civilization, and was clearly established before 800 B.C. It was preceded and then accompanied by an intensification of agricultural practices. Both of these required the accumulation of capital, based on slavery, to which we have referred. The agricultural expansion was originally a shift toward growing emphasis on crops, with decreasing emphasis on pastoral activities. The proportions of cattle, sheep, even horses and all other livestock except goats were reduced. Grazing areas were turned into crops; lands held in common became individually owned; there was a growing pressure on the land, and landownership became increasingly inequitable.

This economic inequality helped accumulation of capital but gave rise to explosive social and political pressures such as those described in the earliest periods of Greek or Roman history. They were relieved, thanks to men like Solon, by diverting both manpower and capital into commerce and city building. These provided full-scale expansion.

3. Expansion

Full-scale expansion, by diverting political and social pressures into peaceful and constructive directions, reduced social conflicts and warfare. It was manifested in the usual four ways, as growth of population, accelerated production, geographic expansion, and increased knowledge. These all occurred in the eastern Mediterranean at least a century before they appeared in the western Mediterranean, so that it is convenient to give slightly different dates for this period in the east and the west. We might say that the Age of Expansion in the eastern Mediterranean was from about 850 B.C. to about 450, while in the western basin it was about 700 to 250 B.C.

The growth of population and of production in the Classical Age of Expansion is beyond dispute. Much of it appeared as the growth of cities in both numbers and size and in the growing specialization made possible by increasing commerce. As Greek colonies were established in grain-growing regions, such as the Black Sea shores or in Sicily, these newer areas began to ship back grain and metal ores to Greece itself, seeking as payment olive oil, wine, and metal products. Of these three Greek exports, two were liquids, a fact giving rise to a demand for pottery containers that could hardly be met by Greek craftsmen. Thus vigorous crafts activities in ceramics and in metals, particularly arms, appeared in the Greek commercial cities. At the same time the shift in agricultural activities from food grains to wool, wine, and oil increased the tendency toward large estates, since these could be produced more effectively on larger than on smaller holdings. This trend toward larger land units continued into the following two stages, the Ages of Conflict and of Universal Empire.

Geographic expansion of Classical civilization in Stage 3 widened ancient geographic knowledge from the narrow area, surrounded by monsters, that was known by the contemporaries of Homer (about 725 B.C.) to the much wider knowledge possessed at the establishment of the Museum at Alexandria in the third century. Part of this increase came from the intense period of colonization before 500 B.C. This was carried on by the Phoenicians as well as by the Greeks. The former established colonies in North Africa (like Carthage), in Sicily (like Utica), and in Spain (like Cadiz). Greek cities, like Miletus, Ephesus, Corinth, and Megara, also sent out colonies. The chief colonized areas were the northern shores of the Aegean Sea, the Black Sea, eastern Sicily, and southern Italy, but there were others outside these limits, such as Naucratus in Egypt and Marseilles in Gaul. In fact, the Greeks penetrated almost everywhere except the Tyrrhenian Sea, including northwestern Italy and Corsica, where they were excluded by the Etruscans, and west of Sicily, where they were excluded by the Phoenicians and Carthaginians.

The conquest of Phoenicia by Persia in 538 B.C. made these great seafaring people a satellite state of Persia, and squeezed the Greeks into the central Mediterranean between

Persian pressure from the east and Carthaginian pressure from the west. Since the Persian fleet was largely Phoenician, this pressure on Classical civilization, from both east and west, was pressure from Canaanite culture. This pressure was greatly relieved in 480 B.C. when the western Greeks, led by Syracuse, defeated the Carthaginians at Himera in Sicily and the eastern Greeks, led by Athens, defeated the Persian fleet at Salamis. As a result of these battles Classical civilization was free to determine its own fate until later it finally destroyed the Persian-Phoenician system (333 B.C.) and the Carthaginian-Canaanite system (146 B.C.).

We have indicated that an Age of Expansion frequently is a period of science and of democracy. This was certainly true of Classical civilization. The rise and fall of Greek and, later, of Roman democracy is a familiar story. Science, on the other hand, had two peaks, both in the Greek period and in no way associated with the shape of the Mediterranean basin or the relationship between core and peripheral areas. These two peaks are generally known as Ionian Science, from about 600 B.C. to about 400 B.C., and Hellenistic Science, from about 350 to 150 B.C. A link between the two was provided by Aristotle's Lyceum.

Any Age of Expansion has strong trends toward rationalism because of the need to make decisions between alternative actions in a period when status is being disrupted and social atomism is prevalent because of expansion. Nevertheless, science (which is, of course, entirely different from rationalism because of its faith in observation) usually flourishes in an Age of Expansion and is killed off by irrationalism in the following Age of Conflict. In Classical antiquity this pattern was not followed. There, rationalism was very strong in the Age of Expansion and began to attack science while this period was still in progress. In the following period, science was destroyed, not by irrationalism, but by rationalism. The reason for this aberration in the pattern lies in the fact that in Classical antiquity rationalism became allied with oligarchy and shared in its victory over both science and democracy. The importance of this on subsequent intellectual history, especially our own, can hardly be overemphasized. It deserves a more detailed examination.

We have already said that reality is not completely rational because it consists of continua. Such continua are nonrational and nonlogical. They can be handled by various techniques all of which ultimately fall back on observation through the senses. Such continua can be dealt with simply by action; so that when a man runs or plays tennis we can say that he is dealing successfully with the continua of space and time. Such activity is based on the use of the senses (observation) plus unconscious (neurological) mental processes. These unconscious mental processes are, of course, nonrational (although not always "irrational") and nonlogical. Or, in the second case, we can deal with such continua rationally and logically by dividing them, as we did with the rainbow, by arbitrary and imaginary divisions into gamuts to which we attach rational labels. We then deal with these labels (or categories) by rational processes, but the verity of the conclusions reached by these processes must be checked through sensual observation. A third method of dealing with reality is by pure rationalism, but before we consider this we must say a few words about the Greek effort to use the second method to develop a scientific approach to reality.

It is generally recognized that science, as we understand it, was born, but never fully developed, among the Greeks. It began to develop among the Ionians about 600 B.C. with the work of men like Thales of Miletus (ca. 624–547). About a century later the optimistic beliefs of the Ionian scientists began to be challenged by a number of thinkers who argued that reality was much more complex than was believed and that its nature varied with the point of view of the observer so that, for example, what seems warm to one observer seems cool to a different observer (or even to the same observer at a different time) so that we cannot say what is really warm or cool. The chief figure in this development of profound doubt was Heraclitus of Ephesus.

Heraclitus was obsessed with the dynamic qualities of observed reality, or, as we should put it, with the inability of man to deal with continua by any processes based on sensual observation. "All is flux," he said. Or again, "You cannot step into the same river twice." By this last statement he meant that the river is always changing. If we step into a river even a second after we stepped into it the first time, it is a different river. The first time we step into it, it is the river-we-have-not-yet-stepped-into, while the second time we step into it, it is the river-we-have-already-stepped-into. These are clearly different rivers, but they are different for other reasons as well. The second time, it is a different river because some of its water has flowed to the sea and been replaced by different water, the fish and plants in it have moved, and its bed and banks have worn away (however slightly). Obviously, it is not the same river. Although our senses can discern the changes only at the end of a long time, it has changed somewhat in any time however brief. Similarly, it changes in space. We walk along its bank and say, "Here is the river." But soon it is very narrow, and we say, "Here is the brook." Yet nowhere can we find a spot or a line which separates the river from the brook or the brook from the rill. We say that John's body is renewed every seven years, its material being completely eliminated and replaced by new material. This process must go on constantly so that at the end of any time, however small, John is a different person. We thus have no right to expect debts to be paid, because we can never find the exact person to whom we made the loan, and anyone has the right to refuse to repay a loan on the ground that it was made to someone else. If we seek repayment after a long interval, say ten years, why should he not say: "You have the wrong person. I do not have in my body a single molecule of the person to whom you made the loan ten years ago"? Of course we might argue, in such a case, that the molecules might have changed but their configuration has remained the same, and the loan was made to the configuration, not to the sum total of molecules. The point of such a distinction between molecules and their configuration, somewhat like Aristotle's distinction between matter and its form, is that matter can be observed by the senses while the form has to be inferred by some mental process. According to these Greek nonscientific thinkers of the fifth century B.C., we can say nothing true or know nothing certain about the physical world of appearances. In this world "all is flux." But behind this material world there must be some nonmaterial unchanging reality that can be found by rational thought. According to Heraclitus this reality behind appearances must be *logos,* a pattern of logical rationality.

On the basis of arguments such as these there arose a

school of rationalists following the teachings of Pythagoras (ca. 580–505 B.C.). To these Pythagorean rationalists the diversity and dynamics of the material world made it unknowable and outside the realm of possible discussion. But behind this "appearance of things," which was really illusion, was reality. Such reality was rational and logical. Accordingly, reality could be found by reason and logic alone, without any appeal to the senses or to observation. In fact, such an appeal to observation would merely distract a person from the unchanging, knowable, unity of rational reality to the constantly changing, unknowable, illusion of appearances. This dichotomy between appearance and reality became basic in the outlook of the Pythagorean rationalists such as Pythagoras himself, Socrates, Plato, or the early Aristotle. They insisted that knowledge could be obtained not by approaching the material world through the senses but by turning away from the material world (which was unknowable illusion) to reality (which was rational and knowable). Reality was to be found by the use of reason and logic alone, because it was rational and logical. This involved the unstated assumption that man's rational and logical mental activities run parallel to reality and reflect it without any physical link between them. According to the Pythagorean rationalists the rational and logical reality behind the world of appearances and found by the use of reason and logic without observation was the eternal, rational, and unified field of mathematics. Our knowledge of these things was not based on observation but on "reminiscence." Learning does not consist of putting anything into the mind but in recalling to the mind from its hiding place in the memory what the mind really knew all the while from some earlier existence or merely from its own structure. This process of remembering mathematics is demonstrated in Plato's *Meno*.

The best known case of an individual starting out as a follower of the Ionian sciences and then becoming a Pythagorean rationalist is to be found in the autobiographical remarks which Plato put into Socrates' mouth in the *Phaedo*. In earlier years, he said, he had been a follower of the natural philosophers (that is, the scientists) and even for a while had accepted the teachings of Anaxagoras, but he soon discovered that the senses were not dependable and that the views of scientists were never in agreement and were always changing. Accordingly he had abandoned dependence on the body and discovered that truth could be found by reason alone. The real philosopher, he felt, should be glad to die, because this would free him from the confusion of the body and the senses. The knowledge of the essence of things must be sought "with the mind alone, not introducing or intruding into the act of thought the sight or any other sense along with reason . . . ; he who has got rid, as far as he can, of eyes and ears and, so to speak, of the whole body, these being in his opinion distracting elements which, when they infect the mind hinder it from acquiring truth and knowledge. . . ." "I decided," he said, "to take refuge from the confusion of the senses in argument and by means of argument alone to determine the truth of reality." The truth thus revealed is recollection, recalled from a previous existence, and its truth is not to be tested, as a scientist would do, by observation but simply by the mathematical rule that all inferences deduced from it are mutually consistent.

We have already mentioned that these Pythagorean ideas

held and propagated by Socrates, Plato, Xenophon, and others were not tenable because long before, while Pythagoras was yet alive, one of his disciples had used the master's own Pythagorean theorem to prove that space was irrational (because it was a continuum). This means that it was possible to prove the irrationality of reality by purely rational (mathematical) arguments and that, accordingly, the fundamental assumption of this school about the rationality and logic of reality was false. Such a discovery should have led any honest seekers after truth to abandon this fundamental assumption about reality and to fall back on some other assumption (such as the scientists' assumption that the senses do give us information about reality).

The continued adherence by the rationalist school to beliefs they knew were false can only be explained on the ground that they had an interest in these beliefs beyond their devotion to truth. Naturally this interest was not stated by these people publicly. At least, no such statement appears in the ancient evidence; so once again we must rely on inference: the key to the thinking of the Pythagorean rationalists lies in their fear of change and hatred of change. Beyond the ordinary change of the physical world they saw the social change that, for centuries, had been spreading political power and economic benefits wider and wider. There can be no doubt that the Pythagorean rationalists resented these political and social changes and wished to deny the possibility and reality of change. Pythagoras himself was the founder of an international oligarchic conspiracy, the Pythagorean Brotherhood, which operated out of Croton, in southern Italy, until it was forced to flee from that city by a democratic uprising about 510 B.C. Thereafter this organization centered in Thebes in Boeotia. In international affairs it operated in support of the oligarchic states and in opposition to the democratic states, like Athens. In intellectual matters it attacked Ionian Science, the sophists, the philosophic nominalists, and the upholders of democracy and of human equality. The latter groups had become allied and, in some cases, identified for logical and historical reasons.

Until the end of the seventh century the Greeks lived in a fairly static society in which each individual's position was based on status rather than on choice or conscious decision and in which it was rare to meet any person with different customs or ideas than oneself. Accordingly, it was but natural for the Greeks to assume that the ideas and customs that they practiced themselves represented intrinsic and innate human nature and absolute truth in a system of absolute and universal values. The growth of commerce and of colonial expansion gave a rude shock to these ideas by showing the Greeks people with ideas and customs different from their own and often antithetical to theirs. The culmination of this educational process is to be seen in Herodotus, who is almost gullible in his readiness to believe that non-Greeks can practice almost any social customs. Experiences such as these could hardly fail to make a thoughtful people begin to examine the basis of their own customs. Can customs be based on essential human nature when different peoples act so differently? Or can there be any absolute value systems or social standards when different peoples have such diverse convictions? From these discussions there emerged, by the fifth century, two quite opposed points of view. On the one hand, the conservatives insisted that there was an absolute system of values and of social behavior and that in this system the customary Greek behavior was the natural inborn behavior of those beings who were fully human; any persons who acted or thought otherwise were at a lower level of this same absolute standard because their natures were not fully human. These conservatives saw the universe of living beings as a kind of hierarchy in which animals acted like animals, barbarians acted like barbarians, Greeks acted like men, and demigods acted like demigods, each according to its "real" nature. From this point of view developed two powerful theories that are still with us today: (1) that all differences between kinds of objects are real, eternal, and objective distinctions, and (2) that all differences between men are equally real, unchangeable, and objective, the result of biological (that is hereditary) differences. The first of these theories led, most obviously, to the corollary that species distinctions are real or, as the philosophers put it, universals are real. This is known as philosophic realism. The second, closely related theory, led to the belief that human personality is identical with human nature, each being based on the individual's biologic heredity and that, accordingly, social distinctions (such as those between noble and worker or between free man and slave) are based on real differences rooted in nature.

The point of view opposed to this absolute thinking was more relativist. It regarded differences in social customs as merely conventional differences indicating no real difference between barbarians and Greeks, between nobles and workers, or between free men and slaves. The external differences between these were merely accidental occurrences, resulting from different environment or upbringing, and signifying no really fundamental differences between the basic natures of the persons concerned. The customs of tribes or the positions of individuals were mere conventions, arising from history, and were thus capable of change in the future as they had changed in the past. In this point of view there was a distinction between nature and personality, the former being presumably the same for all men, while the latter was different merely because each person's history was different. Distinctions were not based on nature but on convention; moreover, if Heraclitus was correct about the dynamic nature of all the universe, then no distinctions between kinds of things were real, but were all equally conventional, drawn by a local consensus and indicated by verbal differences. This point of view led to philosophic nominalism and social, if not ethical, relativism. The chief distinction between noble and worker or between freeman and slave is not any absolute or real distinction but only a verbal distinction based, at most, on superficial and conventional distinctions such as exist between all individuals.

For reasons that should be evident, the absolute point of view based on philosophic realism had considerable appeal to the conservatives and the defenders of oligarchy. It denied the possibility of real change and justified the existing social and economic inequalities as being based on real, eternal distinctions. Furthermore, by insisting on the reality of group differences it reduced the appeal of individualism and justified the domination of the group over the individual.

Parallel reasons made the nominalist and relativist point of view appealing to the egalitarian, individualistic progressives. Nominalism, which recognized the existence of individuals, denied the real existence of groups and thus denied that economic and social inequalities were anything more than accidental and changeable features. This point of view justified individualism as the only reality, insisting that groups or universals were merely conventional collections of individuals to which a common name was given. Such a name was arbitrary and temporary, capable of change and even of complete reversal so that, for example, slavery could be called freedom and tyranny could be called justice, if men merely agreed on the convention to do so.

Thus the sophist Hippias, according to Plato, questioned the reality of the group (the state) by saying, "I believe all of you are kinsmen, friends, and fellow citizens, not by law but by nature; for by nature like is akin to like but law is the tyrant of mankind and often makes us do many things which are against nature." And again the sophist Lycophron questioned class distinctions with the statement, "The superiority of noble birth is imaginary, and its prerogatives are based merely upon a word." The real existence of a slavish nature in conventional slaves was challenged by thinkers like Alcidamas who said, "God made all men free; no man is a slave by nature," and Euripides who wrote, "The name alone brings shame upon a slave, who can be excellent in every way and truly equal to the freeborn man." Another sophist, Antiphon, questioned the real distinction between Greek and non-Greek, saying, "As to our natural gifts, we are all equal, whether we be Greeks or barbarians." According to Plato, Thrasymachus, a sophist, upheld the conventional, arbitrary, and nominalist character of justice by saying that this was merely a word which we apply to whatever the strong impose on the weak.

The nominalist outlook of the sophists was congenial and acceptable to the Ionian scientists, to the democrats, and to most progressive and reforming persons. In many instances, such as Anaxagoras, these "popular" roles were combined in one person. In any case, they were closely allied. This alliance, for a generation (461–429 B.C.), was under the leadership and patronage of Pericles, in whose "kitchen cabinet" Anaxagoras was a prominent member.

4. Age of Conflict

The period of expansion continued until the middle of the third century B.C. in the western half of Classical antiquity, but ended two centuries earlier in the eastern half. We can fix these dates with a good deal of confidence, but the mechanism that caused the change is considerably clearer in one case than it is in the other. The dubious instance is the earlier one, in the mid-fifth century in the Greek-speaking world.

In this earlier case we can see quite clearly that there was a change from a period of expansion to a period of conflict. Before 450 B.C. the four usual kinds of expansion (in production, population, geographic extent, and knowledge) are evident, but after that date they are much less so. On the other hand, three of the four characteristics of an Age of Conflict (decreasing rate of economic expansion, increasing class conflicts, imperialist wars, irrationality) seem to be increasingly evident after 450 B.C. If we move further away from this demarcation date, to compare, for example, 500 B.C. with 400 B.C. or 550 B.C. with 350 B.C., it becomes even clearer that the culture has passed from expansion to conflict.

To be sure there are difficulties, but in some cases, at least, these can be explained away. We must remember that the point at which a civilization (or an area in a civilization) turns from Stage 3 to Stage 4 is the point at which the rate of expansion ceases to rise and begins to decline; it is not the much later point at which expansion itself ceases and is replaced by contraction. There is thus a considerable length of time between these two points during which expansion continues, but with a decreasing rate. In the case of a core area, such as Greece, the difficulty in determining the date is increased by the fact that the rate of expansion itself is still continuing to rise in more peripheral areas (such as the western Mediterranean), and the helpful influence of prosperity there can serve to conceal the less optimistic picture in the older area.

Other sources of ambiguity in demarking the two stages from each other arise from closely related conditions. The ending of geographic expansion and of the growth of knowledge is difficult to establish in the core of any civilization as long as that civilization is continuing to expand in its peripheral areas. In fact, the expression "geographic expansion" can apply only to the society as a whole and could never be established for some limited portion of it. On the other hand, it does seem likely, although the evidence is not available, that the growth of knowledge, for the ordinary Greek, ceased to increase in the fourth century. The wars, insecurity, and general confusion that became endemic in Greek life after 430 B.C. must have made it increasingly difficult for the ordinary Greek (that is, the one who lacked the leisure provided by slaveownership) to obtain information. The established methods by which information was diffused in Greek society, through conversation rather than by reading and thus through such periodic gatherings as the Olympic Games, the Panathenaic festival, and visits to the local agora, as well as the more irregular intercourse provided by visits from foreign celebrities or journeys to places like the Delphic oracle—all these weakened as methods of communication for the ordinary non-slaveowning Greek after 430 B.C. The possibility of becoming literate or of obtaining information from written works may also have decreased about this time, or a little later, for the nonslaveowner. On the other hand, these written sources of information may well have increased in availability for leisured slaveowners for a long time after the fifth century B.C.

If the cessation of the four aspects of an Age of Expansion is difficult to establish for Greece in the fifth century, the advent of at least three of the four aspects of an Age of Conflict is easy to demonstrate. There clearly was a decreasing rate of economic expansion, at least after 400 B.C., for the economic troubles of Greece in the fourth century and later are notorious. The growth of class conflicts seems equally evident. Of course, it might be argued that such class struggles were always present in Greece; and, within limits, that is true. Social tensions had reached a very high peak in the period of transition from gestation to full expansion but had then subsided only to rise again at the transition from expansion to conflict. In Athenian history where our historical evidence is more adequate than elsewhere, there can be no doubt that social tensions reached a high point in the period between Draco and Solon (say 600 B.C.) and then subsided to a low point about 500 B.C. (just before the Persian Wars) only to rise again about 400 B.C. Moreover, the kind of class conflict was different in the earlier period than it was in the later one. In the former the struggle was between the forces of dynamicism of the Age of Expansion and the efforts of the older dominant groups to prevent change and to maintain the static social conditions of the period of gestation. Draco and his supporters wished to maintain the noble-dominated, self-sufficient, largely pastoral economic units of the earlier period, and sought to resist the growth of such innovations as the expanding money economy, the growth of commerce, the development of city life, the rise of a middle class founded on commerce, the shift to a more democratic military force based on infantry from the older system based on the use of chariots by a hereditary nobility, and the resulting modifications of law and justice inevitable with increased social change. This kind of conflict was based on tensions of development in which older ways of providing for human needs resisted the innovation of new methods for providing for these needs. Such tension is endemic in any dynamic society, and, from it, social conflicts can arise at any time.

The increased social conflicts that arose after 450 B.C. were quite different, being caused by tensions of evolution rather than by tensions of development. They did not arise from resistance to change, and even less from unsuccessful resistance to change, but from growing desperation because expansion was slowing up.

Of even greater significance, perhaps, is the fact that in this newer evolutionary crisis the victory was falling more and more to the groups who hated change. This triumph of the reactionaries had occurred occasionally in the earlier period of acute developmental tensions, most notably in Sparta. There the legislation associated with the name of Lycurgus had stopped the development from an agrarian to a commercial economy and had retained local control of political and social life in the hands of the noble landlord class at the price of a renunciation of all commercial expansion. But this local reaction had been overcome in the Greek world as a whole by increased expansion elsewhere, as in

Corinth or Athens. This is, of course, a clear case of geographic circumvention to a local reactionary triumph. But in the period after 400 B.C. in the Greek world there was a general triumph of the forces of reaction. This can be seen in the victories of Sparta, Thebes, Macedonia, and Rome, all of whom supported the oligarchic groups over the democratic groups in each state they attacked.

The growth of class conflict in the period after 430 B.C. can be seen in the writings of the enemies of democracy such as Aristophanes, Xenophon, or Plato, but is most clearly shown in Thucydides. The latter describes the way in which each state became divided into two classes, the democratic group favorable to Athens and the oligarchic group favorable to Sparta. The bloody reprisals these two groups inflicted on each other provide some of the most violent pages in Greek history. In Corcyra, where this schism appeared in one of its earliest and most unhappy examples, the popular party obtained support from the rural slaves by offering them emancipation, while the oligarchic group hired mercenary fighters from neighboring areas, and each group set out, generally successfully, to massacre the other.

Closely related to these growing class conflicts was the increasing evidence of imperialist wars. In the earlier periods there had been political conflicts, but the economic expansion of each state, either intensively (as a shift from agriculture to commerce and handicrafts) or extensively (as colonial expansion), had usually taken place without head-on collisions; but by 450 B.C. expansion was increasingly extensive rather than intensive and was more and more likely to seek political support for its extension because more than one group (each backed by its own state) was trying to expand into the same area, or into an area already occupied by a third group. These two modifications in the nature of expansion are characteristic of the shift from a period of expansion to a period of conflict. When an organization becomes institutionalized, it resists structural changes and thus decreases the amount of intensive expansion (which can be achieved only by structural changes) but still seeks to expand extensively by spreading its institutionalized structure over wider areas of exploitation. When numerous groups seek to do this, the limited number of such wider areas makes conflicts arise. Each group seeks to support its extensive expansion by political force, and the result is imperialist war. Indeed, one of the most notable characteristics of any Age of Conflict is the effort to achieve economic expansion by political rather than by economic means.

Here again Thucydides provides our most reliable evidence. The growing rivalry of diverse economic imperialisms is well shown in his writings, and culminated in the clash between Corinth and Athens in the Adriatic. Athens had come to dominate the commerce of the Aegean in the first half of the fifth century as Corinth dominated that of the Adriatic. When Athens tried to push into the Adriatic, allying with Corcyra to do so, Corinth called upon its ally, Sparta, and the fierce struggle began. It is clear that this Athenian effort to push a fairly primitive commercial economy into an area already occupied by a similar economy was unnecessary and was a result of the institutionalization of that system, but we do not know enough about the Greek economy of the day to say exactly how the system was institutionalized and how it could have been reformed.

We cannot ask of any economic system that it expand beyond the limits of its own technical knowledge or of its own social traits, but we have the right to expect that it utilize these before it seeks to expand by taking wealth from its neighbors. From this point of view it seems quite evident that Greek agriculture was far from exploiting its available resources when the imperialist wars began in the fifth century. At that time grain (usually barley) was grown in a two-field system in which the field was left fallow alternate years; this was equivalent to tilling only half the land each year. The fallow was left to recover the nutritive elements in the soil (nitrogen) and to a lesser extent the moisture. The latter could undoubtedly have been increased to some extent by irrigation, but a lack of private enterprise hampered this. As for the nutritive elements, these could have been increased sufficiently to reduce the fallowing to one year in three or even to eliminate it completely. The Greeks were fully aware of the nitrogen-providing qualities of leguminous crops: clover is mentioned in the *Odyssey*; and alfalfa came from Persia about 480 B.C.; other legumes were known, and their function as green manures was fully known to Xenophon and Theophrastus, yet were rarely used. The use of lime, marls, and various volcanic soils as inorganic fertilizers was also known, above all to Theophrastus. Yet these improvements were generally neglected. The causes of this neglect are to be attributed to a general lack of enterprise associated with a long-established slave system and the growing idea that agricultural labor was a menial activity beneath the dignity of free men. A wider use of legumes and of irrigation could have been made the basis for a more intensive use of livestock and this, in turn, could have led to a considerable increase in the use of meat and cheese in the Greek diet. But, as long as so much of agricultural labor was slaves, and these could be fed on barley and fish, there was little incentive to seek improvements in diet. To some extent such improvements in living were hampered by poor transportation, especially by inadequate harnessing that made it hardly worthwhile to use draft animals, so that heavy work had to be done by slaves. Here again the existence of slavery undoubtedly discouraged innovation: the slaves had to be fed 365 days in the year and had to be kept busy, so there was no real profit in any inventions that would reduce the work of slaves, since their field work in agriculture kept them busy only a small part of the year. Fields were plowed four or five times in a year, and each time were plowed over and over again in many directions "until it was no longer possible to see in which direction the plow went last." The clods were broken up with mattocks. Although this used enormous labor, it was recognized that any increase in efficiency would merely have served to increase the periods in which the slaves were idle. It was difficult to turn slaves to other activities such as vine dressing or olive trimming because these required too much skill for ordinary slaves. In a similar way, deep plowing and drill planting of seed were known to produce superior crops but were not used for lack of enterprise.

On none of these matters can we be very certain of our interpretations, because the facts are rather scanty, but it does seem that the Greek economic system, especially in agriculture, ceased to improve after 400 B.C. even though the knowledge that could have made improvements possible was available. Undoubtedly this had a considerable influence on the growth of imperialist wars, and seems to indicate that slavery had become an institution.

The fourth aspect of any Age of Conflict, increase in irrationality, is lacking in the Greek world after 450 B.C. and was generally rare in Classical antiquity, even when this society was clearly deep in its Age of Conflict. One reason probably lies in the general tendency toward rationality that existed among the Greeks and that we have tried to attribute to their Indo-European heritage. Of even greater significance was the alliance, already mentioned, between rationalism and the triumphant oligarchy.

The critics and enemies of democracy and of the whole Athenian way of life with its emphasis on change, commerce, and social equality formed a motley bloc made up of the philosophic realists, the conservatives and rationalists, especially the Pythagoreans, the defenders of nobility, of oligarchy, and of the state's authority, the admirers of Sparta, and the enemies of science. These groups were broken and disorganized for almost a century after the revolt at Croton (510 B.C.), and were kept off balance by the long series of political and economic successes of the Athenian democracy, but when these successes were followed by a longer series of disasters after 431 B.C., the oligarchic bloc began to organize. It is extremely likely that the nucleus of this revived oligarchic movement came from the Pythagorean refugees in Thebes. In any case, it brought together the diverse groups we have mentioned. The greatest figure in this group was Plato, who, like Anaxagoras a century earlier in the opposing bloc, combined many diverse trends. The writings of Plato remain as the most successful statement of the oligarchic rationalist position, although it is frequently stated even more explicitly elsewhere, as in some of the early works of Aristotle (when he was still a Platonic rationalist), especially the first book of the *Politics*.

The rivalry between these two blocs appeared repeatedly in the public controversies of Athens during the century 450–350 B.C. and even later. The condemnation of Anaxagoras about 450 B.C. was as much an event in this struggle as was the trial and conviction of Pericles in 430 B.C. So also was the execution of Socrates (399 B.C.) and Plato's reaction to this deed by founding the Academy on endowments that continued for 914 years (385 B.C.–A.D. 529).

There were three basic ideas of this oligarchic group: (1) that change was evil, superficial, illusory, and fundamentally impossible; (2) that all material things were misleading, illusory, distracting, and not worth seeking; and (3) that all rationally demonstrable distinctions, *including those in social position (especially slavery),* were based on real unchanging differences and not upon accidental or conventional distinctions. These three ideas together would serve to stop all efforts at social change, economic reform, or political equality.

These ideas, which we might sum up under some such comprehensive term as Pythagorean rationalism, were, of course, not irrational, yet they led, ultimately, to mysticism and served the same purpose of providing an ideology for the vested-interest groups that irrational thinking usually does in the Age of Conflict of any civilization. In the Age of Conflict of Classical antiquity these ideas generally triumphed, although they were challenged, generally with little effect, by the later Aristotle (after 343 B.C.), by Epicurus and Lucretius, and by numerous minor thinkers in the late Hellenistic and Roman periods. When, in the latter period, some of the sophist ideas, such as the conventional nature of slavery, became widely accepted, they were combined, as in Stoicism, with resignation and acceptance of the external appearances of things to a degree that entirely canceled the dynamic and progressive influence they had possessed when advocated by the Sophists.

It might be pointed out at this time that the triumph of the vested-interest groups (the oligarchy) in the struggles of the Age of Conflict of Classical civilization resulted in the social, political, and economic triumph of the oligarchy over the progressive and revolutionary forces. This led to the survival of the works of the intellectual supporters of oligarchy, such as Plato, Xenophon, and Cicero, and to the loss of most of the works of the opposite side, such as the writings of the Sophists and Ionian scientists; the rich were willing to pay for making copies of works favoring their position and would not pay for copying of opposition works. Thus we have today the writings of Pindar and Xenophon, but have lost those of Anaxagoras and Epicurus.

Moreover, it should be pointed out that the oligarchic victory over the forces of progress and equality did not ensure survival to the victors in the long run, or the ending of the opposition's ideology. Quite the contrary. The military tyranny that arose as a consequence of the oligarchy's efforts to maintain slavery and social inequality by force eventually took over the control of Classical society in its own name and liquidated the oligarchy and the Classical culture it had maintained. In a similar way the ideological writings of the supporters of oligarchy survived, but many of the ideas of their nominalist opponents became generally accepted. Thus individualism, the natural equality of all men, the conventional and unnatural character of slavery, and the belief that social distinctions rested on force rather than on real differences became generally accepted in the Stage of Universal Empire, but without in any way destroying the continued existence as institutions of slavery, social inequality, law, or public authority. Of course, in the very long run, with the disappearance of these institutions it might be argued that the ideas that challenged them won out, but this occurred only with the death of Classical society as a whole.

It would seem then that the period after 450 B.C. (in the eastern Mediterranean at least) had the chief, if not all, features of an Age of Conflict. Similarly, the following period in the eastern Mediterranean had many of the features of an Age of Universal Empire. These latter features continued from the establishment of Macedonian supremacy in the seventh decade of the fourth century until the disruption of Alexander's empire and the growing power of Rome threw the eastern Mediterranean back into the belated Age of Conflict still continuing in the western Mediterranean (until 146 B.C.).

The imperialist wars of the eastern Mediterranean's local Age of Conflict continued almost without interruption from the outbreak of the Peloponnesian War in 431 B.C. to the conquests of Alexander the Great a century later. Chief events in this period were the Spartan triumph over Athens in 404 B.C., the Theban victory over Sparta in 371 B.C., and the Macedonian conquest of all Greece at Chaeronea in 338 B.C. The conquests of Alexander the Great during the following fifteen years established a "core" or preliminary universal empire and some of the features of this fifth stage in the evolution of civilization continued, in spite of the subsequent breakup of that empire among the Diadochi. The chief of these features was the creation of a far-flung commercial unity that encouraged distant trade and geographic division of labor. In a full universal empire, such as existed in the Roman Empire under the Antonines, this would have been carried on to include a single monetary system, a unified legal system, and other aspects of unified rule and would have given rise to a period of peace and prosperity to which we apply the term "golden age." In Alexander's system this golden age was never reached because the core empire was disrupted and its temporary beneficial effects were obliterated by the intrusion into the eastern Mediterranean of the Age of Conflict still going on in the western Mediterranean.

The Age of Expansion in the western Mediterranean lasted from the seventh century to the middle of the third century, and thus continued for two hundred years after expansion had begun to decline in the east. It was, on the whole, somewhat different from the earlier expansion in the east, being more agricultural than commercial and more dependent on slavery. Moreover, nonindigenous peoples like the Etruscans and the Carthaginians made very considerable contributions to it. From the Etruscans, for example, came valuable contributions in regard to irrigation and drainage, while the Carthaginians developed the use of plantation slavery, especially in Sicily. Plantation slavery, which refers to the use of gangs of slaves on large estates, was always rare in Greece but became in the west the admired form of agrarian organization. It also became the mechanism by which the slave system was changed from an instrument of expansion to an institution of conflict.

In the earlier period, when agrarian units were still small they were worked by citizen-soldiers, frequently helped by slaves. Hesiod in Greece (about 700 B.C.) and Cincinnatus in Italy would be examples of such farmers. The story of how Cincinnatus was summoned from his plow to be dictator of Rome when it was attacked by the Aequi in 458 B.C. and how he returned to his work after a victorious sixteen-day campaign is significant on two counts. It shows the amateur and temporary status of Roman soldiers at this early period, and it shows that an important citizen worked in the fields himself.

By 200 B.C. the citizen-soldier and the family-size farm were both beginning to vanish from Italy. The ravages of Hannibal in his invasion of Italy during the Second Punic War (218–201 B.C.) had destroyed buildings, equipment, and livestock beyond the ability of the ordinary peasant to replace them. Moreover, these peasants had been away from their farms for years and had difficulty returning to the onerous routine of peasant life. The overseas conquests resulting from the war required a permanent standing army. This was recruited from the uprooted peasants of Italy. The farms of these displaced peasants were purchased by war profiteers or larger landlords who had made money from war contracts or war booty and were in a position to buy the ravaged Italian farms, combine them into large estates, and equip them with buildings and livestock from their wartime profits. The captives taken in the war provided slaves with which these new estates could be worked.

This process was encouraged by a number of other factors. In Sicily, which had been annexed from Carthage in 240, and in Africa, which was acquired forty years later, the Romans found a functioning agrarian system based on large estates. These were copied in Italy and, later, in Spain in accordance with the methods of the Carthaginian agricultural writer Mago, whose works were translated into Latin in the second century B.C. The Roman government was unable to pay off the debts incurred during the Second Punic War except by alienating public lands to the speculators and profiteers who were the chief creditors. Other public lands were transformed into latifundia by tenancy or by simple usurpation. Once Sicily and Africa were acquired,

Italy found it difficult to compete with these new territories in raising grain. Accordingly, the farm lands of Italy were shifted from grain to the production of olive oil, wool, and wine. Grain could be raised on both large and small farms and by persons who had large or small amounts of capital. Olives and wool could be raised only on large holdings and only by persons with considerable capital. Thus the shift from family farms to great estates was encouraged in Italy by the shift from grain to olives and wool.

One last but important factor in this change to large estates was the fact that landownership carried an appearance of aristocracy and social prestige, since the nobility were by law excluded from commerce, and restricted their economic activities to agriculture. As a result, every parvenu who made money in commerce, industry, speculation, or war contracts sought to win public sanction of his rise in the social scale by acquiring a large estate—the larger, the better. In this way many persons with no direct knowledge or interest in farming became owners of latifundia worked by slaves in charge of a steward. In consequence there grew up a pattern of ostentatious display of landed luxury, great debts, and separation of management from ownership.

This new pattern of agrarian organization created a demand for slaves that could hardly be satisfied. No slave system has ever been able to continue to function on the slaves provided by its own biological reproduction because the rate of human reproduction is too slow and the expense from infant mortality and years of unproductive upkeep of the young make this prohibitively expensive. This relationship is one of the basic causes of the American Civil War, and was even more significant in destroying ancient Rome. The normal method for supplying the slave needs of Classical antiquity was by sales of war captives. But even this was not sufficient to meet the demand. It was, however, sufficient to make war an endemic element in Roman life. The supply of slaves had to be supplemented by other means. The senate, which was the chief organ of government and in control of the landed rather than of the commercial classes, permitted piracy to flourish in the Mediterranean because it supplied captives to the slave marts. This continued until the middle of the first century B.C. when the revolutionary threat from the discontented to break up the latifundia forced the owners of these estates to seek support from the commercial groups by wiping out piracy that preyed on commerce. The ease with which piracy was suppressed by Pompey in 67 B.C. is evidence of the lack of effort made in this task earlier.

The supply of slaves was also increased by systematic plundering of the Roman provinces and the territories of allied states. Cicero tells us that each provincial governor had to return after his brief rule with three fortunes peculated from the province: one went to pay the bribes that had obtained his appointment, a second went to obtain acquittal from the charges brought against him on his return, and the third was for himself. A similar behavior was found among lesser provincial officials, especially the tax collectors, who often left an area ruined and depopulated.

Allied territories were not treated much better than provinces. About 104 B.C. Marius called upon the allied King Nicomedes of Bithynia to provide auxiliary troops for services against the Cimbri. The king replied that he was unable to do so because of the depopulation of his country by the slave raiding of Roman officials. When this message reached Rome, the senate ordered that enslaved freeborn citizens of Roman allies who were being held in Roman provinces should be freed, but after eight hundred were freed in Sicily within a few days, the landlords were able to exercise sufficient political pressure to stop execution of the decree.

As a consequence of such methods the number of slaves increased greatly in the period of the late republic, and the danger of slave revolts increased accordingly. William L. Westermann and Tenney Frank agree that at least 250,000 war captives were enslaved in the first fifty years of the second century B.C. Livy tells us that 70,000 slaves participated in the Sicilian slave revolt of 135 B.C.; 20,000 were armed by the rebels in the Social War in 90 B.C.; while Spartacus, who refused help from many, led 120,000 against the city in 72 B.C. In 37 B.C. Octavius Caesar trained 20,000 slaves obtained from his supporters to be oarsmen in his struggle with Sextus Pompeius, and, after his victory, he restored to their owners 30,000 slaves who had been serving with his defeated opponent.

This great increase in the number of slaves after 250 B.C. did not reflect any increase in their productive use. On the contrary, all the evidence indicates that larger and larger numbers were used in quite nonproductive activities: attending their masters, lolling about urban residences, or carrying letters and packages. Moreover, between Cato (who wrote his *De Agri Cultura* about 160 B.C.) and Varro (who wrote his *Rerum Rusticarum* about 37 B.C.) there was a definite shift from a rigorous profit motivation to a more humane and leisurely attitude toward slaves.

Even on the land itself there was a decrease in efficiency. The shift of managerial decisions from an owner on the spot who had a personal interest in efficiency to a freeman overseer who had no such interest does much to explain the mechanism by which the slave-based agricultural system changed from instrument to institution. The owner, of course, had a personal concern in increase of output because each increase accrued to him. But an overseer had an interest in a stable output year by year, something quite different.

If an agricultural unit is operated at peak human efficiency, its output will fluctuate from year to year by a considerable amount, depending on climate conditions. In such a case the overseer of an absentee landlord would have obtained only a modicum of praise in good years (since the high output was attributed to the weather), but would get a maximum of blame in poor years (on the argument that he should have been able to anticipate or compensate for adverse weather conditions) Under such fluctuations the overseer would have a precarious tenure and would frequently have been discharged.

On the other hand, if the farm had a fairly consistent output year after year within narrow limits of fluctuation, the owner would have secured an annual income on which he could depend and the overseer would have a relatively secure tenure. For this reason there was a general tendency for each agricultural unit to approach a fixed annual output. Such a steady output could be obtained only by stabilizing around the output of the poorer years, since it could not be done around the output of the better years. This means that the overseer drove his slaves hard if a year's output seemed likely to fall below his preset annual output figure, but relaxed discipline whenever it became clear that the year's output was likely to exceed the same preset annual output goal. The amount of output lost in the latter years (the meteorologically better ones) was always more than the amount of output gained by driving hard in the years when output would be naturally lower, since the preset annual figure was closer to the lower-output years than to the higher-output years of the farm under efficient management. The net result of all this was a reduction and stabilization of output on large estates of absentee owners. As the number of such estates increased, the output of the whole economy suffered.

This reduction of output for the system as a whole probably did not occur until after the time of Augustus or even later, and was concealed for a long time by the fact that the Roman political system was expanding geographically over larger and larger areas and thus obtaining control of larger and larger absolute amounts of agricultural produce even when the economic system as a whole was not producing more each year but less.

It is, however, very likely that the Mediterranean economic system as a whole reached its highest rate of expansion before 300 B.C. and was operating at a decreasing rate of expansion by 250 B.C. From 200 B.C. to A.D. 200 its absolute output increased only slightly, and by the latter date economic decline in absolute output had begun. Accordingly, the Age of Conflict for the western Mediterranean began by 250 B.C. and the period of decay for the whole civilization began about A.D. 200.

5. Universal Empire

The Universal Empire of Classical civilization was achieved with the establishment of the political supremacy of Rome throughout the Mediterranean in 146 B.C. The rise of Rome had little to do with the Age of Expansion. Rome began as an Etruscan bridgehead on the south bank of the Tiber at a place where several hills on that bank made it possible to defend a ford that crossed the river by way of an island. Thus from its earliest origin the Roman organization was militarized. Its political expansion, coinciding with the decline of the Etruscans, was dominated by military considerations. By 250 B.C., when the shift from an Age of Expansion to an Age of Conflict gave an increased role to any militarized system, Rome was ready to play that role. Until that moment the usual features of an Age of Expansion were obvious: increased production, increased population, increased geographic area for Classical culture as a whole, and increased knowledge. Of the lesser attributes of this period, democracy is manifest, although science is less so.

After 250 B.C. the attributes of an Age of Conflict became clear: class conflict, imperialist wars, irrationality, and declining democracy. All these acted and reacted on the agrarian slave system, increasing the number of slaves and the size of estates. This monopolization of the land led to a depopulation of the Italian countryside. Many peasants decided that they could live on the dole in Rome easier than they could win a living from the soil. As Seneca wrote about A.D. 50, "Country districts which were once the plowlands of whole villages are now worked by a single band of slaves, and the power of stewards is wider than the realms of kings." He also wrote, "Great troops of slaves whom their owner does not know by sight and the slave prisons echoing to the sound of the lash have no attraction for me." Elsewhere the situation was even worse. Pliny tells us that in the time of Nero (A.D. 54–68), six men held half the province of Africa.

Conditions became worse after 50 B.C. when Italy's industry, which had previously produced metal products and tasteless pottery for export, was unable to compete successfully with the industrial activity of the provinces, especially Gaul. One cause of this may be found in the fact that the craftsmen of Italy were mostly slaves, while those of Gaul were largely free. As a result of this, commerce, which had been flourishing under the republic, began to decrease under the empire, the imperial trade being replaced to a considerable extent by local and provincial commerce, except for the trade in luxury goods and in grain. The latter continued to pour into Italy from the provinces, especially from Egypt, which was also the source of papyrus. Under the republic Italy still paid for these imports by metal goods, red-ware pottery, and other products, but under the empire Italian exports decreased in importance, and imports had to be paid for in gold or silver. This began a steady flow of precious metals from Italy, especially from Rome to the provinces. These metals had to be brought back by new conquests extending the frontiers and by ransacking of the provinces by the provincial governors and armies. Thus the army, the imperialist wars, and the corruption in provincial government were necessary for the economic survival of the Roman system. Plunder kept the system functioning until the military weakening of Rome made it impossible to extend the frontiers further, and neither the supply of slaves nor the restoration of specie could be maintained. Thus, by 146 B.C. the Roman state had become the Universal Empire of Classical civilization, although it required another century and a half before class conflicts and imperialist wars were reduced in frequency. The class conflicts led to the so-called civil wars that ended with the triumph of

Augustus Caesar in 31 B.C. The imperialist wars continued as Roman attacks on outside peoples, and led to the conquest of Gaul, of Egypt, and of Britain.

By A.D. 96 the Universal Empire of Classical civilization had reached its golden age, a subperiod that continued for about three generations (96–180) under the "Five Good Emperors." Of this period Gibbon wrote, "If a man were called to fix the period in the history of the world during which the condition of the human race was most happy and prosperous, he would, without hesitation, name that which elapsed from the death of Domitian to the accession of Commodus." But, as Gibbon knew well, it needed but a slight change for this golden prosperity to become the brown of overripeness and decay.

6. Decay

By A.D. 200 Classical civilization had reached its period of decay. With the end of continual warfare and the clear inability of Rome's military forces to extend its frontiers further, the supply of both slaves and booty ceased. The unfavorable balance of payments of Italy became more acute. Trade began to decrease sharply, and a tendency for each province, even each large estate, to move toward economic self-sufficiency began. There was a return to grain growing in Italy. Craft activities began to move from the towns to the estates. The towns themselves ceased to grow, and later declined. The decreasing supply of slaves and the exodus of free persons from the town to the countryside gradually brought about an agrarian reorganization in which the landlords began to work their estates with tenants, requiring payment in kind and labor services on their own holdings as part of the rent. These tenants were called *coloni.*

Efforts to overcome the chronic economic depression by government action led to a much enlarged governmental bureaucracy and to an increased tax burden. This fell primarily on the landlords because of the dwindling commercial and craft activities, because the army was no longer paying its way from the booty of war but remained an expensive financial burden, and because landed wealth was something the tax collector could lay his hands on. The scarcity of manpower and the efforts of tenants to move from one landlord to another seeking better terms gave the landlords an excuse for refusing to pay taxes. To obviate such excuses, laws were passed forbidding the *coloni* to move from their tenancies, making these hereditary, and making the landlord responsible for his tenants' taxes since he could be found by the tax collector more easily than they could and his lands would be surety for payment. Thus the *coloni* tended to become serfs. In time they tended to look to the landlord for protection and for settlement of their disputes. At the same time, as the government became weaker and more remote, the free villagers, or *vici,* also began to look toward powerful local landlords for these same services of protection and justice. The government passed laws to prevent this growing system of patronage but without stopping it.

The decline of slavery led to decreased accumulation of capital, but investment, as we have seen, had declined earlier and more rapidly. The vital issue was no longer expansion but survival. The political disorders of the third century can be measured by one fact: in sixteen years forty-six emperors or would-be emperors met death by violence. Such disorders, intensified in the fourth and following centuries by the barbarian migrations, led to a flight from the towns to the country. Everyone wanted an established relationship to the food-producing land. As all municipal life decreased in vigor, agrarian units increased in self-sufficiency.

The shift of real power from the senate to the armies began as early as 100 B.C., but was not legally recognized until A.D. 195 when, for the first time, an emperor ruled without any senatorial election. Control of the imperial position became a clear power struggle between army commanders. Because such commanders could no longer retain the loyalty of their forces by periodic distribution of provincial booty and foreign slaves, they rewarded them from the chief remaining source of wealth, the landed holdings of their political opponents. This gradual liquidation of the landed class and their replacement by army leaders sprung from the more remote and backward areas of the empire entirely destroyed the town-dwelling landed elite who had been the carriers of the Classical culture. As this aristocratic, clarid, urban, moderate, mundane culture was destroyed, it was replaced by a welter of unprincipled violence, grasping materialism, crass ignorance, crude illiteracy, and narrow, rural provincialism. In reaction against this, there eventually arose a new spiritualism and asceticism, a flight from worldliness, mingled with all kinds of new religious feelings and dark superstitions but also containing much exalted spirituality. Both of these movements were fatal to the Classical ideology. In fact, it became increasingly difficult to find anyone with allegiance to the Classical idea, and certainly no one was willing to sacrifice or die for it. Yet without its ideology no culture can survive.

7. Invasion

As the Classical civilization grew weaker, its ability to maintain its integrity by defending its frontiers decreased. After these frontiers were established along the Rhine, the Danube, the Euphrates, the Red Sea, and the northern edge of the Sahara, they could not be expanded outward. This stopped the supply of slaves and booty that kept the whole economic system functioning. Efforts were made to push Roman rule across the Rhine, or as far as the Tigris, or across the Red Sea, or even across the Sahara, but all such efforts ultimately failed.

As a matter of fact, Rome had increasing difficulty defending these long-established frontiers themselves. This difficulty arose from a number of factors. Rome itself was getting weaker. Its ideology was losing allegiance everywhere; morale was evaporating; the economic system was declining; the political system was finding it increasingly difficult to get its orders obeyed; the social system was disintegrating. Even the army was becoming completely institutionalized, consisting largely of permanent garrisons, recruited from barbarians, with only local interests, and surely no interest in seeking death for the Classical idea or even for the Roman state. At the same time military problems were changing. Originally Roman infantry was pushing into barbarian territory. Later barbarian horsemen were raiding into imperial territory. Ultimately whole barbarian tribes were migrating into the empire itself. The inability of the famous Roman Legion to withstand charging horsemen made Rome indefensible. Rome had not had to face this problem earlier because adequate rain on the Northern Grasslands, century after century, reduced the tendency for barbarians to move. But decreased rainfall after A.D. 200 created a pressure of moving pastoral peoples that became irresistible. The final blow here was the pressure of the Huns out of the Asiatic steppes and on to the horse-riding Germans along the Roman Danubian frontier. The Gothic victory over the Roman army at Adrianople in 378 showed clearly that the final crisis had been reached.

What could be done? The situation both of the Roman state and of Classical culture was hopeless unless the defensive forces could be shifted quickly from infantry to cavalry. This was impossible, not only for the lack of experience in the techniques of cavalry warfare but equally because the weakened Classical economic system could not support a large number of horses. Horses, as grain-eating animals, compete for food directly with men. The inefficiency of the Classical Mediterranean economy, based on an institutionalized slave system, could not produce such a surplus. Yet without cavalry the society could not resist the intruding barbarians.

In fact, the crisis was more fundamental than the simple fact of military defense. No one any longer had faith in the Classical ideology or in the Classical gods. A new ideology and a new religion were needed. Though they were already at hand in Christianity, they could not be fitted into the Classical culture with which they were fundamentally incompatible.

A new technology was needed and was also available. It would be based on deep plowing with properly harnessed draft animals by persons who would have an interest in doing a good job because any additional output arising from increased care would accrue to themselves. But such a technology was much better adapted to the well-watered, heavy soils north of the Alps in the zones of summer crops than it was to the thin, seasonally watered light soils of the winter-growing Mediterranean.

A new military technique was also available. Based on heavy cavalry, armed with impact weapons, and equipped with strong horses, stirrups, and horeshoes, this technique was extremely expensive (in terms of grain consumption) so that one fighting man had to be supported by a hundred or more tillers of the soil. Here again, the areas north of the Alps, with their more productive grain fields and more adequate grasslands, were far better able to support the new system than was the older Mediterranean area.

The bringing together to form a single culture of these various techniques for satisfying man's basic needs required a new society. Classical society could not do it. When these came together north of the Alps, in the peripheral zone of Classical society, there appeared the core area of a new Western culture. But at the same time, in the old core area of Classical society, in the Aegean, sufficiently profound changes occurred in Classical culture to permit a variant of it to survive for another thousand years. This gives rise to one of the greatest puzzles of analytic history: Was Byzantine culture a new society or was it merely a revived Classical culture? Or is it possible that Byzantine culture is an earlier phase of Orthodox (Russian) civilization? In view of the fact that Byzantine culture had a different religion, ideology, social organization, military and economic technology, and almost certainly a different organization of expansion, it seems difficult to regard it as simply a reformed Classical culture. Its relative continuity in politics and law is not that significant. On the other hand, it hardly seems feasible to regard Byzantium as a wholly new civilization. Its brief life of about a thousand years would make it a rival with Hittite society for the position of the shortest-lived of all civilizations. Whatever decision is made in this difficult problem is bound to be unsatisfactory from many points of view, just as a mass of quartz at the junction of two or more crystals cannot be attributed to one or another with any assurance.

On the other hand, the fissure in the West between Classical culture and Western civilization is quite clear. The death of one society and the birth of an entirely new civilization in the peripheral area of a previous one is quite definite. On every level of culture, from the most material technology on one extreme to the most abstract ideology or religion on the other extreme, these two civilizations are different.

10

Western Civilization

The death of Classical civilization and the barbarian migrations that accompanied it left the shores of the Mediterranean Sea and an extensive hinterland behind them in cultural chaos. The area was filled with shattered social groups and cultural wreckage bobbing about on swirls and eddies as if a great ship had sunk in a quiet sea. In the next three hundred years (500–800) these peoples and cultural debris began to integrate to form core areas of three new civilizations. All of these were on the extreme periphery of the older Classical society. To the southeast, in Arabia, appeared Islamic civilization; to the northeast, in the Northern Flatlands, appeared Orthodox Russian civilization; and in the northwest, in France, appeared Western civilization. Each of these had its distinctive outlook and organization, as all societies do, and the relationship between the three became one of the continuing problems of the next fifteen hundred years.

Western civilization presents one of the most difficult tasks for historical analysis, because it is not yet finished, because we are a part of it and lack perspective, and because it presents considerable variation from our pattern of

The Evolution of Civilizations

historical change. The first two of these difficulties are obvious enough. If Western civilization is still in its course, its future is not yet settled and its past is, accordingly, capable of diverse interpretations. Moreover, our own involvement in it handicaps our interpretation because many of its most significant features are so familiar to us that we accept them without statement or even recognition. The importance of these two difficulties will appear in our own analysis.

Moreover, the analysis of Western civilization in terms of the seven stages is difficult because it clearly does not follow the straightforward pattern of seven simple stages. Of course, any student in any society has an inclination to regard his own culture as being in some way exceptional, but in this case, more than others, there seems to be objective justification for such a feeling. No culture has ever exceeded Western civilization in power and extent. Our society now covers more than half of the globe, extending in space from Poland in the east to Australia in the west. In the course of this expansion, most of it during the last five centuries, the power of Western civilization has been so great that it has destroyed, almost without thinking of it, hundreds of other societies, including five or six other civilizations.

As we have already indicated, the history of Western civilization to the middle of the twentieth century is not a simple story of rise and fall, but rather a series of at least three successive pulsating movements of expansion. Each period of expansion has been followed by an Age of Crisis, but in two, and probably in all three, of these crises the organization of expansion has been circumvented or reformed sufficiently to provide a new instrument of expansion and accordingly a new period in Stage 3. We have already given these three periods of expansion the rough dates 970–1270, 1420–1650, and 1730–1929. Each of these ended in an Age of Conflict.

Any such analysis as this is bound to lead to disagreement among students of the subject and, as a consequence, it may be necessary to give in this chapter some references to scholarly research, something we have managed to avoid in the earlier chapters of this book.

Although Western civilization emerged from the wreckage of Classical antiquity, it differed from it in every important aspect of its culture. Even in its first three stages it had a different military system (based on specialized cavalry rather than on infantry), a different technology (based on animal power rather than on slavery), a different economic organization, a different political organization (formed about rural castles rather than around municipal acropolises), and, above all, an entirely different religious system and basic ideology. The only level where a certain similarity between the two cultures could be found is on the social levels where both civilizations began with a two-class society of fighting nobles and agricultural peasantry organized in self-sufficient economic units (*genos* and manor) and slowly changed, in both cases, by the insertion of a town-dwelling commercial middle class between the original two. We have already spoken of this similarity.

The differences between the two societies on most levels of culture are either well known or will be explained in the present chapter. But the most important difference, that on the intellectual level, is too significant to be discussed in this cursory way. In any society the nonmaterial culture is the most significant feature of the whole society, because it is the least capable of being exported and because it is pervasive in all the other levels as well. In this particular case there is the additional necessity for exposition of this aspect, because of widespread ignorance or misunderstanding of it.

We might begin by saying that Western ideology is optimistic, moderate, hierarchical, democratic, individualistic yet social, and dynamic. All these terms refer only to aspects of the whole and do not really get us to its essence. This essence might be summed up in the belief that "Truth unfolds in time through a communal process." Before we attempt to analyze this rather cryptic statement, we should say a few words about the more superficial aspects.

The Western outlook is optimistic because it believes that the world is basically good and that the greatest good lies in the future. This covers all the ideas Etienne Gilson included in the term "Christian optimism." The Classical ideology began by being mundane and ended with a dualism in which it saw the universe as an evil material world opposed to a good spiritual sphere. Western ideology believes that the material is good and the spiritual is better but that they are not opposed to each other since the material world is necessary for the achievement of the spiritual world. The world and the flesh are good because they were both made by God (as in the Old Testament). The material world is necessary to the spiritual in two ways: (1) no soul exists without a body and (2) no soul can be saved except by its own efforts and cooperative actions with other persons, both of which can be achieved only by bodily actions in this world. These ideas appeared clearly in the Christian religion, although they had a very difficult time getting accepted because the dualistic late Classical ideology regarded the world and the flesh as evil and felt that the spirit could achieve full spirituality only by freeing itself from the body, from the world, and from contact with one's fellow man and that such spiritual achievement was a consequence of the individual's own activity alone, without cooperation with his fellow men. This attitude appeared very clearly in Persian thinking about 600 B.C., came into Classical antiquity through the Pythagorean rationalists, and was given a clear, explicit, and influential statement in Plato's *Phaedo* about 385 B.C. Although quite incompatible with the Classical outlook, these ideas became increasingly influential and became the generally accepted philosophic outlook after the third century of our era. This led to a phenomenal outgrowth of anchoritism in the third to sixth centuries. It must be recognized that this philosophic position was basically incompatible with the religious ideas of Christianity. The latter has been threatened ever since by dualistic heresies (like Arianism, Catharism, or Jansenism) derived from this philosophic background.

Western ideology believed that the world was good because it was made by God in six days and that at the end of each day He looked at His work and said that it was good. This meant that the world was a comprehensible place (one of the basic ideas of Western science) and that its existence unfolded in time (not by instantaneous creation or through eternal existence). The body was also good, being made by God in His own image. Man needed others in order to develop his capacities in time, and he needed his body, his fellow men, and God's help, as well as his own efforts to achieve, over time, salvation in the future. This salvation included the body as well as the soul ("resurrection of the body and life everlasting") and could be achieved by *good works* (requiring a body and one's fellow men) and God's grace (granted by God Himself taking a human *body* and living *in time* in *this world*). All of these things were clearly stated in the New Testament, and the objections to them arising from Classical dualism were firmly rejected at the first church council held at Nicaea in 325. The full implications of the injunction to "love thy neighbor" were not completely unfolded in these two steps but continue to be so through the present and into the future.

While the aristocratic Classical culture had put the golden age in the past, more democratic Western culture put it (and salvation) in the future. This optimistic and hopeful attitude applied to most aspects of Western life. Its hierarchical aspect appeared originally in the belief that the spiritual rested on the material (not opposed to it) and also came to apply to much of life. This led to a basic distinction (now largely lost) between necessary and important, in which material things were necessary but spiritual things were important.

The democratic and individualistic aspects of the Western outlook were always present, and go back, like other aspects, to the New Testament. They rest on the belief that all men have souls fit for salvation and, in the long run, have equal opportunity to achieve salvation. These ideas also appear in Christ's concern with the downtrodden and oppressed, in the belief that the first and greatest sin was pride (the sin of Lucifer) and that the greatest virtue was humility, in the Beatitudes and in many parables (such as that of the lost sheep). It is worthy of note that all these points are concerned not only with the individual's relationship to himself and to God but also with his relationship to his fellow men. All these, along with the emphasis on good works and the importance of sacraments, show the significance of the social element in Western thought. The same significance was underlined in the idea that man can be fully man and fully please God only in society. This idea was reflected in religion in the idea of the church (the *societas perfecta*), the belief that salvation could be obtained most readily through the church, the idea of the sacraments (all of which require the presence of at least two persons and most of which require three), the efforts, in the sixth century, to replace anchorites with monks (that is, to replace a late Classical aberration with a system more compatible with Western sociality).

All these different aspects of the Western outlook cluster about the essence of the outlook that we have tried to express in the statement that "Truth unfolds through a communal process." The outlook to which this statement refers lies at the foundation of Western culture and is reflected equally in its religion, its politics, its science, and its economics.

This outlook assumes, first, that there is a truth or goal for man's activity. Thus it rejects despair, solipsism, skepticism, pessimism, and chaos. It implies hope, order, and the existence of a meaningful objective external reality. And it provides the basis for science, religion, and social action as the West has known these.

Second, this attitude assumes that no one, *now,* has the truth in any complete or even adequate way; it must be sought or struggled for. Thus this outlook rejects smugness, complacency, pride, and personal authority in favor of the Christian virtues and a kind of basic agnosticism (with the implication "We don't yet know everything"), as well as the idea of achievement of good through struggle to reach the good. The earliest great work of German literature, *Parzival,* has as its subtitle "The Brave Man Slowly Wise." This is typical of the Western ideology's belief that wisdom (or any real achievement) comes as a consequence of personal effort in time. The same idea is to be found in Dante's *Divine Comedy,* in Shakespeare's tragedies (taken as a whole), and in Beethoven's symphonies.

There are two important ideas here: one is that no one has the whole truth now but that it can be approached closer and closer in the future, by vigorous effort, and the other is that no single individual does this or achieves this, but that it must be achieved by a communal effort, by a kind of cooperation in competition in which each individual's efforts help to correct the errors of others and thus help the development of a consensus that is closer to the truth than the actions of any single individual ever could be. We might call these two aspects the temporal and the social. They are covered in our maxim by the words "unfolds" and "social."

There is also a third idea here; namely, that the resulting consensus is still not final, although far superior to any earlier or more individual version. Thus the advance of mankind or of any single individual is an endless process in which truth (or any achievement, even the development of an individual's personality) is constantly approached closer and closer without ever being finished or reached.

We might mention also another phase of this outlook; namely, the idea that the cooperative effort that unfolds truth through a continuously developing consensus is a competitive process. More accurately it is cooperation through competition, as a game is. This refers to a social process that is superficially competitive but fundamentally cooperative, or, viewed in another way, a situation in which individuals compete and even struggle together for a higher social end (the consensus). This is a dialectic process and is one of the heritages from Classical antiquity, where this idea of the emergence of truth from pluralistic debate in the market place is found in the earlier dialogues of Plato and of other thinkers. It is worthy of note that Plato, while retaining the form of the dialogue, really abandoned its function in his later writings (the *Republic* and those following) by using Socrates as the spokesman of his own ideas that contain the whole truth, while the other speakers contribute nothing to the final achievement since their ideas are erroneous and must be corrected by Socrates.

This idea of the fruitful debate from which truth grows is the basis for the method of medieval intellectual advance (in spite of the erroneous theory so widely accepted that medieval ideas were rigid systems imposed by authority). This conception is of course found behind medieval exposition as in Abelard's *Sic et Non* or Aquinas's *Summa theologica,* but it is much more fully realized in the process by which medieval ideas were reached than in the form in which they were presented. However, in both there was a fundamental assumption that each presentation was temporary and not fully perfect and was subject to improvement in a later revision as a consequence of criticism. The idea, so widely spread today that the *Summa theologica* was a final, complete, and permanent presentation of its subject, was not held at the time by anyone, least of all by Aquinas himself. After all, the Angelic Doctor offered the world at least three versions of this subject—the *Summa . . . contra Gentiles,* the *Summa theologica,* and the incomplete but really much improved *Compendium Theologiae.*

This attitude, to which I have referred by the maxim about the social unfolding of truth, is the basis of the Western religious outlook. This outlook believed that religious truth unfolded in time and is not yet complete. The Old Testament, for example was not canceled or replaced by the New Testament but was supplemented by it. And the New Testament was never, in most of the life of Western civilization, regarded as a literal, explicit, and final statement of the truth. Rather, recognition of its truths have to be developed in time, by social action, from basically symbolic statements. Thus the doctrine of the Christian church was unfolded through church councils (like that at Nicaea) and by conferences of learned doctors and clerics, without ever any feeling that the process was finished. The fundamentalist position on biblical interpretation, with its emphasis on the explicit, complete, final, and authoritarian nature of Scripture, is a very late, minority view quite out of step with the Western tradition.

Closely related to this idea of the unfolding of doctrine through the church is the idea of the development of the individual, both in life and in death, toward the Beatific Vision. The same idea about the social (and dialectic) unfolding of truth is at the foundation of Western science. It assumes that science is never static or fully achieved, but pursues a constantly receding goal to which we approach closer and closer from the competition-cooperation of individual scientists, each of whom offers his experiments and theories to be critically reexamined and debated by his fellow scientists in a joint effort to reach a higher (and temporary) consensus.

The same outlook appears in the basic political ideas of the West. These are liberal and not authoritarian. They cannot be authoritarian because no individual or institution has full and final truth; instead a fuller and more complete truth emerges as a guide to social activity from the free debate in free assembly of all men's partial truths. Thus liberalism in this sense is basic in the outlook of the West and goes back, as we indicated earlier, to the dissociation of state and society in the Dark Ages when the former vanished and the latter continued. In its narrowest version this idea appeared as the theory that all men with different outlooks or contributions cooperate together to form something greater than the partial opinions of any of them. This kind of pluralism is assumed by the *Polycraticus* of John of Salisbury in the twelfth century as much as it is assumed by the United States Constitution in the eighteenth century.

The same kind of pluralist outlook is the real justification of capitalism and of all laissez-faire or pluralist economic systems so typical of the West even in its early period when economic development was taking its first steps. It is the outlook behind the nineteenth century "Community of Interests" that has been exposed to such critical onslaughts in the twentieth century but yet remains as the unstated assumption behind our economic attitudes as they operate in actions.

Thus we see the basic ideology of the West reflected in all aspects of the society, and continuing to influence ideas and actions even after it has been explicitly rejected. It is, for example, behind the theories of such late and "unconventional" thinkers as Darwin or Marx, both of whom believed that the Better emerged from the Good by the superficial struggles of the many to achieve what could never have been reached by any single individual alone. In fact, of these two, Marxist dialectic materialism is rather closer to the Western tradition than Darwin's struggle for existence is. Marx, like his mentor Hegel, was Western in his belief that progress is achieved through struggle, but, like Hegel, he committed the Western sin of pride (the sin of Lucifer) in the intellectual arrogance which expected achievement of a final goal in the material world and in the near future.

Part of the difficulty to be found in analysis of the history of Western civilization arises from the vicissitudes of the "Western tradition." These difficulties were present throughout Western history. In the early period (say up to 1150) the difficulty arose from the fact that the religious outlook and practices of our society were incompatible with the intellectual outlook and philosophy derived from the dualistic ideas of the Platonic and Neoplatonic tradition. Thus, in a figure like Augustine, we find a Christian religious outlook combined with a Platonic philosophic outlook with which it is really not compatible. One consequence of this situation was a great prevalence of dualistic heresies. These were condemned as part of the religious settlement at Nicaea in 325, but they were not really overcome in philosophy until the twelfth century. At this latter time the triumph of moderate realism, as represented by Abelard, Albertus Magnus, or Thomas Aquinas, over exaggerated realism, as represented by St. Anselm or William of Champeaux, represented the achievement, within Christian society, of a philosophy that was compatible with its religious outlook. The official acceptance by the papacy in the early fourteenth century of Thomism, in spite of the attacks of the exaggerated realists, sealed this victory. Such a victory, in accordance with the tradition of the West, was not a victory of one extreme view over another but rather a moderate synthesis of the extremes in a higher unity. Thus the exaggerated realist extremists said that the universal was real and that the individual was an illusion (a position totally incompatible with Christianity and therefore never held, in this extreme form, by any orthodox Christian). At the other end of the spectrum, the nominalists said that the individual was real and that the universal was only a word (or a subjective concept). The Thomistic compromise, which was compatible with Christianity and the Western tradition, said that *both* the individual and the universal were real. This synthesis disrupted very soon into two extremist positions, represented in philosophy by Scotist realism and Occamite nominalism. The same scission into two extremes was found in religion during the late Middle Ages between these who advocated salvation through good works (like St. Francis of Assisi and Thomas à Kempis) and those who advocated salvation through God's grace (the new ascetics, mystics, and ultimately the Protestants), each group tending to place such emphasis on its own path to salvation as almost to deny the other extreme. Or again, within the church appeared a split between those who emphasized it as a temporal organization (and thus corrupted it) and those who emphasized it as a spiritual group, and thus (like Savonarola, Huss, and Luther) tended to deny its organization.

From this it can be seen that the ideology of the Christian West was essentially a moderate one. It was constantly threatened, as moderates always are, by extremism. When these extremists argued for "either-or," the Western tradition answered "both!" But this answer was no sooner given than new appeals by extremists sought to reopen the debate, to destroy the moderates, and to disrupt the synthesis. The extremists from one side (the Left, if you will) based their appeals on individualism, the senses, and materialism, and thus on the Christian insistence on the need of the world and the body. The extremists from the other side (the Right, we might say) based their appeal on society, rationalism, and spirituality, and thus on the Christian emphasis on the soul, God's grace, and the perfect rationality of God. Ultimately, in the history of ideas, the former extreme goes back to the Hebrews and to the Ionian atomists, while the latter extreme goes back to Persian Zorastrianism and to the Pythagorean rationalists, above all, to Plato. Within Western religious history (and the history of the church, which is both temporal and spiritual) these two extremes have been represented by corruption and by dualistic heresy. It is easy for us to see how corruption (that is, too great emphasis on the material and temporal aspect) destroys religion, but it is not so easy for many to see how too great spirituality (that is, too great emphasis on the nonmaterial and eternal aspect) can destroy religion. This condition arises because religion is a linking (from *ligare,* to join together, as in English "ligament" or "ligature") of the two extremes (man and God) that cannot exist if either extremity is absent.

In the history of Western nonmaterial culture, including religion and philosophy, the threat to the synthesized moderate middle ground from the Right has come from dualistic rationalism and especially from the influence of Plato. This influence has worked historically through Augustine of Hippo, who was a Platonist in philosophy although a Christian in religion. In the field of religion itself, this influence has given rise to dualistic heresies of which the chief, as might be expected, have appealed to Augustine. Augustine himself was not a heretic. He said, "Man is saved by God's grace," but he never said, "Man is saved by God's grace *alone.*" Since the orthodox position (the middle ground) was that man was saved by God's grace and his own good works among his fellow men, Augustine's statement was incomplete but not wrong (that is heretical). Only when this partial statement was accepted as a whole, complete, and final statement did it become heresy. But the tendency for the Rightest extremists to do this was very strong, and this tendency was most irresistible among those who were closest to the Augustinian tradition. Thus Luther, who was an Augustinian monk, did believe in salvation by grace alone, and the last great heresy (from the spiritual extremists) was Jansenism, which grew out of Jansen's book the *Augustinus,* a study of Augustine's theology (1632). This spread through figures like Pascal and the Port Royal group and was condemned as a heresy by the papacy in the bull *Unigenitus* in 1715.

Of course, the threat to the Western ideology based on synthetic moderation came equally, if not more easily, from the Left, from the materialists and nominalists. But this is a well known story that needs to be mentioned here only because the loss of the ideology of Western civilization (like the earlier loss of the ideology of Classical civilization) will rest rather on the overemphasis on materialism and selfish individualism than it will on overemphasis of rationalism or spirituality.

In most civilizations, as we have already shown, there is a strong tendency for the basic ideology of the society to become lost and misunderstood during the Age of Conflict and to be abandoned totally in the Age of Decay. Since Western civilization has gone into an Age of Conflict three times, the threat to the society's ideology has been practically endemic. Anyone who wishes to recover this ideology can do so by reflecting on the word "moderation" or the expression "reconciliation of extremes" or, more abstrusely, on our maxim about the "unfolding of truth through social activity over time." When our old professor said of Goethe that he was "conciliatory," he was saying that he was a figure in the Western tradition; but when we say that Hitler was an extremist or a fanatic we are equally clearly excluding Hitler from the real Western tradition.

1. Mixture

The mixture of cultural elements that formed Western society came from four chief sources. One of these was Classical culture, whose greatest influence was in law, government, philosophy, and science. Another was the Semitic influence, which came largely through Christianity and the Jewish people and thus spread its effects largely in the field of religion and morality. The third influence, that of the barbarians, was a very diffused one, and is chiefly notable in social relations and technology; while the last, coming from the Saracens, consists mostly in incidental items and served also as an intermediary in the transfer of Classical influences.

The creation of the new society was a lengthy and painful process in which the most vital changes occurred at opposite ends of the cultural spectrum in the areas of military technology and of religion. The religious influence, which we have already mentioned, served to divorce peoples' allegiance from Classical culture and to focus it on a new ideology for which men were willing to sacrifice their wealth, leisure, and safety. The military influence sprang from the need to find a method by which Christian groups could be defended from the onslaughts of pagan invaders.

A Christian society could arise and maintain itself only if its members could be defended against non-Christian intruders. The older, Classical military tactics had been based

on infantry, fighting in compact masses and highly disci-
plined so that they could not be broken under enemy attack
but rather would remain in alignment and position so that
each individual could be at least partly covered by the shield
and sword of his neighbor. This infantry technique, which
had undergone only slight modifications in the long period
from the Greek hoplites and Macedonian phalanxes to
Roman legions, had become completely obsolete in the
fourth century of our era before the impact of charging
horsemen. The threat from these horsemen rested not only
on their possession of mounts but also on the fact that these
horses could be used day after day without resting because
hoof-wear was prevented by iron horseshoes, and the impact
of their lances on standing men was greatly increased by
the use of stirrups. We do not know exactly when horseshoes
and stirrups were introduced into the West, but it is certain
that they were invented fairly early in the Christian period
in the Northern Flatlands of Asia, probably by one of the
Ural-Altaic-speaking peoples, and were introduced into
Europe during the period of barbarian migrations. It is possible that the Huns had these innovations as early as the
fourth century, and this may well explain the horrors these
people evoked in the West. One of the chief reasons for the
widespread fear of the Huns rested on their ability to travel
very long distances in relatively short periods. This ability
may well have been based on their use of horseshoes.

The new military tactic of mounted men fighting in loose
groups armed with lances or spears required so much skill
and training that fighting men had to be specialists, free to
practice because they were supported economically by
others. This requirement made it inevitable that the new
Christian society must be a two-class society divided into

those who fought from horseback and those who produced the food to support all persons and their animals. The fighting man in this organization was very expensive because his horses (he needed at least two), his arms, and his leisure to practice fighting were expensive. This meant that the ratio, in the society, between soil tillers and fighters would be high, something in the order of a hundred to one. The specialized fighters and the specialized soil tillers in this organization were very unequal in power, although, perhaps, not so overwhelmingly unequal as we might guess. When the organization reached its full development in the late eleventh century, the knight provided all the protection and the peasant (by then usually a serf) provided all the food. The knight needed food as much as the peasant needed protection, but the time ratio between these needs was to the advantage of the knight to such an extent that he could use his power against the peasant in the short run (to enforce obedience) so long as he did not injure the peasant's capacity to produce food in the long run. This power ratio of knight and serf was so great that it was possible for knights to force serfs to contribute to their support beyond the amount necessary for the expenses of protection alone. Accordingly, there was a flow of the economic necessities produced by the serfs into the possession of the knights. Thus the medieval knight became a surplus-creating instrument as well as an instrument of defense, a political power, and the upper class in the social system.

This complex organization on the military, political, social, and economic levels is called feudalism. It was supported by an economic organization of self-sufficient agricultural units called manors, and acted as the surplus-creating organization of the instrument of expansion of Western civilization in its first four stages. The whole system was supported by the economic production of the peasant. This latter relationship was so vital for the existence of the system that the peasant was legally forbidden to leave his position on the land and thus became a serf. On the whole, the peasant did not resist serfdom, since it gave him a secure status that provided protection and justice.

2. Gestation

The period of mixture of Western civilization was merely a continuation of the period of invasion of Classical civilization and lasted from about A.D. 370 to at least 750. It was followed by a period of gestation of about two hundred years. The two periods together had to achieve three tremendous tasks: first, to bring into existence the new Christian society by creating relationships between groups and individuals and by establishing patterns of ideas and activity that would permit a new society to survive; second, to repel invasions of non-Christian cultures or to enforce conformity to the new Christian patterns by those who could not be expelled; and, third, the accumulation and investment functions of the instrument of expansion must begin to operate.

These three tasks were achieved in the order in which we have listed them, the first in the period of mixture, the third in the period of gestation, and the second bridging over both periods. This second was such a gigantic task that it delayed the achievement of the third task and led the society into political ambitions that could not possibly be supported by the economic base available. These ambitions took the form of the Carolingian Empire, whose brief life covered the generation before 814.

The task of repelling invaders from Christian society was extraordinarily successful. To us today it is still a puzzle as to how it was achieved. As late as 732 the Saracen invaders were only fifty miles fom Paris, but as early as 1099 the Christian counterattack on the Saracens had captured Jerusalem. During most of this interval the attacks on the West continued, by Vikings and Northmen in the Baltic and North Sea areas, by pagan Germans and Turkic peoples from the East, and by the Saracens in the Mediterranean area. In one way or another, these peoples were pushed back or were adopted into Western society.

The success of these military achievements, especially by the Carolingians, led to their abortive effort to reestablish in Europe a recreated universal Roman Empire. This was an overextension of military and political ambitions quite unwarranted by the social and economic conditions. In terms of our analysis it meant that surpluses being accumulated by the political and military organizations were being expended in the same levels in an effort to expand on these levels more rapidly than the economic basis would allow. Before any centralized political system such as Charlemagne's could function steadily, it was necessary to achieve a very great expansion and intensification of the economic level by diverting the surpluses being accumulated on the political and military levels into the economic level.

The real difficulties on the political and military levels that made the Carolingian effort fail were in respect to three phenomena: (1) poor transportation, (2) poor communications, and (3) the superiority of defensive weapons. We have already mentioned that the old Roman Empire was supported on the shores of the Mediterranean Sea by the superiority of sea transportation over land transportation, thus binding the shores of the sea to each other more closely than any shore was bound to its own hinterland. The re-creation of a universal Carolingian Empire would have needed a system of land transportation able to bind Europe into a unified whole. No such system existed or could exist in the year 800. Roads were almost totally lacking, and could not be supported in any adequate fashion by the limited output of the economic system. At that time Europe was just obtaining from the East an adequate method of harnessing, including the horse collar and traces, but this method was not yet widely known, and the economic sys-tem was not able to support any large number of horses or men devoted to transportation.

Closely related to the lack of transportation was the in-adequacy of communications, including that basic item, the level of literacy. Literacy has been associated historically with the existence either of a priestly group seeking to keep records or of a commercial group seeking to communicate over a distance as well as to keep records. The transporta-tion inadequacy that led to self-sufficient manors and the political disorder that gave a low level of personal security combined to make commerce almost impossible in the early medieval period. Without a commercial group, literacy thus was a monopoly of the clergy, but even here poverty and disorder led to a high degree of localism and a decrease in communication and in literacy. Without these things no centralized government could possibly function, and the Carolingian effort to establish one proved abortive. It is worthy of note that the subsequent revival of government, after the tenth century, followed very closely the revival of literacy among the clergy and a new commercial class and that rulers made use of these two groups in sequence to count their moneys and handle their communications and accounts.

The third factor in the disappearance of centralized government was the superiority of defensive weapons. For any government to function, it must be able to know what is happening at a distance, to communicate its orders, and to enforce obedience to these. The enforcement of obedience to orders cannot go further than the limit of the superiority of offensive power over defensive power. In the year A.D. 900 there was no such superiority. On the contrary, the defense was superior over the offensive to a degree that has never been exceeded in the historic period, even during its nearest analogy—the Mediterranean world about 1000 B.C.

The military system of Europe about A.D. 1000 is of extraordinary interest because it was built about two "supreme weapons," neither of which could defeat the other. These were the mounted knight and the castle. Quite obviously, a castle could not defeat a knight. And, almost equally obviously, a knight could not defeat a castle. The only way that a knight or group of knights could defeat a castle was by siege, but this was extremely difficult during the early Middle Ages because of the technical difficulty of supplying a besieging force at a distance so that it could starve out the defenders before it starved itself from exhaustion of supplies. Any besieging force had to be stronger than the besieged or it would be driven from the area and the siege broken. But to maintain a superior besieging force placed an almost impossible burden on the available transport. The besiegers could starve out the besieged only if they could supply a larger force at a distance than the besieged had available in their own stores. This was such an unlikely possibility for much of the Middle Ages that a castle remained as a supreme defensive weapon for most of that period. Politically this means that anyone who had a castle could say "no" to any order and could not be forced to submit. This means that every such castle became a nucleus of political independence and, since there were thousands of such castles in Europe about 1000, it meant that Europe was divided into thousands of independent political units and that centralized political power over any extended area was impossible. In this situation the clash of knight against knight was much less significant, for a knight, even when defeated on the field, could not be made to obey if he could retire into his castle.

The defensive superiority of the castle inhibited the growth of larger political units longer than the inadequacy of transportation might warrant because of the intrusion of other factors. One of these delaying factors is to be found in the organization of feudalism itself. Feudal relationships sought to organize over larger areas by subinfeudation. By this process a lord would be owed military service and advice (*auxilium et concilium*) from a large number of vassals, each supported by an economic unit (fief) organized in manors. Efforts to organize these relationships into larger and larger systems led to problems that students of organization call "problems of span." If, for example, the king of France had the right to expect 5,000 knights to answer his summons to military service, he would face an insoluble problem of span if he had to send out 5,000 individual summonses because he had 5,000 separate individual vassals. To avoid this the lord reduced the number of his direct vassals to a manageable span by requiring numerous knights' services from each vassal. Thus the king of France could still summon 5,000 fighting men to service if he had 50 vassals each of whom owed 100 fighting men's services or if he divided up the 5,000 into any two factors whose product would provide 5,000 men. The vassals who owed plural service could obtain the necessary fighting men by subinfeudating the fiefs that supported these fighters to their own vassals, or through them to their vassals' vassals. As these relationships became etablished, each vassal sought to specify what he owed his lord, and thus there gradually arose customary limits on the military service a lord could demand from his vassals. In many areas these limits came to be understood as no more than forty days' military service each year and at no greater distance than two or three days' ride (forty to fifty miles) from the vassal's residencc. These limits made it impossible to besiege a castle successfully within the limits, and this served to extend the defensive invulnerability of a castle against feudal forces even after the period when the inadequacy of transportation had hampered sieges.

The interplay of these influences, and others not yet mentioned, were such as to create three subperiods in the history of castle defense and thus in the history of political development. The first period, when transportation inadequacy was the chief factor, is the period of political feudalism. This political period continued until the late eleventh century because of the importance of limitations on a vassal's military service in feudal customary law. Eventually feudal knights began to be replaced by similar fighters serving for pay rather than for feudal obligation. These mercenary men-at-arms (as they are called) served as long as they were paid, and thus could capture a castle by siege simply by starving it out if transport of supplies was adequate. Since all possessors of castles did not have sufficient economic resources to obtain mercenary men-at-arms, those who did could besiege those who did not and force obedience upon the latter. This led to a reduction in the number of independent political units because it reduced the number who could refuse obedience to orders. Thus the number of political units in Europe became less, and the areas over which their orders could be enforced (or over which their "writ ran," as the saying went) became larger. This led to a second stage in the development of European political organization, known as "feudal monarchy." The number of political units in Europe was reduced from thousands to hundreds.

The next step forward in the development of the political level reduced the number of European political units from hundreds to scores and gave us a new stage in political development to which we apply the name "dynastic monarchy." The military factor that contributed to its growth was the rise of artillery that made the private stone castle obsolete, since guns could shatter the walls of a castle and thus force its owner to submit. Artillery first appeared about 1325, but its effects were not clearly evident for two hundred years. Then they became so clear that when a great lord wanted a residence after 1530 he built a palace rather than a castle. In this way, at the price of political submission to the royal artillery, the lord obtained an indefensible, but much more comfortable, residence at a lower cost.

The number of lords with the financial and economic resources to obtain artillery was, of course, much less than the number who had mercenary men-at-arms, so that the former could enforce obedience from the latter. Political units became fewer in number and larger in area. The possession of artillery became the dividing line between public authority and private power, and later between possession of castles and the lack, as well as between the possession of a royal title and its lack. All these served to demark a period of "dynastic monarchy" in the political level at the rough date 1500.

This period of dynastic monarchy (1500–1800) and even the preceding period of feudal monarchy (1100–1500) are, of course, subsequent to the Age of Gestation of Western civilization, but this examination of the factors necessary for the rise of these later stages of political development will show the futility of the Carolingian effort to create a revived universal monarchy at a time when even the earliest of these factors, transportation, was still in retreat.

As long as transportation was lacking and political disorder continued, the Age of Gestation continued. The demands of political and military life made it almost impossible for the feudal organization to amass surpluses and to direct these surpluses into expansive channels. Only in the final quarter of the tenth century was this situation reversed, and a new period of expansion, the first in Western civilization, began.

3. Expansion

The first stage of expansion in Western civilization lasted for about three centuries (970–1270) and was one of the greatest of such periods in human history. Its instrument of expansion was the feudal system in which a small minority

of fighting men and clergy were supported by a great majority of peasants. The contributions of the latter to the
former were far greater than the costs of protection and
justice they received in return, so that surpluses accumulated
in the possession of the upper class. At first these surpluses
were used for political ends, to build castles or to rebuild
older timbered fortifications in stone. But soon investment
in economic activities began. This appeared either in agriculture or in the encouragement of long-distance commerce in luxury goods. The agricultural expansion was
extensive, and took the form of establishing manors in
untilled areas by clearing wastelands or forests or by draining swamplands. When this was done by secular lords, the
new manors were generally similar to the older manors of
the self-sufficient, balanced three-field type. But increasingly
the manors spread by clerical, above all by monastic, groups
were of a new type producing still the basic needs of their
own inhabitants but adding to this an increasing surplus output of some product for sale off the manor. In grassy or
hilly areas these surplus products from new manors were
likely to be wool, wines, or dairy products (chiefly cheeses),
but in ordinary terrain it might be grain.

The accumulation of surplus in the hands of "the lords
spiritual and temporal" also created a demand for remote
luxury goods derived from commerce. From the eastern
forests opened by Varangians there came, by way of the
Baltic, various forest products such as furs, honey, wax, and
later hemp, tar, and even lumber. From the Levant there
came across the Mediterranean more exotic products, including fine textiles, fine metal products, spices, and dyes. Eventually, links between these two great sea routes were established, the earliest being the Russian river route, then from

Italy across the Brenner to Innsbruck, Nuremberg, and the North German rivers, or across the western Alpine passes to the Rhone, Champagne, and the northwestern rivers to the Low Countries. In the first part of the fourteenth century an all-sea link was opened by way of the Strait of Gibraltar and Bay of Biscay to the Narrow Seas.

The revival of commerce, especially in the twelfth century, gave rise to a new social class isolated from the agricultural process, and living in towns rather than on manors. This new middle class, or bourgeoisie, created such a demand for the necessities of life that a new kind of commerce, of local origin and concerned with necessities, appeared.

These three innovations—commerce, the middle classes, and town life—represented a social and economic revolution in Western society. They led to increased literacy, support for the revival of public authority, new ideas, new morality, and acute religious problems. Taken together these provide a fairly typical example of Stage 3 in a civilization.

The usual characteristics of Stage 3 are easy to identify in the period 1270–1300: increased production, growing population, geographic expansion, and increased knowledge. To a lesser degree, and somewhat belated, can be seen the growth of science, but democratic elements, while present, were unable to develop far because of the continued supremacy of specialized weapons. These kept power securely in the hands of a minority.

4. Conflict

The old view of our grandfathers that the Middle Ages was a static and backward era is now accepted by almost no one, but it is not so generally recognized that medieval expansion was slowing down by the end of the thirteenth century and that the society was entering upon a typical age of conflict. The three hundred years of expansion that were drawing to a close as Aquinas died in 1274 had been financed by the demand of the upper classes for luxury goods of distant origin. In time this demand was reinforced and extended by the demands of the successful commercial groups for both luxuries and necessities. But by 1274 the feudal organization, especially the feudal lords, had become institutionalized into an obsolescent structure with few functions and a powerful determination to resist further change and to defend its own social position. This institutionalized feudalism is called chivalry. As a military system it was being replaced by royal and ducal forces based on mercenary men-at-arms. As a political influence it was being replaced by royal and princely rulers served by clerical or even bourgeois officials. These latter had, for the prince, the great advantage that they could count, keep records, and were literate, and yet had no independent military power of their own. Even as a social group, the feudal nobility were being challenged by persons of other origins, such as royal officials, clerical leaders, and wealthy bourgeoisie. The nobility had no desire to continue the process of change that had brought them to this situation, but they were in no position to stop continued development.

One of the chief consequences of these economic changes was the advent of a money economy. As a result of this, all relationships in society developed a tendency to become expressed in monetary terms. This was true of the relationships that each noble lord had with his vassals in the feudal system and with his serfs in the manorial system. The aid and counsel owed by the vassal in the former case, as well as the dues and services owed by the serf in the latter, were, sooner or later, transformed from obligations to pay in kind to obligations to pay in money.

Each change was made at the going rate of value, so that the nobles ceased to have fixed incomes in kind and began to have fixed incomes in money. But the steady rise in prices up to 1300 meant that the value of fixed-money incomes was steadily reduced; every year a fixed income would buy less. This rise in prices and equivalent fall in the value of money occurred because both the amount of money in circulation and the speed with which it circulated increased faster than the increase in the volume of goods available (although this was also increasing).

The reduction of noble incomes by the decreasing value of money meant that less could be saved from these incomes. Thus there was less and less available for investment. If we consider that the price level was about three times as high in 1300 as it had been at the end of the tenth century, we shall see that a noble who commuted his income into money at the earlier date would have only one-third as much real income at the later date. No one, of course, was quite this badly off, for the simple reason that no one commuted as early as the tenth century, and the later the commutation the less the loss, but by the end of the thirteenth century most nobles were being reduced to desperation. This situation was made even worse by the fact that the institutionalization of the nobility led to customary and legal restrictions on their activities that made it very difficult for them to supplement their decreasing real incomes. On the Continent generally (but not in England), they were forbidden to engage in commerce or to marry nonnoble girls. These restrictions made it impossible for the nobility to obtain access to incomes from the commercial class (as was done in England, where there were a peerage and an aristocracy but no nobility).

The result of all these noble misfortunes was that the only feasible way in which a noble could supplement his income was as a mercenary soldier or, possibly, as a royal bureaucrat. The latter was unlikely because writing and counting were not noble skills. Thus a noble was inclined to seek to supplement his income from war. This need became the basis for the imperialist wars of the Age of Conflict that began at the end of the thirteenth century. English wars against the Scots, Welsh, Irish, and French; French wars with the English, Burgundians, and others; the almost endless struggles among the princes, both lay and clerical, of Italy and Germany; all these, as well as civil struggles such as the Wars of the Roses, the struggles of the Armagnacs, or the Sicilian Vespers, helped to provide jobs for the impoverished feudal nobility.

The economic crisis that emerged from the decrease of feudal spending was delayed only briefly by the continuance of saving and investment by commercial groups. The economic life of the towns, including both commercial and crop activities, became institutionalized in the fourteenth century largely by the activities of the guilds. As demand ceased to grow, these adopted restrictive regulations, preventing admission of new workers to most activities and, under the pretext of protecting the quality of the products, curtailed output and increased prices. At the same time towns placed all kinds of restrictions (generally known as municipal mercantilism) on business activities. These included restricting commercial exchange to set times and places (the market), putting restrictions on nontownspeople in the town market, forbidding purchases for later sale in the same market, hampering or taxing export of goods from the town, and so forth. All such regulations, embodying what is technically called "a policy of provision," had a very adverse influence on technological advance for most of the fourteenth century.

The decrease in expansion arising from the growth of economic institutionalization was accelerated by a number of other factors. One of these was a fall of prices after 1300, accompanied, within a half-century, by a scarcity of labor. The fall of prices probably began with the decrease in demand arising from institutionalization, but it was greatly accelerated by the scarcity of bullion. By the year 1300 the accessible silver mines and scanty gold resources of Europe had been systematically exploited for about four centuries and most of the easily obtained bullion had been extracted. Mines were becoming exhausted or were going deeper than could be operated easily by the available technology. The problem of keeping water out of the deeper mines was rapidly becoming insoluble. The ordinary lift pumps known at the time would not take water higher than about thirty feet, since they worked by air pressure, so that depths greater than this had to be pumped out in multiple stages. Problems of ventilation and of removing ores were also rising rapidly. As a consequence, after about 1320 the annual increase in the bullion supply and thus the increase in the volume of money were less than the increase in production of goods, and the long rise in prices was reversed. Costs, particularly wages, did not fall so rapidly as prices, with the result that profit margins (price minus costs) were reduced or wiped out completely. This discouraged production. The situation was alleviated for a short time just at the middle of the fourteenth century because the outbreak of the Hundred Years' War in 1338 helped to strengthen prices, but profit margins hardly benefited at all, because the shortage of labor resulting from the onslaughts of the Black Death after 1348 raised wages. Even today, when wages constitute a smaller portion of total costs, nothing will curtail production faster or more completely than rising wages in a time of falling prices. One rather paradoxical consequence of this situation was that incomes were distributed somewhat more equitably, and the standards of living of the poorer groups frequently improved in spite of the general economic decline. This meant that aggregate incomes, as a whole, were decreasing, but the share of the total income going to the working people was rising and the share of the upper classes was falling quite rapidly. As a consequence of this, both saving and investment (which were upper-class activities) decreased even more rapidly, and the depression worsened.

This economic and social crisis of the fourteenth and early fifteenth centuries is well documented in the historical records. Josiah C. Russell tells us that the British population was 1.1 million in 1086 and rose very rapidly until about 1240, then increased more slowly during the next century and achieved a peak of about 3.7 million in 1348; it then decreased to 2.23 million by 1377 and to 2.1 million in the early fifteenth century and was still at no more than 3.2 million in 1545. M. M. Postan tells us that all the towns of England, except Bristol and London, lost population from the fourteenth century to the fifteenth century. A similar pattern was being experienced on the Continent. E. Baratier and F. Raynaud report the population of Marseilles fell by at least 75 percent in the period 1263 to 1423. Similar trends have been reported from most of western and central Europe. C. M. Cipolla says that the crises of the early decades of the fourteenth century were comparable in their gravity to those that struck the modern world in 1929–35. In his study of Italian businessmen, Y. Renouard says that economic enterprise was replaced by warfare after 1330 as the accepted method for making one's fortune. An old work of R. Davidsohn's gives us fairly specific figures for the manufacture of woolen cloth in Florence in the fourteenth century: 100,000 pieces in 1309, only 70,000 in 1339, falling to 30,000 in 1373, and reaching 19,000 in 1382.

Various explanations have been offered for these misfortunes, such as the plague, growing public disorder, increased religious controversy, and others, but, however these factors may have acted and reacted on one another, there can be no doubt that by the year 1380 Europe was in the kind of crisis we call an Age of Conflict.

Naturally there were growing class conflicts as part of these crises. In England we have the plaints of Langland and uprisings led by men like Wat Tyler and John Ball; in the Low Countries we find many similar disturbances even earlier (especially 1323–28); in France occurred the revolts of the Jacquerie and other disorders; while in Germany (as a semiperipheral area) these outbursts came somewhat later, culminating in the Peasants' revolts of 1524.

All these hardships and disorders led to a growth of irrationality, one of the most typical examples of this to be found in any Age of Conflict. All kinds of irrational heresies, like the Flagellants or the Beguines, became rampant in Europe; witchcraft, astrology, even devil worship, dances of death, necromancy, and all degrees of despair and emotional desperation were prevalent. The tone of the age is clearly revealed in a man like Villon and well described by modern writers like Johan Huizinga or Millard Meiss.

The geographic expansion of Christendom, which reached its peak with Marco Polo (1271–95), largely ceased with that achievement and was only resumed a century later with the exploits of the Portuguese in a new Age of Expansion.

5. Second Expansion

The debasement of Europe's material, social, and spiritual life which had continued for over a century and a half was reversed, quite suddenly, just before the middle of the fifteenth century. About 1440 new life began to spring up, with new hopes and renewed ambitions. This new growth was based on the activities of a new instrument of expansion, commercial capitalism, a complete circumvention of the previous feudal organization that had originated the older period of expansion in the tenth century.

This new instrument of expansion, which we call commercial capitalism, was a circumvention of feudalism, but it could just as well be regarded as a reform of the commercial organization of the Middle Ages. In the earlier period, demand, originally of feudal origin, had given rise to a commercial system whose symbols are Bruges, Venice, and Nuremberg. In the new age of expansion which began about 1440, the original demand came from princes and dynastic monarchies, and gave rise to a new commercial organization whose symbols are Cadiz, Antwerp, and London. One aspect of the change is the shift from institutionalized Mediterranean commerce to instrumental Atlantic commerce. After the original impulse (feudalism or dynastic monarchy as the case may be) both organizations were capitalistic and commercial. By capitalism we mean "an economic system motivated by the pursuit of profits within a price structure." Such profits can be derived either from the exchange of goods (as happened in commercial capitalism) or from the production of goods (as occurred in the third period of Western expansion, which began about 1720). Either type of capitalism can become institutionalized, in which case profits are sought not from exchange or from production of goods but from restrictions on exchange and restrictions on production. This restrictive capitalism arose because profits (which are the real motive of any capitalistic system) are the margin between selling prices and costs. As long as a capitalistic organization is an instrument, it seeks to increase profits by reducing costs rather than by increasing prices; but when a capitalistic system becomes an institution, it shifts its efforts to trying to increase profits by increasing prices. Such increases in prices can generally be achieved only by reducing the flow of goods (either by restricting exchange or by restricting production). An effort to make this the chief method for maximizing profits indicates institutionalization of the organization. We have three different names for institutionalized capitalist systems which were dominant in the three Ages of Conflict of Western civilization. These are municipal mercantilism in the period 1270–1440, state mercantilism in the period 1690–1810, and monopoly capitalism in the period 1900 and after.

The new Age of Expansion after 1440 lasted until near

the end of the seventeenth century. It is very familiar to all students of history and is frequently called the ambiguous term "Renaissance." Even a neophyte in the study of history is aware that this period possessed the qualities we have listed as typical of any Age of Expansion: increased production, rising population, geographic expansion, growth of knowledge, and intermittent impulses of science and democracy. Except for geographical expansion and science, all these were probably less extreme, in a quantitative sense, than history textbooks might lead us to believe, but I think there can be no doubt that they existed sufficiently to justify the name "expansion" for the period as a whole. The two most dramatic aspects of the period, however, are to be seen in science and in exploration and colonization. In science the period from Copernicus, or even Leonardo, to Newton is recognized as one of the most brilliant in all history, while in geographic expansion the age of Vasco da Gama or Magellan is no less famous. In both of these fields, and in the others as well, the period of a century or more after 1690 is one of much more modest achievements. Only in the nineteenth century, with the surge of a new Age of Expansion, were the achievements of the sixteenth and early seventeenth centuries generally exceeded.

The successive stages of expansion and conflict that we are trying to distinguish in the past thousand years of the history of our own civilization are even less definitely demarked than similar stages in other civilizations. In addition to certain difficulties already mentioned, such as the inevitable lack of perspective occurring when we study our own society, there are other difficulties that arise from the cyclical character of these stages. Cultural lag and aberrations that emerge from the contrast between core and peripheral zones are especially troublesome in a civilization that repeats stages.

We have already mentioned the problems that arise in demarking stages from the fact that such stages tend to be somewhat later in peripheral areas than they are in core areas. When stages are repeated, as in Western civilization, this gives rise to particular difficulties because peripheral areas could, in theory, fall one full stage behind the core area and thus mask the fluctuating process in the civilization as a whole. Fortunately, Western civilization did not have a full stage lag in its peripheral areas, but the lag was sufficiently prolonged to provide a masking influence on the demarcations of stages. In general, the core of Western civilization could be regarded as the northern half of Italy, France, the Low Countries, extreme western Germany, and England without its Celtic fringes. The masking effect arose because of continued expansion in Germany and in the New World after this core had already moved into the next stage. There can be little doubt that the shift from expansion to conflict that occurred in the core of Western Europe at the end of the thirteenth century arrived somewhat later in Germany. Again, when Western Europe resumed expansion about 1440, Germany continued in the period of conflict for another century. And, finally, when the second stage of expansion reached its end in Western Europe in the late seventeenth century, it continued in Germany and in Mexico for several generations more. On the other hand, about 1840, when England, France, and, above all, Belgium were expanding vigorously in the third occurrence of expansion of Western civilization, Germany and Mexico were just about to resume expansion.

The masking effect between stages to which we refer was intensified by cultural lag. This means that in any single area, be it core or not, all aspects of the society do not start, stop, or proceed at the same times and rates. In general, change or innovation was earlier in the military and economic aspects than it was in the political, social, legal, or intellectual aspects. This can be seen quite clearly in the early sixteenth century and again in the late eighteenth century.

The last imperialist war of the first Age of Conflict was the series of struggles called the Italian Wars (1494–1559). These began with an excuse rather than a cause, just as the earlier Hundred Years' War (1338–1445) had done. The cause of both of these was the need for the institutionalized feudal system to wage war in order to make a living. In other words war had become an end in itself, as is usually the case with any institution. The excuse given in 1338 for the English invasion of France, like the excuse given in 1494 for Charles VIII's invasion of Italy, was no more than that— just an excuse—a flimsy dynastic claim to a distant throne. But in each case hordes of unemployed nobles were eager to support such a claim, no matter how flimsy, for the sake of booty and payment for military service.

The first imperialist wars of the new Age of Conflict were the wars of Louis XIV, which began in 1667 and which continued, with interruptions, until after Waterloo in 1815. The excuses that Louis XIV gave for his wars were just about as flimsy as those which had been offered in 1338 and 1494 in the earlier Ages of Conflict, and were repeated in the last of these wars by Napoleon.

As far as our analysis goes, the Italian Wars of 1494– 1559 should have been followed by a period of peace such as followed the Napoleonic Wars of 1803–15, since, in each case, a new period of expansion had begun. Let us note that expansion had fully begun even before these last imperialist wars commenced, since the second Age of Expansion began about 1440 and the third began about 1730. This was simply a result of cultural lag, and reflected a situation where older institutions continued to work for a war that newer instrumental developments had made unnecessary and unrewarding. A similar and parallel situation may be existing now, at the middle of the twentieth century, if we are endangered by imperialist war at a time when new instruments and techniques of peaceful expansion have already begun to function.

In the period 1815–1914, of course, there was an absence of imperialist war, and Europe was generally concentrating its resources and energies on expansion, and did so because the fact of expansion, especially the new industrialism, was too obvious for anyone to ignore the fact that it was more feasible to get ahead by peaceful methods than by warlike ones. But in the period of expansion from 1440 to 1680 this was not nearly so clear, chiefly because of cultural lag of behavior and thought patterns from the earlier Age of Conflict.

We have said that the Italian Wars began in 1494 as a typical imperialist aggression by the institutionalized feudal system. But the war changed its character after about twenty-five years, and became a balance-of-power struggle against Hapsburg hegemony. In 1494 the king of France was the aggressor; by 1520 the king of France was fighting for survival against a dynastic monster that had come into existence through a series of circumstances, some of them accidental, which had made the Hapsburgs the overwhelming power in Europe. Among these circumstances were the family arrangements that accumulated by inheritance a large number of important dynastic claims in the hands of Charles V of the Holy Roman Empire. Of almost equal importance was the accidental circumstance that the same Hapsburgs, as rulers of Mexico and Peru, were able to tap the immense resources of bullion of America at a time when the existence of mercenary armies made money equivalent to soldiers and thus to power.

The influx of American bullion that made the Hapsburgs a great military and political power without an economic or social system capable of supporting a hegemony of Europe had several results. By raising prices rapidly it completed the ruin of the older nobility and any other persons on fixed incomes. At the same time this price inflation gave a great spur to economic (especially commercial) expansion and to the growth in wealth and influence of the bourgeoisie and richer peasants. Moreover, the revelation that the possession of money could make a dynasty powerful even without a sound economic and social system to support it fastened the mercantilist system, in a broader, more exploitative, way upon Europe. Political power supported by mercenary soldiers was used to regulate economic activities so that a favorable balance of trade would bring in sufficient money to hire mercenary soldiers and thus expand a dynasty's ability to control more taxpayers, get access to larger numbers of mercenary recruits, and to increase the favorable balance of payments.

These obsolescent ideas, which continued as a cultural lag during the course of the new, second Age of Expansion, ensured a continuance of imperialist wars even in the period of expansion. The struggle against Hapsburg hegemony that began after 1519 was ended with the Hapsburg political defeat in the Thirty Years' War (1618–48); the struggle against French hegemony in Europe that began in 1667 continued until 1815. But the interval between these two struggles, which should have been a period of peace, was not, because of economic struggles, such as the three Anglo-Dutch Wars, which were justified by institutionalized mercantilist ideologies.

Moreover, only local and sporadic movements toward democracy appeared in this period of expansion because the organization of military force and of political power was not such as to permit democracy to function. The Italian Wars of 1494–1559 were like a caldron in which a great variety of military ideas and tactics were thrown together and tested. Among these were the old mounted knight, the new infantry of English crossbowmen or Swiss pikemen, the even newer infantry of arquebusiers, the light cavalry (reiter) armed with "horse pistols," primitive artillery, and even a Spanish revival of the Roman legionary. From the competition of these various arms there emerged by 1559 a tactical combination of pike and arquebus that held the field for over two centuries. In this combination the pikemen defended the arquebusiers against charging horsemen, while the arquebusiers defended the pikemen against forearms. At first, slowness of reloading, which left arquebusiers in jeopardy from cavalry for long intervals, required a high ratio of pikemen in the unit, but the slow increase in rate of firing and the invention of the ring bayonet (which made each musketeer able "to act as his own pikeman") in 1690 led to the reduction and eventual elimination of pikes. But the use of muskets, either with pikes or bayonets for defense against cavalry, supplemented by artillery, remained a skilled task as long as guns remained muzzle-loading, spark-ignited weapons. Such skill could be obtained only from professional mercenary soldiers in the relatively small numbers that could be paid by dynastic monarchies in the mercantilist period. In this period this organizational feature of small, professional mercenary armies was reinforced by the fact that arms were handmade on a piece-by-piece basis and were thus too expensive for the average private citizen to obtain or for the public fisc to purchase on a mass basis. Accordingly, it is not surprising that political power remained concentrated in a narrow group who controlled this limited supply of weapons and did not spread to that majority who were relatively isolated from war and weapons and thus had no basis on which to establish any claims for participation in governmental functions.

This narrow basis for military activity in the sixteenth, seventeenth, and eighteenth centuries fully sustains the narrow distribution of political power in the same period. Accordingly, it became relatively easy for the vested interest groups to defend the *status quo* and to prevent structural changes when the new period of crisis began at the end of the seventeenth century.

6. Second Age of Conflict

The second period of expansion in Western civilization was transformed into a second Age of Conflict when the instrument of expansion became an institution. The two phases of this organization are generally called commercial capitalism and state mercantilism. The preceding period of mercantilism, which we called municipal mercantilism, generally had been regulated by municipal political units rather than by the wider monarchical political units of the eighteenth century; it had been dominated by the interests of the consumer and had reflected this concern in a "policy of provision" that put restrictions on exports but not on imports, and tried to regulate craft activities to protect quality. By 1400 this policy had become very restrictive. The second phase of mercantilism was organized on a different basis with different aims, since it was generally regulated by dynastic monarchies and generally sought to protect the interests of commercial groups. As such, it had no interest in restricting either imports or exports, but rather sought to make goods go through the territory so that fees of handling and the profits of exchange could be ensured to the citizens. This is frequently called "the policy of the staple," and contrasts both with the "policy of provision" of the first Age of Conflict and with the "policy of protection" of the third Age of Conflict (that associated with monopoly capitalism after 1900). These three policies represent the interests of three different aspects of the economic system. Any economic system must provide production, distribution, and consumption. Each of the three Ages of Conflict of Western civilization sought to protect the vested interests of one of these aspects, but in the reverse order so that the consumer was dominant in the first period (about 1400), the trader was dominant in the second (about 1750), and the producer was dominant in the third (about 1930). Any effort to make means into ends or to make one section or aspect of a process the dominant interest of the whole process is a clear indication of institutionalization.

This process of institutionalization can be seen as a kind of general stagnation of Western civilization during most of

the century from 1650 to 1750. The geographic expansion
that had spread in such a phenomenal way in the period
1450 to 1650 began to hesitate. In North America the
colonies remained east of the Appalachians or, in some
areas, below the fall line; in South America the incredible
explorations of the earlier period, which, for example, had
seen the continent crossed from west to east by way of the
Amazon, were not repeated until the nineteenth century. In
the history of Africa we find a similar situation. In most
areas of the Dark Continent there were widespread explorations and missionary activities, even a transcontinental
journey, in the sixteenth century, but then nothing similar
occurred again until the nineteenth century. Expansion into
India and the Far East shows a similar, but less drastic,
hesitancy.

The same cycle can be seen in legislation, which devoted
itself, after about 1650, to the defense of the *status quo* or
to the effort, by political action, to obtain a larger share
for oneself of what was regarded as a static and unexpand-
able body of the world's wealth. This can be seen in the
navigation acts that the English colonies in America so
resented in the period after 1765 but that were first enacted
after 1649. These acts sought to prevent economic innovations in the colonies and to force their trade and commodities to go through England and English hands whatever
their ultimate destination. At the same time, within England,
technical innovation was discouraged, work became an end
in itself, and laws were made to preserve existing markets
as they stood. In a semistatistical study, *Change and History*,
published in 1952, Margaret T. Hodgen found three periods
of technical innovation in Western history. These were the
eleventh century to the fourteenth century, the sixteenth

century, and the nineteenth century. Governments did all they could to discourage such innovation in the late seventeenth century in contrast to the late sixteenth when they still sought to reward it. In England the patent power was used to prevent new techniques rather than to encourage them. As early as 1623 the Privy Council ordered destruction of a machine for making needles; cloth buttons (rather than bone) were forbidden in 1698, while Indian calico was forbidden in 1686. A law of 1666 ordered all persons to be buried in wool rather than in the traditional linen. Every effort was made to prevent new techniques in the textile industry and thus, in effect, to hamper the growth of cotton textiles. In France these efforts culminated in the crafts codes of Jean-Baptiste Colbert. Issued in seven volumes of 2,200 pages over the period 1666–1730, these sought to prescribe every detail of the established craft techniques and to proscribe innovations in these. Economic aims and economic values were distorted and frequently reversed so that consumption was condemned as an evil, abundance abhorred, work praised as an end in itself, exporting encouraged, and poverty regarded as a good because it was the only way to keep people working. The esteemed Sir William Petty (1662) believed that a country could get richer and richer by exporting more and more and that it would be a good thing "if the products of the labor of a thousand men could be burned" since these men could then keep their skills by having to make the goods over again. Charles Davenant in 1698 wrote. "By what is consumed at home one loseth only what another gets and the nation in general is not all the richer, but all foreign consumption is a clear and certain profit." More briefly in 1673 Becker wrote, "All selling is good, all buying bad," while in 1677 John Houghton drew a logical conclusion from these ideas by suggesting that England could get richer by inviting foreigners to come in to "consume our corn, cattle, cloths, coals, and other things." It was suggested that an enemy in wartime could be greatly weakened if he could be flooded with goods and, as late as 1810, that last great mercantilist, Napoleon, issued licenses to smugglers to carry goods into England secretly. De Mandeville praised vice because it was unproductive, while Defoe praised a law forbidding a more efficient canalboat able to do the same work with fewer men.

It can hardly be expected that ideas and statements such as these could be fitted together to provide any self-consistent and convincing economic theory, but even as they stand they reveal a determination to defend isolated vested interests such as prevail in a period of institutionalized organizations.

As might be expected in such a period, the century 1650–1750 was one of imperialist wars, of class conflicts, of flattening population expansion, of softening prices, and of irrational confusions. Of these the class conflicts and imperialist wars continued until 1815, although a new Age of Expansion had begun as early as 1730. Napoleon was the culmination of this Age of Conflict, seeking to establish a universal empire (and almost succeeding in the core area by 1811), seeking to enforce his mercantilist conceptions with the full authority of his imperial system, and quite convinced that he was living in a limited world in which one share could be increased only if another were curtailed.

In these wars Napoleon was fighting "the wave of the future" with the methods of the past. This can be seen quite clearly if we merely look at four or five aspects of the new nineteenth century of expansion.

In financial matters one of the great problems of Western civilization from the earliest period had been fluctuations and, above all, limitations on the volume of money. So long as money was in the form of specie there could be no close correlation between the volume of money available and the economic need for money as a medium of savings and exchange. The volume of money was strictly related to the supply of bullion except for minor influences (like hoarding, flows of specie to India and the East, and such), but this supply was in no way related to economic needs. We have seen that the supply increased too rapidly in the three centuries 1000–1300, then increased far too slowly (because of exhaustion of existing mines within the framework of the existing technology) for the next century and a half (1300–1450), then was expanded in a spectacular and accidental way, quite out of relationship to economic need, by Spanish access to the bullion stores of Mexico and Peru (1450–1650), but that the diffusion of these stores left the economy of Western civilization on an inflated price level that could not be sustained by any continued increase in bullion supplies. Thus, by the late seventeenth century and much of the eighteenth century, the flow of bullion was not sufficient to satisfy either the demands of an expanding economic system or those of a mercantilist political system supported by a mercenary military system. This inadequacy began to be remedied at the very end of the seventeenth century, notably by the establishment of the Bank of England in 1694. This remedy rested on the use of banknotes backed to only a fractional part of their value by specie reserves. This was a partial solution of the problem of money for two reasons: (1) it permitted a great increase in the volume of money when the supply of bullion was increasingly inadequate and (2) it permitted the volume of money to fluctuate to some extent in response to changing needs for money in the economy.

This new technique of monetary manipulation became one of the basic factors in the great Age of Expansion in the nineteenth century and made the fluctuations of economic activity less responsive to the rate of bullion production from mines, by making it more responsive to new factors reflecting the demand for money (such as the interest rate). This new technique spread relatively slowly in the century between the founding of the Bank of England and Napoleon's creation of the Bank of France in 1803. The Napoleonic Wars, because of the backward, specie-based, financial ideas of Napoleon were, on their fiscal side, a struggle between the older, bullionist, obsolete system favored by Napoleon and the new fractional reserve banknote system of England.

A similar situation existed in regard to food production. No very impressive economic expansion was possible in the eighteenth century without some new agricultural techniques capable of increasing the output of food. No such increase could be expected so long as the medieval three-field system with its unenclosed scattered strips and free-ranging farm animals continued. This medieval system had been a great success in its day, greatly superior to the old classical two-field, slave system, and capable of supporting the new Western civilization through its first two Ages of Expansion, but by 1650 its output per man-day of work was not sufficient to support any notable increase of the proportion of the population in crafts and trade, and it was, of course, quite incapable of providing the food or raw materials for industrialism.

This medieval organization of agriculture was fully institutionalized by 1650 and had become a great obstacle to continued expansion. Just at that point, however, there became available in western Europe the elements of a new agrarian system fully capable of supporting a new period of expansion and destined to do so in the nineteenth century.

The new organization of agriculture is usually known as the agricultural revolution. In essence it abandoned the three-field system for a leguminous-rotation system in which a leguminous crop was put in place of the fallow stage in the older three-stage cycle. Such a leguminous crop (like alfalfa or clover) put much more nitrogen in the field than any fallow year ever could, but it required a major reorganization in livestock handling. Animals had to be fenced *in* rather than fenced *out* of the arable field as in the older system, because the fallow and, to a lesser degree, the stubble, on which medieval livestock had foraged, were gone. Fencing in of animals (or enclosure) had three important results: (1) selective breeding could be practiced, with a great improvement in the quality of farm animals; (2) animal manure was now available in quantity to be used where its fertility was most needed; and (3) feed had to be supplied to the animals, thus providing a use for the leguminous crop that had been put into the fallow stage of the older cycle. There was thus a drastic increase in size, quality, and numbers of farm animals as a consequence of the agricultural revolution. As an index of this we might note that the slaughter weights of farm animals tripled at Smithfield Market in England during the eighty-five-year period ending in 1795.

The agricultural revolution did not cease with the factors we have mentioned, but included a number of other significant items. Enclosure ejected a considerable number of subsistence peasants from the agrarian system and led to larger holdings and some degree of rural depopulation, thus providing manpower for increased commerce and industry. It also made possible numerous other technical advances, many of them associated with the ideas of rural eccentrics like Jethro Tull (1711). These included planting of seed in rows, in holes in the ground, by use of a seed drill instead of broadcast surface sowing as in the Middle Ages. This encouraged seed selection and the use of horse-drawn cultivators.

The agricultural revolution was the basis of the new Age of Expansion that began in England about 1730 but that had not yet reached France a generation later. This fact was perfectly clear to Arthur Young when he traveled in France just before the French Revolution. As a consequence the Napoleonic Wars were, from this point of view, a conflict between the older three-field fallow system and the newer enclosed leguminous rotation systems (frequently called, in France and elsewhere, the "Norfolk System").

There was also a third important element in this situation. This was the shift from a craft system of manufacture to an industrial system. The vital point about this shift is not so much the growth of the factory system or the growth of an urban proletariat that did not own the tools it used, as the shift from an economy in which production was achieved by energy released in living bodies (man- or animal-power) to one in which production was achieved by energy released through nonliving mechanisms (water power or steam engines). This shift, which permitted great increases in production of manufactured goods, would never have been possible without the agricultural revolution that preceded it and possibly without the advent of a fractional-reserve banking system as well. The change, which is usually called the Industrial Revolution, was in full development in England but was largely unknown in France during the Napoleonic Wars. In this regard, also, these wars represented a conflict between a newer organization for fulfilling human desires and an older, obsolescent one.

There is a fourth way in which the Napoleonic Wars represented a struggle between the new and the old. On the Napoleonic side we find ranged all the forces of mercantilism, meaning the theories and the vested-interest forces that believed that economic life had to be regulated by the government and regulated for largely political ends. This system played a very significant role in Western civilization in the period 1200–1800, but by the latter date it was clearly obsolete, and had to be replaced by a more advanced system. This newer system of economic management is known as laissez-faire and, as is well known, it was associated with the period of expansion of the nineteenth century. What is not so well known, however, is what the shift from one to another really entailed.

Every economic system has to be regulated. That is, somehow, decisions must be made as to what is produced, how much of it, and who gets it. In the early Middle Ages and again in the late nineteenth century, the European system of management was an unregulated, automatic one. That is, no centralized decision making occurred in either. But the two were entirely dissimilar in the ways that this came about. In the medieval system, economic regulation was automatic through medieval custom: what was produced, how much, and who got it were established on the basis of what had been done at an earlier date. Custom ruled.

In the nineteenth century, once again, Europe had an automatic management of economic life, but now it was a dynamic economic system, not the static one of the earlier Middle Ages, and, as a dynamic system, it could not be regulated by custom. Instead, it was regulated by the market. The market is a place where buyers and sellers come together to exchange their goods. In an automatic laissez-faire market numerous sellers compete with each other, thus forcing prices downward, while simultaneously numerous buyers compete with each other, thus forcing prices upward, and, finally, during all this, buyers "higgle" with sellers. As a consequence of these three forces operating in the market, a price is reached at which goods are exchanged for money in terms that will clear the market of both.

Such a market mechanism is fully capable, as we all know, of determining, without centralized control, what will be produced, how much will be made, and who will get it. But no laissez-faire system can do this unless a market exists, and no such market can exist unless both transportation and communications are so highly developed and so free that people know what is going on and both goods and money are free to move where each is more valuable. Neither transportation nor communications were adequate to this purpose when the customary system of the static medieval economy began to break down from the introduction of dynamic economic influences about the year 1000. Thus there was no market in the year 1000, and there was still no market, although a myriad of small markets, in 1700. These small markets existed from the inadequacy of both transpor-

tation and communication, and were "small" in the sense
that the numbers of buyers and the numbers of sellers in each
market were too small to prevent monopolistic or oligopo-
listic prices and to achieve competitive prices. To prevent
this and to protect the consumer from exploitation, municipal mercantilism grew up and dominated economic regulation during the period 1200–1500 approximately.

As improvements in transportation and communications
appeared in the period of medieval expansion, there was a
tendency for the numerous small markets regulated by
municipal mercantilism to flow together to create fewer and
larger markets. These larger markets, drawing from areas
larger than the areas of municipal control and similarly
supplying goods to larger areas, could not be controlled by
municipal authorities. Still, these authorities continued to
attempt to do what was technically beyond their powers to
do. These efforts, aiming at the defense of established vested
interests rather than at the protection of consumers as originally intended, are part of the institutionalized structure of
the first Age of Conflict.

As a consequence of the inability of municipal authorities
to regulate the newer, larger markets created by improved
transportation and communications, this task was taken
over by the emerging dynastic monarchies. We have already
shown how changes in weapons, political organization, and
political ideology had created these newer political structures with power to regulate economic life over larger areas.
This newer economic regulation by dynastic monarchies is
known as state mercantilism. It aimed to protect traders
rather than consumers or producers. Much of the expansion
of the second period of expansion arose from its efforts.

By the eighteenth century, state mercantilism had become in its turn a structure of vested interests serving to hamper economic life rather than to help it. This was as true of traders as it was of consumers and producers. This shift of state mercantilism from an instrument to an institution was based on two chief features. On one hand the organization was no longer used for an economic purpose but had become an end in itself with largely political purposes. It was used to increase state power rather than for economic life. On the other hand, by the late eighteenth century, transportation and communication were again beginning to improve so rapidly that continental and even world markets were coming into existence. These were, of course, much wider than the areas of power of the dynastic monarchies and, accordingly, could not be controlled by them. The continued efforts of governments to exercise such control in the portions of markets that fell in their respective power areas merely served to create restrictions on economic life and hampered production, exchange, and consumption alike. This situation was shown by Adam Smith in his book *The Wealth of Nations* in 1776. Clearly markets were now large enough to be regulated by supply and demand, by competition and higgling, and any movement to allow this would be economically progressive. From this point of view, also, the Napoleonic Wars represented a struggle between an older and a younger system.

Thus from four points of view concerned with finance, agriculture, manufacturing, and economic regulation, the political struggles between England and France in the Napoleonic period reflect a contest between the future and the past. There are, of course, numerous other factors involved in this contrast. Some of these will be mentioned in the next section, but these four should be sufficient to show that

Napoleon represented an outmoded system and that he was the last phase of a fairly typical Age of Conflict.

The other marks of such an Age of Conflict, with one notable exception, are fairly obvious or have been mentioned already. The exception is in intellectual history, where an Age of Conflict usually is a period of irrationality. This is, of course, not a term that could be applied to the eighteenth century where the more usual label (at least for the generation 1730–90) is "Enlightenment." This discrepancy is but one indication of a situation that is far too complex to be discussed here; namely, that the periodization of intellectual history is quite different from the periodization of other aspects of society. In these other aspects we can distinguish five successive stages on each level over the period from A.D. 950 into the future, but on the intellectual level, as shown in the chart (page 389), we have at least nine stages over the same time. To some extent this can be explained by cultural lag, but there are other influences quite as significant, including the much weaker degree of integration between one theory and another, even at the same time, or between a theory and any other aspect of the society, than exists between the more concrete aspects of culture.

At any period it is possible for a thinker either to accept a theory which is morphologically compatible with his age or to reject it. In such cases the ideology of the age must be sought in the generally unstated assumptions made both by conformists and nonconformists. In the eighteenth century the Enlightenment was nonconformist to the other levels of the society, and this is, indeed, one of the chief causes of the French Revolution. The rational, orderly, organized qualities of the Enlightenment were quite incompatible with the irrational, disorderly, and disorganized society of the day,

STAGE →	950 Gestation	1050 Expansion	1150	1250 Conflict	1350	1450 Expansion	1550	1650 Conflict	1750	Expansion	1850	Conflict	1950	?
INTELLECTUAL	Neoplatonic Dualism			Medieval Synthesis 1200	Nominalism 1300	Irrationalism and Humanism 1400		Scientific Dualism 1600	Enlightenment 1720	Romanticism 1800	Scientific Materialism 1850	Irrational Activism 1890		1950
RELIGIOUS OUTLOOK	Augustinian Christianity			Thomistic Catholicism 1200	Confusion 1300		Erastian Dogmatism 1550		1780	Critical Skepticism			Revival of Religion 1950	
SOCIAL GROUP (Dominant)	Lords			Balance of Power Royal Bureaucracy, Nobles, Clergy, Burghers 1200–1400				Bureaucracy		1800 Bourgeoisie			Managers 1950	
ECONOMIC CONTROL	Custom		Municipal Mercantilism 1150		1300		State Mercantilism			Laissez Faire 1820		Planning 1935		
ECONOMIC ORGANIZATION	Manor 1000		Revival of Commerce 1280	Crisis 1300		Commercial Capitalism 1440			Industrial Capitalism 1770		Monopoly Capitalism 1900	Pluralist Economy 1950		
POLITICAL	Feudal		Feudal Monarchy 1100		1400	Dynastic Monarchy				National State 1800			Ideological State 1960	
MILITARY	Knight and Castle 1200			Mercenary Men-at-Arms			Professional Pikes and Muskets Artillery 1550			Mass Citizen Army 1800			Army of Specialists 1934	

and thus gave rise to tensions that, reinforced from other directions, provided the energy motivating the French Revolution. The irrationality to be associated with the second Age of Conflict might be sought either in the intellectual stage that preceded the Enlightenment or with the romantic movement that followed it. In the former case it would be associated with such items as the political theory of Hobbes and with Jansenism, while in the latter case it would be associated with the literary movements that began with Richardson or Macpherson's *Ossian* and developed into Rousseau, *Sturm und Drang,* Wordsworth, and others, or with the political theories of men like Burke, Fichte, Bonald, or DeMaistre, and the religious movements represented by Methodism. On the whole, it seems preferable, without being dogmatic, to associate the latter intellectual stage with the irrationalism we expect from an Age of Conflict. But, at any rate, the subject is too complicated to be discussed in any satisfactory way here.

7. Third Age of Expansion

The third Age of Expansion lasted from about 1730 to about 1929, although indications of a new Age of Conflict began to appear as early as 1890. Its instrument of expansion remained capitalistic, but operating in fields other than those that had become institutionalized in the earlier Age of Conflict of the late seventeenth century. The reappearance of expansion clearly resulted from circumvention of this previous organization. Again the period of expansion can be divided into substages that make the process of expansion appear as a series of steps or surges. We might list these steps as follows: (1) the agricultural revolution from 1730; (2) the Industrial Revolution from 1770; (3) financial capitalism from 1850; and (4) monopoly capitalism from 1900. Naturally the dates listed are very rough, because the advent of these steps is quite different in various areas.

We have already indicated the nature of the agricultural revolution as a reform of the institutionalized medieval three-field fallow system. Its roots go back many generations, but it began to operate as a significant, expansive force in England about 1730. It is, of course, one of the most important events in modern history.

Two revolutionary events of the later eighteenth century contributed a good deal toward the new Age of Expansion. These were the transportation revolution, which began about 1750, and the population revolution, which began about a generation later. The transportation revolution consisted of a series of innovations that provided (*a*) an effective traveling coach; (*b*) hard-surfaced, all-weather roads; (*c*) canals; (*d*) telegraphic communication; and (*e*) railroads. All these appeared in the century 1750–1850. In the following century the revolution in transportation and communciations continued with the advent of (*f*) high-speed printing presses; (*g*) the internal-combustion engine, leading to automobiles and airplanes; and (*h*) electricity, leading to radio, the motion picture, and television.

The population revolution began about 1780 with the use of vaccination for smallpox. It continued with the discovery of germ infection and the invention of antiseptics by Pasteur and Lister, as well as improvements in surgery such as the discovery of ether. Advances of this kind have continued with accelerating rapidity and have given rise to a population "explosion" resulting from a drastic reduction in death rates far sharper than the slight decreases in birthrates.

The transportation and population revolutions occurred most conveniently between the agricultural and Industrial revolutions in Western civilization, each of the four providing a sound basis for the next. This was quite different from the experience of the non-Western world where these, and other, revolutionary advances diffused in a quite different sequence that was far better fitted to raising problems than to solving them.

The Industrial Revolution, which we have defined as production by energy coming through nonliving mechanisms (that is, from water power or steam rather than from men or animals), is familiar to all of us. Accordingly, we shall refer only to certain organizational features that help to distinguish its early period of owner-management from its second period of financial capitalism. In the former the typical pattern of organization was the private firm or partnership with both capital and decision making supplied by the owners. In the latter the typical form of organization was the limited-liability corporation and the holding company, in which capital came from the owners but decision making came from the management. As is well known, the Industrial Revolution first flourished in textiles using either water power or steam engines. Even when it spread into mining and ironmaking, the older form of proprietorship or partnership continued to prevail. But gradually it spread into the activites of the still-expanding transporation revolution. There, in canal building and, above all, in railroad building, it became impossible to continue to use the partnership form of business organization because the needs for capital were far greater than could be satisfied by the savings of any group of partners. The corporate form of enterprise was adopted for these activities because it could mobilize the savings of many in the control of a few and do so with limited liability for the many. First used on a large scale in railroads, it soon spread into coal mining, iron-making, and machine building.

This change led to the period of financial capitalism that began about 1850 and died a violent death about September 1931 with the collapse of the international gold standard. As the period developed, the need for capital by corporations became so great that specialized capital-raising organizations appeared. These investment bankers, in return for their services, obtained representation on the boards of directors of corporations and sufficient influence to direct their companies' financial services and purchases toward other corporations where the particular investment bankers concerned had interests. From this there grew up a network of interlocking directorships and banking influences and, finally, an elaborate system of holding companies and financial firms. These growing monopolistic influences were centralized by the joint concern which all financiers had in keeping the value of money high (or "stabilized," as they called it). This joint concern was reflected in the appearance of a joint organization, the central bank, which held the gold reserves that became the central feature of the monetary system. The international gold standard became the chief mechanism by which the supply of money could be kept low and its value, accordingly, kept high. A high value of money, which implies a low supply of money, was chiefly advantageous to creditors, to whom obligations were owed in money terms. But such a high value of money clearly meant low prices of goods, and was a disadvantage to debtors and to manufacturers of goods.

Thus there appeared a dichotomy between bankers and industrialists, with one eager for a high value of money and high interests rates, while the other was eager for high prices of goods (thus low value of money) and low interest rates. For a long time the dichotomy between the two did not come into the open because bankers succeeded in befuddling industrialists on financial matters, presenting them as abstruse subjects in which the industrialist's wisest course would be to follow his banker's advice. As long as the industrialist was dependent upon the banker for capital, he had to use that advice, even when he sometimes suspected that the interests of the two were not identical. But few industrialists before Henry Ford even realized that the interests of bankers and industrialists were opposed.

This opposition of interests between the two appeared most clearly when there was an insufficient supply of money for the growing industrial structure. This insufficient supply of money was based on the insufficient supply of gold, since the bankers controlled the supply of money through the mechanism of the gold standard. The bankers called the use of the gold standard "stabilization," and insisted that it provided a stable value to money; it did no such thing, but rather provided stable foreign exchanges (for all currencies based on gold) and a growing value to money. The growing value to money on the gold standard occurred because the supply of money could not increase as rapidly as the supply of goods when the former was based on output of the world's gold mines and the latter was based on the much more expandable industrial system. Accordingly, the overall tendency was for prices to soften during the whole period 1770–1931 except when there were sudden increases in the world's gold supplies (notably in 1848–52 and 1896–1904) or when political events, such as wars, made it necessary to suspend the gold standard or to destroy quantities of goods, as in 1792–1815, 1861–72 and 1914–19. Outside these exceptional events, the general tendency of the price history of the third Age of Expansion was deflationary (as was evident in 1816–48, 1872–96, 1920–33). This tendency led, in each deflationary substage, to growing depression and to increasing agrarian and labor unrest associated with such historic labels as the "hungry forties," the "Populist movement," and the "great world depression." The tendency generally benefited bankers and injured industry by increasing the value of money and the costs of credit and making profitable industrial operations more difficult (since falling prices force businessmen to incur costs on an earlier and higher price level than that on which they must subsequently offer their product for sale). In these deflationary periods, as low prices drove corporations to bankruptcy, bankers were able to assume control of them, to consolidate them into larger units of monopolized industry, and to reap the profits of reorganization and refloatation of securities. Although industrialists and businessmen generally accepted the bankers' justifications of these events, debtors (especially farmers) and workers (who suffered unemployment) were increasingly resentful. The first deflationary period, leading to the disturbances of the late 1840s, and the second, leading to the disturbances of the early 1890s, were both ended by the discovery of new gold supplies, in California and Australia in 1848–50 and in South Africa and the Klondike in 1897–1900. In addition, the supply of gold, in the second case, was increased by new methods of extracting gold from its ores. But none of these occurred in the third deflationary period, 1919–31, and financial capitalism, long threatened by its own creation, monopoly capitalism, perished in 1931–33. As a consequence, the domination of economic life by financial figures, such as Rothschild, Morgan, Mirabaud, Baring, Montagu Norman, or even Ivar Kreuger, was ended and replaced by great figures of monopoly capitalism like DuPont, Melchett, Leverhulme, Rockefeller, Ford, Nuffield, and others. In this connection, however, it should be pointed out that the typical figure of monopoly capitalism is not the individual "captain of industry" of the earlier period but the anonymously managed superfirm like United Shoe Machinery, I. G. Farbenindustrie, Unilever, DuPont Chemicals, Hartford-Empire, Alcoa, Volkswagen, Pecheney, General Motors, General Electric, or General Dynamics. It should also be noted that the generally deflationary character of the nineteenth century had certain beneficial aspects, such as wider distribution of goods at lower prices and, above all, the drastic need to lower costs of production by greater productive efficiency in order to ensure continued profits in a soft-price era. These two aspects of the period explain why the nineteenth century remained an Age of Expansion in spite of its adjustment difficulties.

It is not necessary to point out that the general characteristics we have posited for an Age of Expansion were in full flower during the nineteenth century. Geographic expansion was resumed so that Africa, the polar regions, the Matto Grosso, and New Guinea became familiar areas; population soared; production increased, even in periods of falling prices; knowledge expanded beyond any one person's comprehension; even democracy and science reached their greatest victories. Indeed, the nineteenth century in terms of our description of an Age of Expansion could be the Age of Expansion *par excellence.*

In the military and political levels the third Age of Expansion was associated with such familiar historical developments as the mass citizen army, the national state, and democracy. The shift to these from the older stages of these levels generally occurred during the era of the French Revolution and Napoleon. The reasons for these changes should be examined because, while often mentioned, they are rarely analyzed.

The second Age of Conflict had been associated with the professional mercenary army, the dynastic monarchy, and authoritarian government. On the economic and social levels it had been associated with mercantilism and the supremacy of the bureaucracy. As is well known, these last two stages were replaced, on their respective levels, by laissez-faire and the bourgeoisie in the nineteenth century. Any analysis of the process that gave rise to these extensive changes on all levels of culture might well begin with the military situation.

In the second Age of Conflict the best available weapons in Western civilization were artillery, muskets, and pikes (or bayonets). These were difficult to use and usually expensive to obtain. As a result they could be used only by trained men and could be bought only by a relatively well-to-do entity. Such trained men had to be professional users of weapons, and the weapons had to be provided by the state or by the wealthy. All of this taken together meant that weapons were available only to a small minority of the population and that the majority must expect, as a general rule, to yield to the authority of the minority that controlled these weapons. Thus it followed, almost as a matter of course, that the political level had to be authoritarian. The organization of that authority into a dynastic monarchy was a consequence of the governmental traditions of Europe. As the system operated, it was expected that allegiance and loyalty would be given to the family of the ruling monarch, in order to assure succession to his heir. This loyalty was not really expected from all persons, but only from the significant ones —the clergy, the nobility, the chief bourgeoisie, and all guild members and possibly from well-to-do independent peasantry, but the ordinary peasantry and the guild apprentices, as persons of little significance, were not subjects of much concern about their allegiance of loyalty. The operation of mercantilism and the social superiority of the royal bureaucracy were also dependent, if less directly, on the organization and control of the military level. Thus the structure of all four levels (military, political, economic control, and social) was based on the military organization of professional mercenary soldiers.

In the age of Napoleon and just after it, this military organization was modified greatly into a quite new system that survived for over a century. This innovation was the mass citizen army fighting for patriotism rather than for pay. The new organization was made possible by a series of innovations in weapons and tactics, and in military, as well as political, organization. In weapons the arrival of the Industrial Revolution and of mass-produced firearms based on interchangeable parts lowered the cost of weapons at the same time that the general economic expansion was raising standards of living. These two intersecting factors made it possible for the average man, in areas where these factors were operating, to obtain guns at a cost that he could afford to pay (that is, no more than his earning power over a few weeks). These guns were becoming easier to use by the shift from spark ignition to percussion ignition and breechloading. All these innovations made it possible to arm large masses of men at relatively low cost. At the same time the shift to such a mass army was made possible by changes in political organization.

The political organization that we have called dynastic monarchy could continue only so long as the best weapon available in the society could be obtained only by a minority. As soon as a majority could obtain the best available weapon and use it with little training, it became impossible for any minority to enforce obedience on a majority and, accordingly, the authoritarian structure of political life began to crumble. A reorganization of political life became necessary.

This reorganization of the political structure had a double aspect. On the one hand it became necessary to shift from minority rule to majority rule, and on the other hand it became necessary to find a new political organization that could place its appeal to allegiance on a basis that could be used for the majority of the society. This new basis was nationalism, and the new organization, which succeeded the dynastic state in the early nineteenth century, is known as the national state (prevalent from about 1800 to about 1950).

The political shift from dynastic monarchy to national state and the shift in weapons from a professional mercenary army to a mass army of citizens allowed the cost of a man's service to be reduced (since he fought for patriotism instead of for money) and permitted a great change in military tactics (since patriotic men were more willing to die than were mercenary soldiers). The older tactics of the dynastic monarchs had favored wars of maneuver with limited forces for limited aims. By "wars of maneuver" we mean tactics in which enemy forces were dislodged from their positions by cutting their communications and supplies rather than by assault, with battles occurring only rarely and chiefly from accidental collisions during shifts of position. Such wars were long drawn out, with few battles, and could be ended at any time by negotiation because of the possibility of compromising the combatants' limited and concrete goals.

The advent of patriotic mass armies made it possible to force the enemy from his position by assault rather than by maneuver. The new tactics, worked out by Napoleon in the period 1795–1815, organized this assault in three steps: artillery barrage, bayonet attack by infantry, and cavalry pursuit. All three steps were innovations, but the greatest change was in the second where the bayonet was entirely transformed from its earlier role as a defensive weapon against cavalry to an offensive weapon against opposing infantry. It was the nature of this second, and central, step in the new tactics that made necessary the innovations in the use of artillery and cavalry in the two other steps.

The possibility of heavy casualties in the second step of the new tactics, in which bayonets were sent against fire-power, made it necessary to obtain very high morale from citizen soldiers. This high morale could not be obtained so long as the aims of war remained, as in the earlier period, limited and concrete; they had to be made unlimited and idealistic ("saving the revolution" or "civilization," "making the world safe for democracy," "freedom of the seas," "rights of small nations," and similar unobtainable abstractions). Such goals could not be compromised, and, accordingly, battles had to become conflicts of annihilation in which the survival of the contending regimes was at stake.

Such battles of annihilation led to a series of brief "one battle" wars such as the French-Austrian War of 1859, the Prussian-Austrian War of 1866, the Franco-Prussian War of 1870, the Russo-Turkish War of 1877, and the Spanish-American War of 1899. Even as this pattern was being established, however, new forces were arising that laid the basis for quite a different pattern in the twentieth century. These new forces were (1) the growing importance of ideological forces, which made it less likely that a people would accept the consequences of defeat in a single battle, and (2) the growing strength of the tactical defensive, which made it less necessary to yield to such a defeat in one battle. The growing ideological influence was clearly evident in the American Civil War, the struggle with the French guerrillas, and the Paris Commune after Sedan in 1871, the Boer War of 1899–1902 and, above all, World War I. The growing importance of the defensive made the second step of a Napoleonic battle, the bayonet offensive, less and less likely to be decisive and made it less and less possible that the outcome of the battle itself could be decisive. The growing strength of the defensive rested on the rapid growth of firepower after the invention of the machine gun about 1862 (this made both bayonet and cavalry obsolete), the increasing use of field fortifications (this reduced the effectiveness of both artillery barrage and of offensive firepower), the invention of barbed wire about 1879 (this hampered the infantry charge of the second step and the cavalry pursuit of the third), and of the airplane in 1903 (this took from the cavalry its only surviving role as reconnaissance). The tactical changes made necessary by these innovations were not recognized by military men until after they had inflicted the almost unbearable casualties of 1916–17, but these changes (such as use of tanks, infiltration, aerial bombardment, and the like) made weapons once again so expensive and so difficult to use that it became increasingly needful to replace the mass citizen army by an army of specialists. Such a change, by reserving instruments of force to a minority, reversed the trend on the political level to a new development from democracy toward authoritarian government. The date of this reversal might be fixed in 1934, the year that the German general Guderian read de Gaulle's book *Army of Specialists*. At the same time it became clear that rapid improvements in weapons, communications (radio), transportation (trucks), and organization made it possible to enforce obedience to orders over geographic distances far greater than those covered by any national groups. Accordingly, appeal to political allegiance on nationality grounds became obsolete and it became necessary to make such an appeal on some much wider basis. The new basis, now in process of being discovered, was common ideological outlook. Accordingly the stage of the national state began to be replaced by the stage of the ideological state (or bloc) on the level of political organization, and the area covered by a single political unit widened from the nation to the Continental bloc. The inability of Hitler to make such a shift from a nationalist to an ideological (or other wider) basis at a time when his factual power was so much wider geographically than the area of Germanism was but one of his fatal errors.

This change has been recognized in popular discussion and carried, perhaps, to a degree not justified by the actual facts. We are told that we now live in a "two-power world," although the power of the United States and of the Soviet Union is not in fact hemispherical. Each of these superpowers can, it is true, obtain obedience in most matters over about forty percent of the earth's surface, but this leaves a buffer area between, amounting to about a fifth of the earth. This "buffer fringe" lying between the Soviet "heartland" and the peripheral, and ocean-linked, Western civilization is occupied by the shattered remnants of dying civilizations or the hopeful efforts of incipient new civilizations. The hope of the future does not rest, as commonly believed, in winning the peoples of the "buffer fringe" to one superpower or the other, but rather in the invention of new weapons and new tactics that will be so cheap to obtain and so easy to use that they will increase the effectiveness of guerrilla warfare so greatly that the employment of our present weapons of mass destruction will become futile and, on this basis, there can be a revival of democracy and of political decentralization in all three parts of our present world This possible development in military and political matters would, of course, require the development of decentralized economic techniques such as could arise if sunlight became the chief energy source for production and the advance of science made it possible to manufacture any desired substance by molecular rearrangement of such common materials as sea water, plant fibers, and ordinary earth.

Hopes such as these are far in the future and could be fulfilled only if (1) a showdown conflict between the Soviet bloc and the Western bloc is indefinitely postponed and (2) the structural problems of Western civilization and the no less critical problems of the Soviet Union are solved. Here we shall consider only the situation in our own society.

The third Age of Expansion of Western civilization began to draw to its close at the end of the nineteenth century. By 1890 the rate of general expansion had begun to decrease, giving rise to acute crises in industry, agriculture, labor relations, political action, and international relations. These crises culminated in the beginnings of a new, third Age of Conflict in Western civilization.

8. Third Age of Conflict

The third Age of Conflict of our society began to display the ordinary marks of such a stage about 1890. At that time, in the principal industrial countries it became clear that the rate of expansion had reversed itself. This led to a frenzied effort by businessmen to organize in cartels and trade associations in order to keep prices above competitive levels and to share shrinking markets rather than to compete, as formerly, for new ones. Along with this went loud demands for tariff protection and all kinds of restrictive agreements, tacit or explicit, restricting new investment or entry of new enterprises into an activity. Increased pressure was put on governments to favor industrialists, and business organizations were formed to fight labor demands for any larger share of the goods being produced.

At the same time, labor and agriculture were reacting in a similar fashion, forming political pressure groups or even political parties, and seeking common action to raise prices, divide markets, exclude foreign competition, and to strike back at organized industry, finance, or transportation.

While these activities were occurring as symptoms for the usual decline in the rate of expansion and of the growing class conflicts associated with an Age of Conflict, the other marks of such a period were no less obvious. Imperialist wars developed from epidemic to endemic status in our culture, beginning perhaps with the Boer War and the Spanish-American War, but rapidly expanding into a cycle of international stress and crises in which we still live. At the same time, on the intellectual level occurred a great upsurging of irrationality. This latter development is associated with the eager acceptance of the theories of men like Freud, Bergson, or Sorel, and culminated in the utterly irrational activism of Hitler, Mussolini, and many lesser persons. All the characteristics of an age of irrationality began to appear on all sides—increased gambling, increased smoking, the growing use of alcohol and narcotics, a growing obsession with sex and with perversions of sex, an increasing mania for speed, for nervous tension, and for noise; above all, perhaps, a growing tendency to regard violence as a solution for all problems, be they domestic, social, economic, ideological, or international. In fact, violence as a symbol of our growing irrationality has had an increasing role in activity for its own sake, when no possible justification could be made that the activity was seeking to solve a problem.

All these characteristics of any Age of Conflict are too obvious to require further comment. They arose, as is usual in an Age of Conflict, because the organizational patterns of our culture ceased to function as instruments but had become institutionalized. This process was evident on all levels of culture. Religious organizations no longer linked men to God but adopted diverse mundane purposes. Our intellectual theories no longer explained anything or made us at home in the universe. Our social patterns no longer satisfied our gregarious needs, even when we fled from the lonely anonymity of the city to the rat-race uniformity of suburbanism. Our political organizations increased the burden of their demands on our time, energy, and wealth but provided with growing ineffectiveness the justice, public order, education, protection, or incidental amenities we had come to expect from them. And, on the military level, costs rose at an astronomical rate without being able to catch up with our increasing danger.

The core of our problems could be placed in any one of the levels we have mentioned. Indeed, there might be good grounds for arguing that the root of our problem was our success in making life an end rather than a means to something higher. But, in this civilization as in others, it will be convenient to discuss the problem of our Age of Conflict in terms of the institutionalization of our instrument of expansion.

In an earlier chapter we discussed this phenomenon as an example of the process in general (chapter five). At that time we said that the economic organization had become institutionalized by taking on purposes of its own separate from the purposes of the organization as a whole. The purpose of any economic system is to produce, distribute, and consume goods. If it can do this at an increasing rate (within limits), so much the better. Our economic system performed these functions more effectively than any other in history by organizing itself around "a profit motivation within a price structure." As it became institutionalized, profits became an end in themselves to the jeopardy of production, distribution, and consumption. The change arose because profits could be maximized only by increasing the margin between selling prices and costs of production. But high selling prices and high profit margins with low costs of production tended to reduce consumption of goods. And low consumption of goods, at a time when production figures were constantly setting new maximum records, could only result in rising inventories and an indigestion of distribution that was bound to make goods back up to the factories to smother production.

This situation arose from a number of factors. During the nineteenth century, production had been emphasized in such a way as to distort the economic system as a whole, since such a system must also include distribution and consumption. Moreover, within the productive system the pursuit of profits had been emphasized to the neglect of any of the other necessary parts of the productive process. Put briefly, profits had become an end rather than a means. One consequence of this failure in coordination of the economic system as a whole and the even greater failure to coordinate the economic system in the civilization as a whole had been the growth of a very inequitable distribution of the wealth produced by the economic system. Such an inequitable distribution of wealth was a very excellent thing as long as lack of capital was prevalent in the economic system, but such a maldistribution of income ceases to be an advantage as soon as the productive system has developed out of all proportion to the processes of distribution and of consumption. In the United States, according to the National Industrial Conference Board, the richest one-fifth of our population received 46.2 percent of the national income in 1910, 51.3 percent of it in 1929, and 48.5 percent in 1937. In the same three years, the share of the poorest one-fifth of the population fell from 8.3 percent to 5.4 percent to 3.6 percent. Thus the ratios between the portion obtained by the richest one-fifth and that obtained by the poorest one-fifth increased in the three years mentioned from 5.6 to 9.3 to 13.5. If, instead of one-fifth, we examine the ratios between the percentage obtained by the richest one-tenth and the poorest one-tenth in the same three years we find that this ratio was 10 in 1910, was 21.7 in 1929, and reached 34.4 in 1937. To some extent this situation was made worse by the growing separation, in the more advanced industrial areas, between ownership and control of corporations, since this led to an increased accumulation of undistributed profits held by the corporations in control of the management rather than distributed as dividends to the owners. Such undistributed profits became savings with no possibility of serving as consumer purchasing power.

These factors and a number of others that we have not space to mention here led to a situation where increasing proportions of the national income were going to those persons in the community who would be likely to save and decreasing proportions were going to those persons in the community who would spend their incomes for consumers' goods. This situation could continue as long as all the savings made by the former group were invested in new capital or otherwise spent, because these actions would distribute such savings to persons who would use their incomes to buy goods. Only under these conditions (that all savings be invested or spent) could all goods produced be sold.

The last statement can be expressed in a simple arithmetical relationship. In any single firm the total selling price of the goods produced is equal to the sum of their costs of production and their profits. In the economic community as a whole the aggregation of the selling prices of all firms will be the sum of aggregate costs plus aggregate profits. The incomes of the community as a whole are the same as the aggregate of the selling prices of all goods because the profits and costs of each firm are the incomes of those to whom they are paid. If savings are held back from these incomes, the purchasing power available to purchase the goods being offered for sale will be reduced below the prices being asked. Thus:

Total prices = total costs + profits

Total incomes = total costs + profits

therefore

Total prices = total incomes

But available purchasing power = incomes — savings + investment. Accordingly, the purchasing power available to buy the goods being offered at the prices being asked will be inadequate unless all savings are invested.

During the world depression of 1929–38 all savings were not invested because there was no point in spending money on new capital plant so long as the goods being produced by the existing capital plant were going unsold because of the inequitable flow of incomes into the control of persons who wished to save rather than into the control of those who wished to consume.

This crisis of the system was intensified by a number of other factors, notably the deflationary influence of a monetary system tied to a limited supply of gold under conditions of power production of goods. As a consequence the crisis was accompanied by a drastic price deflation that eventually led to a banking crisis and the end of the international gold standard. The date of this last event could be fixed at September 21, 1931, when sterling, which had been the center of the whole world's financial network for more than a century, went off gold. Succinctly, the banking crisis arose when prices of goods fell so low that the banks could not liquidate collateral fast enough and at high-enough prices to provide sufficient funds to meet the demands made on their reserves. As confidence in the banking system decreased, demands rose, reserves fell, and the liquidation of collateral could not keep up with either. Accordingly, banks could not fulfill their obligations and had to close their doors, go bankrupt, or call upon governments for help. The net result was the end of financial capitalism.

This shift from financial capitalism to monopoly capitalism was made possible by the very means that bankers developed for their control of business firms. As we have seen, business firms came to bankers to obtain capital and were bound to remain under banking influence as long as their need for outside capital continued. To ensure continued banking control of these firms, bankers used such mechanisms as interlocking directorships, holding companies, consolidations, and controlled banking services. But these methods of banking control, by reducing competition between firms, made it possible to seek profits by raising prices rather than by decreasing costs and thus made it possible for such firms to become self-financing of their own capital needs and, accordingly, to be freed from banking control. In the earlier period a firm could not seek profits by raising prices because both competition with other firms and the limited supply of money anchored to the limited supply of gold made it difficult to raise prices of any individual product. Accordingly, profits (which are the margin between prices and cost) had to be sought by reducing costs. This need, incidentally, placed the interest of labor in opposition to management, since wages formed the chief item in costs. Management thus, in the periods of industrial capitalism and in the following period of financial capitalism, was almost inevitably opposed to the unionization of labor. But once financial capitalism had brought considerable elements of monopoly into the picture (as J. P. Morgan did when he organized the United States Steel Corporation), decreased competition made it possible to increase profits by raising prices faster than costs. This made it possible for firms to become self-financing out of their own profits, to dispense with bankers' flotations and biased advice, and to reduce management's opposition to unionization of labor. As industry became more heavily capitalized, wages became a decreasing portion of costs, and the value of uninterrupted use of the expensive capital plant made it advisable to avoid labor disputes and labor stoppages by allowing unionization of labor and higher wages, recovering the increased costs of higher wages by raising the increasingly noncompetitive prices of the products. Thus highly capitalized monopolistic industry became an exploitation of the absent consumer by management and labor jointly. At approximately the same time, the end of the international gold standard freed the supply of money from its dependence on the limited supply of gold (and from the maldistribution of gold arising from the bankers' mismanagement of the gold standard) and thus made it possible for prices to be raised, perhaps indefinitely by joint labor-management actions. And finally, in the same context of events, the pressure to raise wages was increased by the desire to provide increased purchasing power to buy the growing flood of goods being produced.

The shift from financial capitalism to monopoly capitalism made possible a new period of expansion in Western civilization, but before that new mechanism could be used for expansive purposes the institutionalization of the previous organization of financial capitalism had thrown the whole society into an Age of Conflict. It is not yet clear if the society will be destroyed as a consequence of this or if it will be able to straighten itself on a new course of expansion. The structure of the new system is entirely different from that which existed in the period of financial capitalism before 1929.

In that earlier period the two chief differences were (1) that the whole economic system was dominated by bankers and financiers, especially by investment bankers, and (2) that, as a result, the system had a financial mechanism that was basically deflationary because the volume of money was determined, in the final analysis, by the limited supply of gold. As a consequence of the first of these characteristics, the lines of prestige and influence in the system passed from financiers to heavy industry and then to light industry and commerce, after which they were diffused among petty bourgeois clerks, farmers, laborers, bureaucrats, and service workers. As a consequence of the world depression, finance was reduced to a subordinate role and a struggle arose about the arrangement of the other groups. In fascist states, industry, commerce, and petty bourgeois, by abolishing any forms of political democracy, sought to establish authoritarian regimes in which industry with its allies could exploit farmers, laborers, and consumers in general in order to favor producers in general. In "New Deal" and democratic states this did not occur, but instead labor, farmers, commercial groups, and to some extent consumers in general were strengthened and all groups (including reduced finance) became satellites around the governmental system. The control of money supply, which had been one of the chief attributes of the banking group before 1929, became an attribute of the government after 1945, and the government exercised its control under pressure from the shifting alliances and alignments of the great economic power blocs that surrounded it. These blocs came to include: (1) finance, (2) heavy industry, (3) light industry, (4) commercial and service groups (such as real estate), (5) civil servants, (6) the armed services, (7) labor, (8) farmers, (9) transportation, and others. If any one or several of these blocs become too obviously exploitative of the others, the others form an alignment to pressurize the government in another direction. The chief consequence of such alignments and pressures has been to increase government spending and thus to increase inflation. In general all these pressures have sought to achieve some redistribution of economic resources among the three chief claimants to these resources; these three are consumption, capital accumulation, and government services (including defense). In the financial capitalist system before 1929, the great danger had been the great diversion of resources toward capital accumulation to the jeopardy of the two others. In the new pluralistic system that has arisen, the great danger in many countries has been toward increasing consumption to the jeopardy of capital accumulation and public service. This danger has frequently appeared as a tendency toward inflation that would destroy capital accumulation by destroying savings.

At the present time it is too early to judge if the present crisis of Western civilization will resolve itself into a new, fourth Age of Expansion, or will continue through an Age of Conflict to a universal empire and ultimately to decay and invasion.

In any case the immediate future seems to offer to Western society a culture in which, on various levels, an army of specialists serves an ideological state, supported by a pluralist economy regulated by planning (both public and private) in a society in which the dominant social class is made up of managers (rather than owners, bankers, voters, or others). In this culture the nature of the intellectual and religious levels will depend on whether the whole system continues in a period of conflict or turns toward a new Age of Expansion.

Conclusion

What is the point of all this? Looking back over our discussion, it seems to me that at least six chief points readily emerge.

In the first place, I have sought to emphasize the difference between knowledge and understanding in the field of history. To know is not too demanding: it merely requires memory and time. But to understand is quite a different matter: it requires intellectual ability and training, a self-conscious awareness of what one is doing, experience in techniques of analysis and synthesis, and above all, perspective. Moreover, perspective requires a familiarity with the units of social aggregations and a recognition that understanding can be achieved only if we tackle societies and that it cannot be reached if we try to deal with social groups determined by geographic areas, political units, religion, nations (linguistic or "cultural"), or by intellectual categories such as veterans or middle class. To obtain knowledge we must use such groups, but to obtain understanding we must use the only group that is comprehensible: the society.

There is nothing very original in this first point, since it is, among others, advocated by Toynbee in the first volume of his *A Study of History,* but it has not been accepted by historians, who, in practice, continue to deal with noncomprehensible units such as states or nations. Moreover, Toynbee never defined his terms, and constantly violated his own precepts in his own practice.

The second major point is the recognition that civilizations pass through a process of rise and fall. This is, of course, one of the oldest clichés in any "philosophy of history," and no claims to originality on that score could be made for this present book. But I have sought to go beyond the mere recognition of "rise and fall" to seek to find the mechanism of the process. Here I do not feel entitled to make any claim to startling originality because the process I describe—the institutionalization of social instruments—is clearly what was at the back of the minds of a number of earlier writers on the philosophy of history. I have sought to make the process explicit, so that it can be recognized and analyzed more readily and so that turning points in the process can be established with greater confidence. At the same time I have given, I hope, sufficient warning that this process is neither rigid nor single in any society, but rather that each civilization is a confused congeries of such processes in all types of human activities and that the explicit recognition or description of one such organization as the independent factor in a medley of mutually dependent factors is not a description of the reality (which is far too complex for any historian to describe it adequately), but is a technique for dealing with an irrational process similar to that used by a mathematician who deals with the irrationality of change by the use of a calculus based on untrue assumptions involving finite increments or on an assumed distinction between an independent variable and dependent variables. For the historian, as for the mathematician, I should advise that the chief task must not be a vain search for the factor that is independent but an explicit recognition that we are assuming the independence of one variable.

A third conclusion, derived from the second, is concerned with periodization in history. It has been clear for a long time that the periodizations now used are unsatisfactory. The division of ancient history into a Greek period, a Hellenistic period, and a Roman period makes no sense at all, can be maintained only by making the second period (connecting two linguistic divisions) vague and undefined, and clearly requires numerous violations of chronological order. Attempts have been made to get around these weaknesses in the customary division by efforts, such as Sanford's (in a textbook) to divide the Classical world into several geographic areas that advance chronologically side by side; these have been far from successful. In European history the same problem of periodization has been causing even greater dissatisfaction. The existing division into medieval, Renaissance, modern, and contemporary history has pleased no one (and has been most displeasing to the specialists on the Renaissance), but no substitute for these long-established divisions has been found. The greatest problem has arisen in the Renaissance period because of its wholly ambiguous relationship to the medieval period, a relationship that remains ambiguous because of the mistaken effort to treat the Middle Ages as a single period. As a consequence we find medieval history, to nonmedievalists, represented by a welter of contradictions called "renaissance of the twelfth century," "Age of Authority" (or Faith), "Dark Ages," and other totally misleading verbal tags. My division of the mil-

lennium 400–1400 into the four stages of Mixture, Gestation, Expansion, and Conflict solves many of these
difficulties, provides tools with which to analyze aberrations
like the Carolingian revival, and, above all, provides a
vocabulary for dealing with the problem.

On the whole, the division into seven stages is largely my
own except that I have used Toynbee's ideas, if not his
nomenclature, with reference to the last four or five stages.
The great advantage that my seven stages provides over
Toynbee's recognition of the last five of them rests in my
insistence that any division into stages must be based on
analysis of the process of "rise and fall" that is being discussed. It is not sufficient merely to describe and to devise
name tags for stages based on such description. This is
what Toynbee has done, and this is why Toynbee is so
notably unsatisfactory in dealing with the earlier stages of
any civilization's evolution. Toynbee's process of "Challenge
and Response" explains nothing, is based on a mistaken
Darwinian biological analogy, and provides no technique
for analyzing a society or for communication with others
about it. It is true that societies are challenged and either
do or do not respond to these challenges. This is so true as
to be quite unhelpful. The important point is *why* a society
responds or fails to respond, how we can judge the likelihood
of either beforehand, and what is the consequence of either
alternative. Moreover, Toynbee's failure, already sufficiently
emphasized, to correlate his process with his division into
stages is a major weakness.

Toynbee's failure to provide a satisfactory analysis of
process explains his failure to understand, or to provide
stages for, the first part of a civilization's existence. The
whole process of mixture, gestation, and incipient expansion

is of vital concern to us today when the buffer fringe between the Western and the Soviet blocs, from Morocco to Indonesia, offers a real challenge in this very regard. Here Toynbee has almost nothing to offer, either to the peoples of those areas who are struggling to establish viable societies or to us who are trying to understand what is happening there.

A fifth contribution I have tried to make is concerned with vocabulary. This contribution has two parts. On the one hand, I have tried to provide a vocabulary sufficiently well defined to allow communication between students of these problems, yet sufficiently realistic to assist explanations of what is happening or did happen in any society. On the other hand (and this is a major point), I have tried to establish some degree of sophistication in the use of historical vocabulary so that awareness of the subjective nature of most intellectual categories dealing with historical facts will be maintained. I am sure that my vocabulary is far from perfect; this is inevitable. The real point is that my vocabulary is *fruitful:* fruitful in research projects, in arousing original questions and interpretations, and in making communication between historians more helpful. No vocabulary is perfect; like everything else it is an instrument that becomes an institution, serving eventually to hamper thought and communication about these important matters. When that occurs, the old vocabulary of clichés must be circumvented or reformed. As it is now, the vocabulary of periodization and the vocabulary of analysis (by aspects or "levels") hamper historical understanding, particularly by encouraging specialization, either by period or by subject, in areas that are unreal, defunct, and much too narrow. The best histories of the future will emerge from work that straddles the older, obsolete, and unrealistic boundary lines.

In fact, it is possible today to attract favorable attention simply by pointing out the artificial nature of these older boundary lines.

All this leads to the sixth contribution offered by this book. It tries to provide techniques for dealing with history or with social problems in general. For years I have told my students that I have been trying to train executives rather than clerks. The distinction between the two is parallel to the distinction previously made between understanding and knowledge. It is a mighty low executive who cannot hire several people with command of more knowledge than he has himself. And he can always buy reference works or electronic devices with better memories for facts than any subordinate. The chief quality of an executive is that he have understanding. He should be able to make decisions that make it possible to utilize the knowledge of other persons. Such executive capacity can be taught, but it cannot be taught by any educational program that emphasizes knowledge and only knowledge. Knowledge must be assumed as given, and if it is not sufficient the candidate must be eliminated. But the vital thing is understanding. This requires possession of techniques that, fortunately, can be taught.

The historian who is on an executive level rather than on a clerical level because he can make decisions and understands the materials with which he deals must have techniques of analysis, of morphological understanding, of developmental processes, and of evolutionary changes. I have tried to suggest, in an introductory fashion, the kind of techniques that might be used. Tensions and social conflicts can be analyzed in terms of the struggle between instruments and institutions, or of the morphological relationships between levels, or of the relationship, which I hardly mentioned, between fact and law. Clashes between areas and between groups must be analyzed in similar terms. Failure to use such techniques leads to childish judgments on historical events just as, among practicing politicians, it leads to childish decisions in world problems.

An example of how such techniques may be used in history might be helpful. For years I have been teaching students that historians come up against four kinds of problems. These are: (1) informational problems; (2) logical problems; (3) analytical problems; and (4) chronological problems. Techniques, capable of being taught, can be devised for dealing with each of these. The use of such techniques not only provides a method of attack on such problems; even more valuable is the fact that it makes us aware of the distinction between the problem and our approach to it; it becomes possible to judge the degree of inadequacy in our own performance or the degree to which our method of attack determines the kind of answer we get. Probably the achievement of such sophisticated self-awareness is the chief value to be derived from awareness of one's techniques, their adequacy, and their character.

The techniques I have discussed as instruments for dealing with the past have value outside the study of history, for they are equally useful in dealing with the present or the future. I sometimes demonstrate this to my students by imagining that one of them is called upon to lead a United States government commission of inquiry to Brazil, a country of which he knows little. I show how the techniques of analysis applied by me to past history can be used to approach this task by helping the leader to decide which experts he should take with him, how their assignments should be set on their arrival in Brazil, and how their results, at the end, should be coordinated to provide an adequate picture of a functioning Brazil beset by actual problems.

The value of these techniques, since they seek understanding rather than knowledge, is constantly high and has, if anything, increased in recent years. These years have seen, since Sputnik, a dramatic increase in the prestige of science and in the use of scientists in dealing with world problems. I should be the last person to regret this development, but, as a scientist, in the social sciences, I know that the problems of the world are not solved by the use of the natural sciences alone. Indeed, the direction and the coordination of scientific activities with respect to world problems require guidance and supervision by persons with a wider perspective than that provided by specialization in the natural sciences. Such perspective can best be found in the study of the past. With such perspective the techniques I have described in this volume as instruments for the study of the past can be used to guide natural scientists and other workers in dealing with the problems of the present and the future.

Selective Bibliography
By William Marina

The following is not intended as a complete listing of all of the writings of Carroll Quigley. A definitive list should be completed after a careful examination of the more than thirty boxes of materials which he left to the library at Georgetown University, and which are still being organized. Rather, this listing contains some of his more readily available writings which might be of interest to the reader who has enjoyed *The Evolution of Civilizations,* as well as citations to several reviews of his two major works.

At the time of his death, Quigley was at work on a study which had occupied him for years and which might be called the sociology of weaponry; that is, the way in which the structure and development of civilizations are to a considerable extent a reflection of the weapons systems and military organization prevalent within a society. Drafts of this study, some two thousand pages in length, are in the papers

Dr. Marina is Professor in Business, Communications, and History at Florida Atlantic University in Boca Raton. He is coauthor of American Statesmen on Slavery and the Negro *(1971), author of* Egalitarianism and Empire *(1975), and associate editor of* News of the Nation: A Newspaper History of the United States *(1976).*

left at Georgetown. His own feelings about this work are perhaps best conveyed by a comment made in delivering the initial Oscar Iden Lecture at the School of Foreign Service at Georgetown University only a few weeks before his death:

> Another thing which may serve to point out the instability of the power system of the state: the individual cannot be made the basic unit of society, as we have tried to do, or of the state, since the internalization of controls must be the preponderant influence in any stable society. . . .
>
> Also related to the problem of internalized controls is the shift of weapons in our society. This is a profound problem. I have spent ten years working on it throughout all of history, and I hope eventually to produce a book if I can find a publisher. There will be endless analyses of Chinese history and Byzantine history and Russian history and everything else, and the book is about nine-tenths written, I'd say, in the last ten years. The shift of weapons in any civilization and, above all, in our civilization, from shock weapons to missile weapons, has a dominant influence on the ability to control individuals. . . .
>
> In our society, individual behavior can no longer be controlled by any system of weaponry we have. In fact, we do not have enough people, even if we equip them with shock weapons, to control the behavior of that part of the population which does not have internalized controls. One reason for that, of course, is that the twenty percent who do not have internalized controls are concentrated in certain areas. I won't go into the subject of controls. It opens up the whole field of guerrilla resistance, terrorism, and everything else; these cannot be controlled by any system or organized structure of force that exists, at least on the basis of missile weaponry. And, as I said, it would take too many people on the basis of shock weaponry. We have now done what the Romans did when they started to commit suicide: we have shifted from an army of citizen soldiers to an army of mercenaries, and those mercenaries are being recruited in our society, as they were in Roman society, from the twenty percent of the population which does not have the internalized controls of the civilization.[1]

---

[1] "Public Authority and the State in the Western Tradition," pp. 34–35.

I deeply appreciate the efforts of Professor Quigley's widow, Mrs. Lillian Quigley, a fine scholar and writer in her own right, to make available to me her husband's work relating to the philosophy of history, the sociology of weaponry, and its influence on civilization. To borrow a phrase from Quigley's title, *Tragedy and Hope,* his death was a tragedy which deprived us of the full measure of his brilliant analyses about the development of civilizations. My examination of his papers also suggests hope, for he left in manuscript a vast addenda to what he had earlier begun. I am certain a great deal of this material will eventually find its way into print, but *The Evolution of Civilizations* is the indispensable first step toward understanding Quigley's interpretation of human action and history.

Books

The Anglo-American Establishment: The Conspiracy from Rhodes to Cliveden. New York: Books in Focus, Inc. 1982.

The Evolution of Civilizations. New York: Macmillan, 1961; Indianapolis: Liberty Fund, 1979.

La Evolución de las Civilizaciones. Mexico City: Hermes, 1963.

A Evolucao das Civilazacoes. Rio de Janeiro: Editora Fundo de Cultura, 1963.

See the reviews of the English edition in the *American Historical Review* 67 (July 1962):987; *Christian Science Monitor,* January 8, 1962; *Kirkus Review,* September 1, 1961, p. 838; *Library Journal,* November 1, 1961, p. 3788; *School and Society,* October 6, 1962, p. 321; and *Social Education* 26 (April 1962):219.

Tragedy and Hope: The World in Our Time. New York: Macmillan, 1965.

Weapons Systems and Political Stability: A History. Washington, D.C.: University Press of America, 1982.

The World Since 1939. New York: Collier Books, 1968. A reprint of the last half of *Tragedy and Hope.*

Among the reviews are: *American Historical Review* 72 (October 1966):123; *Annals of the American Academy* 368 (November 1966):244; *Best Sellers,* February 15, 1966, p. 434; *Book Week,* January 16, 1966; *Choice* 3 (June 1966):348; *Library Journal,* August 1965, p. 3284; *New York Times Book Review,* January 23, 1966, and Quigley's reply to same, with the reviewer's rejoinder, in the February 20, 1966, issue; *Saturday Review,* February 12, 1966, p. 34; and *Virginia Quarterly Review* 42 (Spring 1966):301.

Articles

"Falsification of a Source in Risorgimento History." *Journal of Modern History* 20 (September 1948) : 223–26.

"The Origin and Diffusion of Oculi." *American Neptune,* July 1955; and rejoinder in *ibid.,* January 1958.

"Aboriginal Fish Poisons and the Diffusion Problem." *American Anthropologist* 58 (June 1956):508–25.

"Comparative Cultural Developments." *The Community Development Review* (December 1957).

"French West Africa." *Current History* 34 (February 1958): 91–98.

"Education in Overseas France." *Current History* 35 (August 1958): 102–11.

"The French Community and Western Security." *Current History* 39 (August 1960): 101–7.

"French Tropical Africa: Today and Tomorrow." *Current History* 40 (February 1961):77–87.

"Belgium"; "France"; "Italy"; "North Atlantic Treaty Organization"; and "The Netherlands." In Funk and Wagnalls, *New International Yearbook*. New York: Funk and Wagnalls, 1961, 1963.

"The Round Table Groups in Canada, 1908–1938." *The Canadian Historical Review* 43 (September 1962):204–24.

"The Brazzaville Twelve." *Current History* 43 (December 1962):346–53.

"Weapons Control as Seen from Abroad." *Current History* 46 (June 1964).

"The Creative Writer Today." *Catholic World* 206 (December 1967):111–17.

"France and the United States in World Politics." *Current History* 54 (March 1968).151–59.

"Needed: A Revolution in Thinking." *National Education Association Journal* 57 (May 1968):8–10.

"Lord Balfour's Personal Position on the Balfour Declaration" (ed.). *Middle East Journal* 22 (Summer 1968):340–45.

"Major Problems of Foreign Policy." *Current History* 55 (October 1968):199–206.

"Our Ecological Crisis." *Current History* 59 (July 1970):1–12.

"Youth's Heroes Have No Halos." *Today's Education* 36 (April 1971):46–48.

"Assumption and Inference on Human Origins." *Current Anthropology* 12 (October–December 1971):519–40; and discussion in *ibid.* 14 (October 1973):499–502.

"General Crises in Civilizations." American Association for the Advancement of Science news release, 1972.

"Cognitive Factors in the Evolution of Civilizations." *Main Currents in Modern Thought* 29 (November–December 1972):69–75.

"The Search for a Solution to the World Crisis." *Futurist* 9 (March 1975):38–41.

"America's Future in Energy." *Current History* 69 (July 1975):1–5.

"Public Authority and the State in the Western Tradition: A Thousand Years of Growth, 976–1976." *The Oscar Iden Lectures.* Washington: School of Foreign Service, Georgetown University, 1977.

Index

This book was Linotype set in the Times Roman series of type. The face was designed to be used in the news columns of the London *Times*. The *Times* was seeking a typeface that would be condensed enough to accommodate a substantial number of words per column without sacrificing readability and still have an attractive, contemporary appearance. This design was an immediate success. It is used in many periodicals throughout the world and is one of the most popular textfaces in use for book work.

Printed on paper that is acid-free and meets the requirements of the American National Standard for Permanence of Paper for Printed Library Materials, Z39.48-1992. ∞

Cover design by Erin Kirk New, Watkinsville, Georgia
Book design by JMH Corporation, Indianapolis, Indiana
Typography by Weimer Typesetting Co., Inc., Indianapolis, Indiana
Printed and bound by Sheridan Books, Inc., Chelsea, Michigan